Anglicisms in Russian and German Blogs

Hallesche Sprach- und Textforschung

Herausgegeben von Alexander Brock und Annette Schiller

Band 10

PETER LANG
Frankfurt am Main · Berlin · Bern · Bruxelles · New York · Oxford · Wien

Julia Balakina

Anglicisms in Russian and German Blogs

A Comparative Analysis

PETER LANG
Internationaler Verlag der Wissenschaften

Bibliographic Information published by the Deutsche Nationalbibliothek
The Deutsche Nationalbibliothek lists this publication in the Deutsche Nationalbibliografie; detailed bibliographic data is available in the internet at http://dnb.d-nb.de.

Zugl.: Phil. Diss. an der Philosophischen Fakultät II
der Martin-Luther-Universität Halle-Wittenberg 2009
unter dem Namen Naumova, Julia

3
ISSN 0941-4134
ISBN 978-3-631-61517-1

www.peterlang.de

Contents

List of Tables

List of Figures

Introduction

My doctoral thesis examines three languages: English, German and Russian. Russian and German appear to have more differences than commonalities in terms of their language history, graphical peculiarities, etc. Nevertheless, given the rapid development of cross-cultural communication, the gap between the languages is narrowing. They are tending to 'look alike' due to the bulk of foreign vocabulary, mainly English, trickling down to them. In both Germany and Russia, there is an acute awareness of the need to preserve the national language. However, only very few scholars have compared languages with regard to the incoming stream of anglicisms. In particular, very few studies have addressed the emergence of common tendencies in the process of integration or the defining factors that play a decisive role in adopting foreign vocabulary. Accordingly, it is vital to find out how English loans are integrated into the systems of German and Russian and to determine the common tendencies, peculiarities and deviations as well as to dwell upon linguistic and extra-linguistic reasons for the process of borrowing. Moreover, Internet language was chosen for the present research, the primary reason being that nowadays life without the Internet would be almost unimaginable. Because so many people of different origins and social backgrounds spend their time communicating with each other online, it comes as no surprise that a special Internet culture has appeared with its own idiosyncrasies. Therefore, studying Internet language enables the development of certain rules and tendencies concerning language on all levels (including graphical, grammatical and lexical) to be traced – which is why it is not just interesting but also highly relevant to involve Internet language in the present research. In particular, blogs were chosen for the present analysis as they reflect the peculiarities of Internet language, for they consist of spontaneous texts created by common users. This is why the lexis used (anglicisms in particular) can be regarded as belonging to the vocabulary of the user and not as inserted on purpose, which makes the results of the present research very reliable. Moreover, it is almost always possible to glean some personal information about the author of a particular blog, i.e. their age and sex, allowing sociolinguistic analysis. The present work also includes a historical overview of scholarly research into anglicisms.

German definitely has a longer tradition in the study of anglicisms than Russian. This is probably attributable to these countries' history, as in Soviet times research concerning anglicisms was almost inconceivable until the 1980s. The most significant contribution to the research of anglicisms in present-day German was first conducted by Zindler. His book *Anglizismen in der deutschen Presse nach 1945* is actually the first research paper undertaken after World War

II to tackle anglicisms. A book by Broder Carstensen entitled *Englische Einflüsse auf die Deutsche Sprache nach 1945* contains a detailed classification of loans. In fact, Carstensen's contribution to the research of anglicisms cannot be overestimated, for he was one of the leading linguists to devote themselves to exploration in the field of anglicisms.

In addition, the following linguists should also be mentioned for their significant contribution to research into anglicisms in German : Duckworth (1979), Karin Viereck (1980), Wolfgang Viereck (1980), Fink (1995, 1997, 2000), Busse (1993), Yang (1990) and Sörensen (1994), along with younger ones such as Adler (2004), Bohmann (1996), Gester (2001), Glahn (2002), Kupper (2003), Nettman-Multanowska (2003) and Zürn (2001).

As far as Russian is concerned, the initial basic research papers were the books written by Aristova, the first one being *Английские слова в русском языке* (1978), which deals with problems of language contacts, forms of borrowings and the evolution of English loanwords in Russian, and the second *Англо-русские языковые контакты (англицизмы в русском языке)*. Numerous articles devoted to the issue of anglicisms in Russian have been published by for example Volodarskaya (2001, 2002), Zelenin (2003), Krisin (1965, 1998 and 2004), etc. Furthermore, the book by Timofeeva (1995) *Новые английские заимствования в русском языке. Написание. Произношение* should be mentioned in this context as well as it deals with the integration of borrowings into the graphical and phonological system of the Russian language in greater detail. Moreover, a large number of articles dealing with questions of anglicisms in both Russian and German can be found on the Internet.[1]

Generally speaking, while the problem of anglicisms has been exhaustively discussed in German, the lack of research in Russian is apparent. Moreover, insufficient research has been conducted in the area of contrastive studies in both languages.[2] Despite the presence of current research into Internet language and different forms of communication, there is still a lack when it comes to the study of online diaries or *blogs*. Therefore the goal of the present research, namely the comparative analysis of anglicisms in Russian and German taken from *blogs,* seems very necessary, new and important.

---

1 See References.

2 One more contrastive project which reflects the main tendencies in the adoption of anglicisms in both Russian and German should be mentioned here: A dictionary of European anglicisms: a usage dictionary of anglicisms in 16 European languages, Manfred Görlach, ed., Oxford: Oxford Univ. Press, 2001.

The Goals of Research and Hypotheses

As mentioned above, the Internet is gaining in popularity and is of particular interest to reseachers, especially linguists. A large number of loans of English origin can be found on the Internet, the majority of them relating to computer technology and the Internet.

Moreover, besides the well-known forms of communication like chats and forums, new forms are appearing on the Internet, such as *blogs*. It would hence be very interesting to describe and define a *blog* as a new form of communication and as a new text type, apart from analysing the anglicisms presented in *blogs*. The present research is based on online diaries written in both German and Russian. The aim is to establish whether there are any common tendencies in the integration of anglicisms in the two languages and also what factors influence the use of anglicisms on the Internet and namely in *blogs*.

The following goals are to be tackled in conjunction with this study:

- Defining and describing a *blog* as a new text type;
- Searching for anglicisms in both German and Russian *blogs* (a personal homepage that consists of posts in reverse chronological order and contains links to other websites and comments);
- Comparatively analysing the material gathered in terms of phonology, morphology, grammar, semantics and stylistics for German and Russian and ascertaining whether there are any common tendencies concerning the adoption of anglicisms;
- Classifying anglicisms;
- Identifying identical loans in German and Russian and comparatively analysing similar loans (with respect to morphology, grammar, semantics and stylistics) because due to the peculiarities of the structure of German and Russian some of the loans are transformed;
- Pinpointing possible linguistic and extra-linguistic reasons for the borrowing of similar lexical units in both languages;
- Conducting sociolinguistic analysis to determine whether the age and sex of the writer influence the anglicisms they use.

The following hypotheses are to be confirmed or rejected in the present paper:

- The number of loans in one language exceeds that in the other in particular topics;

- The number of anglicisms in topic-oriented *blogs* exceeds the number of anglicisms in non-topic-oriented *blogs*;
- The age of the producer influences the number of anglicisms used (i.e. the younger the producer, the more anglicisms are used);
- The age and/or sex of the producer affects the choice of anglicisms used;
- Subject matter (according to gender preferences) influences the use of anglicisms.

Overview of the Paper

The first chapter 'Blogs' will describe the phenomenon of a *blog* and define the term. The history of the term and the phenomenon will then be outlined together with some statistical data. Also, it is very important to compare an online diary with its prototype, the handwritten diary, in order to define common features as well as the differences that have emerged. Finally, a *blog* will be defined as a new text type worthy of the present research. The chapter entitled 'Borrowings' will cover the varieties of loanwords and the reasons for borrowings. The term 'anglicism' will also be defined.

In the chapter 'Corpora', all the common tendencies concerning types of corpora in contrastive linguistics and the process of their composition will be reviewed. Furthermore, the structure of the corpora for the present research will be described. In the next chapter entitled 'Anglicisms in *blogs*', the hypotheses mentioned above will be verified with the help of the statistical data collected.

In the chapter 'Graphical adaptation', a comparative analysis of Russian and German will not be performed owing to the major differences in their graphical systems. However, general tendencies concerning the integration of loans into the graphical systems using the examples taken from the corpus analysed will be identified. The next chapter 'Morphology' will be devoted to a comparative analysis of the processes concerning the integration of anglicisms into the morphological system and will address word-building processes, gender assignment, declension, the conjugation of verbs, etc. Also, numerous examples of anglicisms of the same origin found in German and Russian will be analysed.

In the next chapter, 'Semantics', all types of meaning will be described. Also, changes taking place upon the adoption of anglicisms, both qualitative as well as quantitative, will be surveyed and illustrated with numerous examples. In addition, the interesting relationship between anglicisms and their native correlates will be studied. Moreover, the influence of context on the meaning of an anglicism will be discussed along with the connotative part of meaning. In this chapter, various stylistic devices involving anglicisms will be presented as along with the stylistic interference of anglicisms. All this will be backed up by numerous examples taken from the corpus analysed.

1. Blogs

1.1 The Term *Blog*

Nowadays we live in a high-tech world where new technologies are appearing every day, and something which seemed outlandish last week may become commonplace tomorrow. For example, the so-called *'new medium'* that entered our lives more than ten years ago, the Internet, is gaining more popularity and has become part of our everyday life. These days, having an Internet connection at home is as common as having a washing machine. Even so, new functions, possibilities and phenomena are being discovered on the World Wide Web with every passing day. The possibility *to blog* can be also referred to as one of the relatively new phenomena that have appeared on the WWW. Although the history of *blogs* will be addressed in the next part of this chapter,[3] at this point it is important to define the term *blog* and to state why *blogs* have become so popular among different social and age groups in such a short period of time.

The secret of this popularity lies in the unprecedented accessibility of *blogs* that makes it possible for each ordinary user to share their feelings and ideas with the whole world. Striving for acknowledgement and fame and the need for self-expression are the primary motives that prompt people to write *blogs*. Blogging is sometimes the only way for an average person to demonstrate to others what they are worth. The Internet provides a real opportunity for everyone to gain their share of public acknowledgement without any racial, sexual or any other type of discrimination. No one can say exactly how many *blogs* exist at this time but there are certainly millions of them – and their number is growing daily.[4]

The term *weblog* was first coined by John Barger in December 1997 on his website *robotwisdom.com* while the shorter version, *blog*, appeared just two years later and was coined by Peter Merholz on *peterme.com.* He broke the word into the phrase *"we blog"* reflecting the essence of *blogs* as a united medium between users all over the world. There is one more meaning hidden in the term

---

3 See Item 1.2.

4 According to statistical data presented in «Количество блогов в интернете достигло 35 млн.» Полит.Ру. URL: http://bilingua.ogi.ru/culture/2006/04/18/blogs.html (18 April, 2006), and in «Количество блогов в интернете удваивалось каждые полгода», E-news: Новости Украины и Мира. URL:http://e-news.com.ua/print/147600.html in April 2006 (15 May, 2006) there were approximately 35.5 million blogs, a figure which had risen to 72 million by the beginning of 2007. In March 2005, 500,000 blogs appeared daily, while in March 2007 the quantity totalled 1.4 million.

that could be defined as a *"web log"*, i.e. *"to log on the web"*. That is the aim of the *blogs* – to record anything possible without any restrictions on the WWW.

Despite the fact that *blogs* are a relatively new phenomenon, a number of different definitions have appeared. Some of them are listed below.

- *Weblogs (blogs)* – frequently modified web pages in which dated entries are listed in reverse chronological sequence. (Herring 2004:1)
- A *weblog* is usually defined as a personal or non-commercial website that uses a dated log format (usually with the most recent addition at the top of the page) and contains links to other websites along with commentary about those sites.[5]
- A *weblog* (usually shortened to *blog*, but occasionally spelled as *web log*) is a web application presented as a webpage consisting of periodic posts, normally in reverse chronological order.[6]

Having summed up the definitions above, we can define the term *blog* as follows:

A blog is a personal homepage consisting of posts in reverse chronological order and containing links to other websites and comments.

It is also important to mention that blogs are connected to each other through links forming blogrolls and then a blogosphere. The blogosphere comprises all existing blogs. Such a close connection between blogs and users contributes to the social significance of blogs, where everyone can receive feedback on everything they publish.

To finalise the matter, blogs can be regarded as a new model of communication where each reader can be both author and journalist simultaneously. Weblogs should be treated like media for the masses with the following pattern: to inform – to publish – to create a network. Weblogs have changed the phenomenon of information, its access, control and value. Due to blogs, information is now appearing in unparalleled quality and quantity. Here it would be appropriate to cite Peter Schlobinski (2006), who defines the idea of blogs as follows:

> Ein Blog ist schon für Privatpersonen mehr als ein Persönliches Tagebuch. Es ist ein Rednerpult. Ein Raum für Zusammenarbeit. Eine politische Bühne. Ein Ventil für Nachrichten. Eine Sammlung interessanter Links. Ihre ganz privaten Gedanken. Notizen für die Welt.[7]

---

5 "Ask Yahoo!" URL:http://ask.yahoo.com/ask/20021115.html (15 November, 2002).

6 Sanjay Das. "About Blog".
URL: http://blogchronicle.blog-spot.com/2005/05/about-blog.html (17 May, 2005).

7 Peter Schlobinski URL: http://www.blogger.com/tour-start.g/ (25 May, 2006).

1.2 The History of Blogs. Statistics

Although *blogs* seem to be a new phenomenon, if we take a look at their history we find that they are already more than ten years old. This chapter outlines the history of *blogs*.

Mosaic's What's New page, which appeared in 1993, is often called the first *blog.*[8] It gave a list of links people considered worth sharing. Then in 1994 *Justin Hall* created *Justin's Homepage* that was also full of links. In 1997 *Dave Winner* began publishing *'Scripting News'*, which is considered the prototype of *news weblogs.*[9] But it was not until December 1997 that *John Barger* coined the term *weblog*, ushering in the history of *blogs.*[10]

In 1999 there were only a few sites identified as *weblogs. Jesse James Garrett* compiled a list of sites he found on the web that looked like *blogs*. The list comprised twenty-three sites at that time.[11] The real *blog* boom started with the creation of *free blog software*, which made the creation of *blogs* accessible to everyone.

The first application named *Blogger* was released in August 1999. Since that time, the number of *blogs* appearing has grown from day to day. By October 2000, *blogger* users were creating 300 new *blogs* a day, by March 2005 this figure had increased to 500,000, while by March 2007 it totalled 1.4 million. Since then, many other applications have appeared that allow users to create and design *blogs* any way they like, including *PostXING, Scoop* and *Igloo.*

The statistical data taken from *technorati.com* and *robotwisdom.com* show that nowadays there are about 35 million *blogs.* Sixty-six per cent of them have not been updated in the past two months, while a million *blogs* consist of just one or two entries. According to the existing data, only around a million *blogs* are active and continuously maintained. As far as the Russian and German *blogosphere* is concerned, there are about 454,000 *blogs* in Russian and some 200,000 in German.[12]

---

8 John Barger. "Weblog resources FAQ" (September, 1999). URL:http://www.open.ge/el/?base=www.robotwisdom.com/&view=0&url='weblogs/index.html/ (23 May, 2005).

9 Александр Птица . «Дневники, «Живой Журнал», блоги и все, все, все» (01 June, 2002), ITC.UA URL:http://www.itc.ua/articles.phtml?ID=10097/ (12 October, 2005).

10 See Item 1.1.

11 Михаил Бекетов. «Интересное интервью про блоггинг». Деловой Квартал. URL: http:// www.dkvartal.ru/beketov/6847/comments/ (12 July, 2007).

12 At the time of compilation of the corpus.

It can therefore be stated that, having appeared about ten years ago, *blogs* are nowadays reaching the peak of popularity, as can be clearly seen from the statistical data presented in this chapter.

1.3 Bloggers

It is not only *blogs* that are relevant for the present research; the authors of *blogs* (*bloggers)* are equally important. There are evidently no age or sex restrictions as far as *blogging* is concerned; anyone who is able to use the Internet is able to *blog*. This claim is backed up by the following statistical data presented on the webpage *webstrannik.net*:

- 51.5% of bloggers are aged 13–19;
- 39.6% are 20–29;
- 5.8% are 30–39.[13]

As far as the sex of *bloggers* is concerned, no clear trend is apparent. Some sources say that females make up 56% of *bloggers*; some claim 67%. In some cases it is reported that one in five women are interested in blog sites.[14] On the other hand, "Wie ich blogge? Erste Ergebnisse der Weblogbefragung 2005"[15] states that in all age groups over 20, men outnumber women, although among teenagers females dominate by two to one, the overall proportions of *bloggers* being 54% males and 46% females.

The question of anonymity has also been discussed in various surveys.[16] It has been stated that the majority of users write under their actual names or give details about their real life, while just under a third use a pseudonym or reveal no information at all. The reason for these results probably lies in the need for self-expression and self-realization the authors of *blogs* tend to have; it is more logical to write under one's real name or give some information about oneself so that people know whose 'masterpieces' they are reading. This is also the reason

---

13 Note that the statistical data refer to the time when this chapter was written.

14 See webstrannik.net.

15 Jan Schmidt, Martin Wilbers. "Wie ich blogge?! Erste Ergebnisse der Weblogbefragung 2005" (Januar 2006), Forschungsstelle "Neue Kommunikationsmedien". URL: http://www.fonk-bamberg.de/pdf/fonkbericht0601.pdf/ (10 February, 2006).

16 See also Schlobinsky 2005, Jan Schmidt, Martin Wilbers. "Wie ich blogge?! Erste Ergebnisse der Weblogbefragung 2005" (Januar 2006), Forschungsstelle "Neue Kommunikationsmedien". URL: http://www.fonk-bamberg.de/pdf/fonkbericht0601.pdf/ (10 February, 2006).

for making *blogs* accessible to everybody; only ten percent of *bloggers* close their *blogs*, marking them 'for friends' use only'.[17]

The results of the research concerning personal information in Russian *blogs* are shown in the table below (Schlobinski, Siever 2005: 234).

Table 1: Personal information in Russian blogs

Name	76.6%
E-mail	63.3%
Profession/job	36.6%
Date of birth	30.0%
Photo	26.6%
Address	20.0%
ICQ number	16.6%

Similar research has been conducted into German *bloggers*.

Table 2: Personal information in German blogs

Address	86.6%
Date of birth	60.0%
Name	40.0%
ICQ number	33.3%
Hobbies	30.0%
Job/profession	10.0%

It can be seen from the tables above that Russian bloggers are more willing to publish their names and information about their jobs/professions than Germans. This probably has something to do with national character. Moreover, as far as job and profession are concerned, most Russian *bloggers* are claimed to be office managers, businessmen, writers or programmers.[18] Accordingly, mentioning one's profession in the personal information field in a *blog* is a question of prestige.

17 Ibid.

18 Such conclusions were drawn on the basis of the analysis of personal information given by *bloggers* on www.livejournal.com.

On the other hand, Germans are keener to share information about their date of birth and address. Then again, women tend to conceal information about their age. In Russia this tendency is stronger owing to age prejudice. The same can be said about address: only 20 percent of Russian *bloggers* inform their readers of where they live. As living in the provinces is not 'prestigious', unlike Germans most Russian *bloggers* do not fill in the field 'address'.

Bloggers can also be classified as:[19]

- *Personal bloggers* – individual writers who normally create *blogs* of a personal type, online diaries that may sometimes be focused on some particular subject or topic;
- *Business bloggers* who blog to promote products and services. Their *blogs* have to offer real, usable information to readers like reviews, comments, links to relevant articles and similar resources;
- *Organizational bloggers* – blogging to communicate with fellow-employees, students and colleagues;
- *Professional bloggers* who are hired and paid to write *blogs.*

Personal bloggers are relevant for the present research. A *personal blogger* can be of any age, sex or level of education. On the whole, the average *blogger* is a teenager keeping an online journal of what goes on in their private life.

1.4 Reasons for the Popularity of Blogs

Above all, the question "So what makes people *blog*?" arises. The table below shows the results of a poll carried out in Germany.[20]

Table 3: Reasons for keeping a blog

For pleasure	70.8%
Because I like writing	62.7%
To record ideas and experiences	61.7%

19 "Just about anyone can use a blog!"
URL: http://weblogs.about.com/cs/we-blogs101/f/whoblogs.htm/ (13 June, 2006)

20 For more details see Jan Schmidt, Martin Wilbers. "Wie ich blogge?! Erste Ergebnisse der Weblogbefragung 2005" (Januar 2006), Forschungsstelle "Neue Kommunikations-medien". URL: http://www.fonk-bamberg.de/pdf/fonkbericht0601.pdf/ (10 February, 2006).

To discuss my ideas and experiences with the others	49.0%
In order not to keep my feelings to myself	44.5%
To share my knowledge of some particular subject with others	33.4%
To stay in touch with relatives and friends	33.2%
To find new friends	27.2%
Professional interest	12.7%
Other reasons	10.7%

Simply writing for oneself at home cannot be compared to publishing things on the Internet, where everyone can read them. Even those who had probably never written a line before began deriving pleasure from writing a *blog*.

The next category of answers is closely connected to people's feelings and private experiences that are important. The best way to preserve them or to understand them better is to share them with others. Sharing the knowledge one has means showing what one is worth.

Finding new friends or keeping in touch with them is one more reason for keeping a *blog*. Writing e-mails is currently passé. Whenever your friends wish to know how you are, they read the entries in your *blog*.

What makes *blogs* really popular is primarily the need for self-expression. By blogging, people develop a feeling of being able to write everything they want to. This very feeling could be characterized as one of complete freedom and impunity. These are the psychological reasons for *blogs* being so attractive. Moreover, the accessibility of the Internet and the ease of creating *blogs* add to their growing popularity.

Peter Schlobinski points out ten reasons for the success of *blogs* (Schlobinski, Siever 2005:16ff):

- From passive audience to active user

It means that every user can combine several roles at once: being the author of a *blog*, just a reader, or a writer of comments on the entries. This makes everyone part of the communication process.

- From media to content

Anything new attracts the immediate attention of the audience, especially the Internet audience. The successful cooperation between the new media, the Internet and software which are easy to use enables users to concentrate on the content of their creations and to obtain a deeper insight into the essence free from technical obstacles.

- From mono medium to multimedia

Blogs are not just texts – they can be enhanced with pictures, videos and music to prevent readers from getting bored.

- From periodical edition to real-time mode

By writing entries or reading them, one can get the feeling of being inside somebody else's life and following it in real time.

- From deficiency to redundancy

This point deals with information sources that with the appearance of *blogs* have become very popular among users as alternatives to traditional new sites. The reason is that they enable readers to get the information prefiltered by the *blogger* and to choose exactly what they are searching for.

- From 'edited by' to direct

Publishing whatever you want and how you want is the motto of *blogs*.

- From the distribution of access to the possibility for users to search, surf, navigate and decide for themselves

It is the feeling of freedom that comes from surfing on the Internet, where most of the pages are accessible, that makes *blogging* so popular.

- From one-way communication to interactivity

Nowadays the standard roles with news being delivered to – and passively received by – the public are no longer hard and fast. Anyone can take any role they wish.

- From linear to hypertext

It has become possible to switch to other sites and information channels with just one click of the mouse. Texts need no longer look boring; they can be made to attract readers' attention and to make navigation easier and more interesting.

- From data to knowledge

The continuous exchange of information contributes to the creation of worldwide knowledge.

The reasons mentioned above disclose the essence of the phenomenal popularity of *blogs* as a genre that grants self-realization to any average user. It is well known that the need for self-realization is at the top of the hierarchy of human needs which every individual tries to satisfy.

1.5 Classification of *Blogs*

Over time, *blogs* have been changed and modified, and many different types have appeared. They include the following:[21]

- *Business blog* – aims to promote or defame businesses, to argue about economic concepts, to disseminate information and more;
- *Cultural blog* – discusses music, the theatre, sports, popular culture, etc;
- *Gossip* – contains news and rumours of celebrities;
- *Link blog* – shares links to other resources with the reader;
- *Political blog* – aims to discuss politics and is normally news-driven;
- *Topical blog* – concentrates on some particular topic or subject matter;
- *Travel blog* – aims to share information and experiences gained during holidays;
- *Corporate blog* – is kept by members of corporations or other institutions to exchange information, news, etc;
- *Friend blog* – composed of short, frequently updated messages written by friends connected through similar interests.

Besides, there are the *community blog, moblog, science blog, spam blog, legal, directory, media, advice, religious blog,* etc. *Blogs* can also be classified by the type of media involved, such as *photo blogs* where the authors publish pictures, or *video blogs* containing numerous videos and the like. *Blogs* can take many forms as can be seen from the list of different types of *blogs* given above. New technologies allow users to choose between different interfaces to customize their own *blogs*. But as Meg Hourihan puts it: "If we look beneath the content of *weblogs*, we can observe the common ground all *bloggers* share – the format."[22]

---

21 Wikipedia, the free encyclopedia. URL: http://en.wikipedia.org/wiki/Types_of_blogs/ (15 May, 2003).

22 Cited from Carolyn R. Miller "Blogging as Social Action: A Genre Analysis of the Weblog." URL:http://blog.lib.umn.edu/blogosphere/blogging_as_social_action_a_genre_analysis_of_the_weblog.html (4 November, 2004).

However, common form does not necessarily mean common content. The posts of a *blog* differ greatly in size and content. "Ein Blogeintrag kann alles sein, vom Smiley über das Zitat eines anderen und einen Aphorismus bis hin zum Roman" (Alphonso, Pahl 2004:39). Although there are no limits on the content of entries, it is important to mention that entries reflect the subjective opinion of the author and allow the readers to form their own opinion. Personal thoughts are combined with links and comments in original *blogs* that are normally written in the first person singular.

But of course, not every *blog* contains all the forms and content mentioned above; moreover, *blogs* differ in regard to the aims behind them. Rebecca Blood, in particular, distinguishes three main types of *weblogs* according to their function: *filters*, *personal journals* and *notebooks* (quoted from Herring 2004:2).

- *A filter blog* is a prototype of weblogs.

The first page that was identified as a blog belonged to a filter type. The author or blog editor creates a list of links to other blogs or web sources they find of interest. Also, they provide comments and opinions on the news and current events. This type of blogging can be called external because the content deals with external information in regard to the author. The major goal is to help readers find their way in the flood of information on the WWW. Examples of this kind of blog are http://generatorblog.blogspot.com/ and http://www.mark-simonson.com/category/Links/.

- *Personal journals* are, on the contrary, internal in type.

They represent the author's inner world, their attitudes, feelings, experiences and the like.

These *blogs* being updated typically several times a day were instead a record of the blogger's thoughts that include the ones made on the way to work as well as notes about the weekend or a quick reflection on some subject. [23]

Parts 6 and 7 of this chapter will dwell upon this type of *blog* in detail. This particular type of *blog* is relevant for the present research. It should also be mentioned that the aim of such *blogs* is self-expression. The most popular sites where personal journals can be found are: *livejournal.com, mytagebuch.de, webblog.ru, technorati.com,* etc.

---

23 Rebecca Blood. "Weblogs: a history and perspective" (07 September, 2000), Rebecca's Pocket. URL: http://www.rebeccablood.net/essays/weblog_history.html/ (15 May, 2005).

- *Notebook* type is a kind of combination of the two types mentioned above.

The content may be either internal or external, with the entries being normally longer and topic-oriented. A good example of this kind of *blog* is www.pabspotpourri.blogspot.com.

As already mentioned, *filters* were the first types to appear while nowadays the second type of *blogs*, *personal journals*, prevail numerically, comprising 80% of all *blogs*.[24] Confusing the two terms *online journal* (or *diary*) and *blog* is fairly common. Someone who writes a journal on the Internet *is logging his life and not the Web*[25] while *weblogs* are primarily intended to log what is happening on the WWW. Nevertheless, as the number of online journals is growing and evidently exceeds the number of other *blogs,* the majority of users associate the term *blog* only with the journal type. This statement has found empirical support in the research findings of Susan C. Herring (2004:6). The vast majority of the *blogs* in this research were found to comprise the personal journal type (70.4%). It is relevant to mention that typical journal sites such as LiveJournal.com and Diaryland.com were excluded from the research presented, making the results even more striking. Therefore, in the next chapters the term *blog* will be used to identify the journal type relevant for the present research.

As mentioned above, *blogs* can be classified by the media involved, function, aims, etc. At this point it is relevant to introduce one more interesting classification suggested by Krishnamurthy.[26] He offered a classification of *blogs* that implies four different types according to two basic dimensions each with two values: personal vs. topical, and individual vs. community. This classification is illustrated in the diagram below:

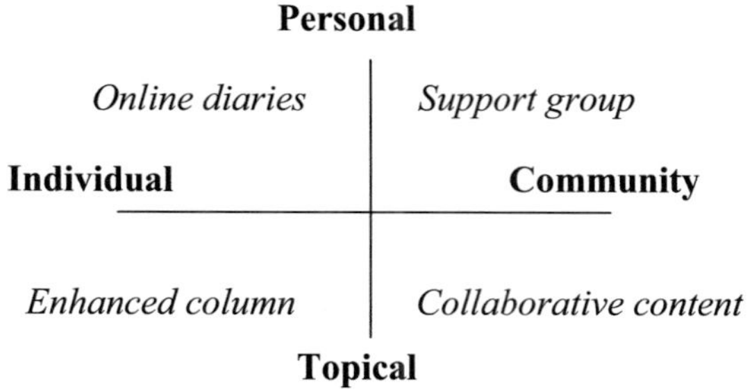

24 See statistical data presented on http://www.webstrannik.net/.

25 "What are blogs and how did they become so popular?" Ask Yahoo! (15 November, 2002). URL:http://ask.yahoo.com/ask/20021115.html (18 June, 2005).

26 See Susan C. Herring (2004:6).

As seen from the diagram above, *online diaries* are treated like highly personal, individual creations that make them closer to the prototypical diary genre.[27] Going back to the question of content, *blogs* can be classified in other ways depending on their content. First of all, they can be subdivided into *topic-oriented blogs* and *non-topic-oriented* ones.[28] *Topic-oriented blogs* are devoted to some particular subject. Good examples are *music blogs, computer blogs, sport blogs,* etc. The author may devote all the entries or just some of them to some definite subject. As far as *non-topic-oriented blogs* are concerned, they are not connected to a particular subject but instead are a potpourri of everything.

Topic-oriented blogs, where all the entries are devoted to some particular subject, contribute to forming communities. They are designed to attract as many readers as possible and often kept by several authors simultaneously. They could also be contrasted with the individual entries that are devoted to some particular topic and are considered to be incidental. The latter do not affect the individuality or personality of the blog.[29]

The main *blog* types are shown in the diagram below:

Figure 1: Classification of blogs

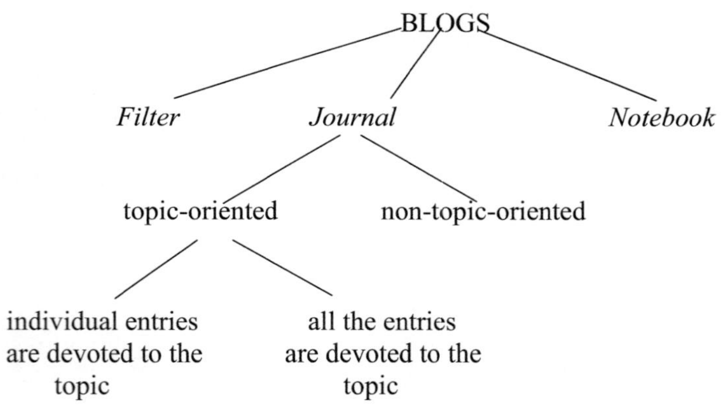

27 The comparison of two genres is made in Item 1.6.

28 See also Rebecca Blood "Weblogs: a history and perspective" (7 September, 2000), Rebecca's Pocket. URL: http://www.rebeccablood.net/essays/weblog_history.html/ (24 July, 2005).

29 For the present research topic-oriented blogs where only single entries are devoted to some particular subject, were chosen.

In the present paper, journal-type *blogs* will be analysed. They will be further subdivided into *topic-oriented blogs* (in which only individual entries are devoted to any particular topic) and *non-topic-oriented blogs*. These types of *blogs* appear suitable to help test the hypotheses mentioned above.

1.6 Online Diary vs. Handwritten Diary

The diary emerged as a separate genre long ago. It could also be considered one of the most popular genres ever because of its accessibility. One need not be a professional writer in order to keep a diary. A stereotypical or 'traditional' diary could be defined in the following alternative ways:

- "a personal record of daily events, appointments, observations, etc";[30]
- "a book in which you write down the things that happen to you each day";[31]
- "a diary or journal is a book for writing discrete entries arranged by date. It can be used for recording in advance appointments and other planned activities, and/or for reporting on what has happened over the course of a day or other period [...] Diaries run the spectrum from business notations to listings of weather and daily personal events through to inner exploration of the psyche, or a place to express one's deepest self".[32]

It should be mentioned at this juncture that the two terms 'diary' and 'journal' exist side by side with some still strictly differentiating between them. In this paper both concepts will be used synonymously. Moreover, it is important to say that this paper deals with the diaries that only contain personal records concerning the author's experiences over some period of time, as well as their feelings, attitudes, etc, not with entries reflecting lists of appointments and planned activities. Summing up the definitions of a diary mentioned above, the following features can be singled out:

- A diary is written by one person;
- A diary includes notes on one's private life;
- The notes are placed in chronological order;
- The information described in a diary is truthful;[33]

---

30 Collins Concise English Dictionary (2006:404).

31 Longman Dictionary of Contemporary English (1995:372).

32 From Wikipedia, the free encyclopaedia. URL:http://wikipedia.org/ (15 May, 2003).

33 The dubious points concerning the degree of truthfulness will be discussed further in this chapter.

- A diary is written for oneself.[34]

The following definition of a diary may be suggested here:

A diary is a list of personal notes arranged in chronological order concerning one's private life that usually contain truthful facts and are written mainly for oneself.

Discussing this topic in greater detail, first of all, a diary is a product of one person; collective writing is not typical of a diary. As such, it should possess such features as intimacy. Everything that could be found in a stereotypical diary deals with the private life of its author. Secondly, the chronological order of the notes is also an important feature of a diary. An author describes day-by-day events that happen in their private life, their reactions, their feelings, etc. Everything that an author is not willing to share with others finds its home in diary notes.

Finally, sincerity is also an important feature of a diary. Only true events and feelings are to be found in a stereotypical diary, which is why diaries are intimate items which are kept hidden from external readers. One normally writes a diary for oneself, although some celebrities publish their diaries in order to make their private life accessible to the masses.

Nowadays, the still-popular traditional handwritten diary has an online counterpart, the *'weblog'* or just *'blog'*.[35] This combination seems paradoxical as the diary has always been regarded as representing an intimate side of one's private life while everything connected to the mass media is usually associated with publicity. The numerous definitions of *blog* were mentioned in the previous section. Now it is important to compare a traditional handwritten diary with a *blog*, identifying both the features that bring them closer to each other and those that constitute the major differences in order to understand how and why they diverged.

Blog is a combination of genres "that straddles and confuses ideals of the literary and non-literary, public and private." (McNeill 2006:1) On the one hand, it can be treated as an embodiment of the Internet genre, or as a popular forum where everyone who has read a diary entry can comment on and discuss it with other users or just chat.[36] But on the other hand it has preserved some of the features of a printed diary. Attempting to transfer the stereotypes and the rules of a

34 As in the case of truthfulness, this point will be discussed later in this chapter.

35 The definition and the main characteristics of a blog were given in Item 1.1.

36 Ibid.

printed diary to new surroundings, the writers themselves strive to invent the rules defining how a *blog* should look and be dealt with.

Normally, the entries in a *blog* should not be changed afterwards, and that makes it similar to a printed diary. Readers expect the entries to be written once and for all like those in a printed diary. Expectations have not been altered despite the new tendencies introduced into the genre by the Internet.

Furthermore, the readers of a *blog* expect the author to be truthful; they expect to find in online entries a truthful reflection of offline life just as they would in a traditional diary. As Laurie Mc Neill mentions: "Readers still expect texts that are personal, even intimate, even while they hope to become part of a community through the shared experience of reading these 'private' texts." (McNeill 2006:8) This rule only partially holds for *blogs* because the authors, wishing to impress their readers, often spice up their entries to make them more interesting.

Thirdly, the entries are placed in chronological order. In the case of *blogs* chronological order is preserved, albeit in reverse, with new entries being placed at the beginning. The subject matter of a *blog* is partly the same as that of a diary: a description of events and sharing feelings, although in some *topic-oriented blogs* a wide range of different subjects described can be found as well. That is the main idea that is shared by both a *blog* and a diary.

When writing entries in a *blog*, the author seeks a response from the readers while a diary does not. "While writing to an actual reader in a print diary may be viewed as breaking general 'rules', doing so online is not just expected but demanded."(McNeill 2006:4) By introducing a number of rules for readers, authors anticipate possible negative reaction and misunderstandings that allow keeping supposed new readers. The style of a *blog* – the lexis the author uses – is important to him; the aims of an online diarist are to be appreciated by the readers and as a result to –build up a community. If the author fails to attract readers, this is due to his incapacity to "perform the genre" (McNeill 2006:4). The author of a print diary, on the other hand, does not pay any attention to the form; their creation is not normally intended for an external reader. Hence the style is not really important. All the features concerning a handwritten diary mentioned above are generalized, as each diary is unique and deviations from the norm described are possible.

The last but still the most important feature based on the above is the communication formula. For a written diary it could be formulated as follows: "One typically writes for himself, but when it comes to a *blog*, one writes for many." This is the feature which poses many questions as a number of different opinions exist. For example, T. Mallon states that "…writing for self does not exist in any real sense.... Ultimately all discourse is intended for an audience other than the self who is doing the writing" (1984:66; quoted from Miller, Shepherd 2004) whereas Elbow disagrees by pointing out that "writing can be private and the self can constitute the sufficient audience." (Ibid.) Diaries have often been published throughout history. This fact argues for writing for a potential audience, but on the other hand authors of a diary, despite probably keeping in mind some potential unknown readership, still hide it from those around them at the time of writing. This could be the main feature of writing for oneself: the author of a diary addresses everybody and nobody in particular at the same time, just as a *blogger* does. "Why it's OK to have millions of strangers look at your journal, but not your Mom, is beyond me." (Mister Bad 1999; quoted from Miller, Shepherd 2004) This statement brings the two genres closer to each other.

On the other hand, it was stated that if a person was asked to simultaneously keep two diaries, one traditional and the other posted on the Internet, the entries would drastically differ from each other.[37] In the first place, this difference can be rooted in the audience the author is anticipating or the absence of such. The following statement seems optimal for resolving the problem concerning the communication formula: a traditional handwritten diary is normally kept for oneself or for potential strangers while a *blog* is written for actual strangers. The audience, be it expected or existing, sometimes even consisting of just oneself, is what brings the two genres closer to each other and yet constitutes the major difference between them.

The following diagram depicts the relationship between a *blog* and a diary in a general sense. The doubtful points concerning a diary and a *blog* are shown on a scale.

Figures 2.3: Blog vs. Diary

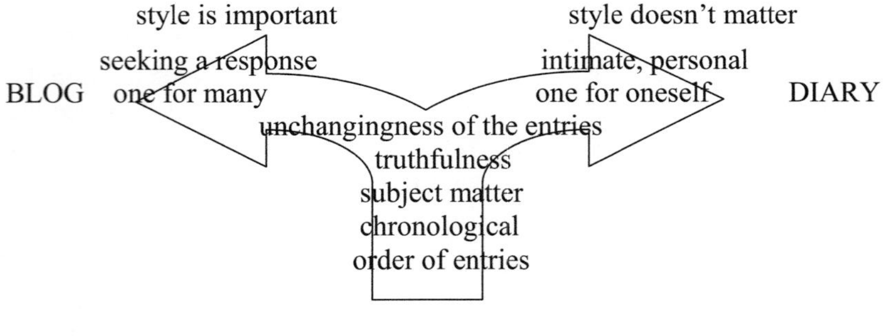

37 See Валерия Бескаравайная "Повседневность: век спустя..." URL: http://sociologist.nm.ru/articles/beskaravainaja_01.htm/ (15 June, 2005).

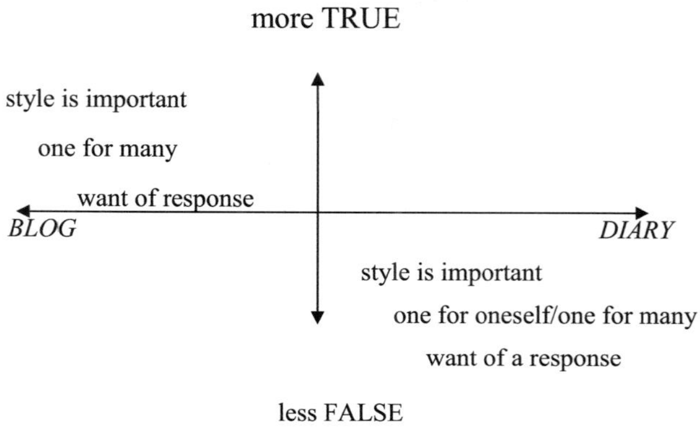

Bearing in mind that authors of diaries write not only for themselves but also for potential readers, characteristics of blogs such as 'style is important', 'want of response' and 'one for many' could be also partially applied to diaries – which explains why these characteristics lie somewhere between 'true' and 'false' on the scale.

In conclusion, the reasons for diaries undergoing such drastic changes from intimate to public are to be found in the evolution of moral values, technical progress and other societal changes. Thanks to the Internet, many normal people have found a way to gain public acknowledgment. The best way for an ordinary person to demonstrate their 'significance' and attract attention is to publish a diary and make it accessible to readers. By contrast, others lock up their diaries – which arouses readers' curiosity. The number of those who wish to share the details of their own private life, truthful or sometimes embroidered, is increasing exponentially, making the whole issue of *blogs* more popular and more important from day to day.

As far as the relationship between a handwritten diary and a *blog* is concerned, Laurie McNeill (2006:6) acknowledges that, "Perhaps we can read the *blog* as simply as another kind or fiction of the diary genre, one particularly well-suited to contemporary diarists." In other words, *blogs* serve as a bridge between the Internet and a printed culture that is a result of cooperation between writers and readers. It should also be mentioned that the latter reflects the state of things in modern society and culture.

1.7 The Blog as a New Text Type

The problem of text types and text typology has been exhaustively discussed elsewhere.[38] In the present paper, an attempt will be made to describe *blogs* as a new text type by dwelling on the unique characteristics that make them different from neighbouring text types such as personal homepages and diaries.

1.7.1 Terminology

First of all, we need to state what is actually meant by a text type. We should distinguish between speakers' general knowledge about text types and theoretical linguistic knowledge intended to provide text typology.[39] As Heinemann (2002:141) puts it, "Textsorten gehören zum Alltag und zum Alltagswissens der Kommunizierenden." Every speaker is able to distinguish between text types (varieties) that belong to their everyday life. They are able to not only recognize but also produce them. Nevertheless, being a part of everyday knowledge, text varieties do not exist in reality. As noted by prominent scholars, only knowledge of them exists, in contrast to specific examples representing text varieties in reality (Heinemann 2002:140).

On the other hand, there is theoretical knowledge of text types that is applied in text linguistics:

> Texttyp hingegen wird als eine theoriebezogene Kategorie zur wissenschaftlichen Klassifikation von Texten verstanden, die auf eine Erscheinungsform von Texten bezogen wird, die im Rahmen einer Text- bzw. Gesprächstypologie beschrieben und definiert ist. (Heinemann/Viehweger 1991:144)

Here we deal with text varieties (text types) as a part of general knowledge and text types as a subject for text analysis. In order to clearly distinguish between the two phenomena, it would be appropriate to give Isenberg's definition (1983):

> Den Ausdruck Textsorte verwenden wir als bewußt vage gehaltene Bezeichnung für jede Erscheinungsform von Texten, die durch die Beschreibung bestimmter, nicht für alle Texte zutreffender Eigenschaften charakterisiert werden kann, unabhängig davon, ob und auf welche Weise diese Eigenschaften im Rahmen einer Texttypologie theoretisch erfassbar sind. Im Unterschied hierzu gebrauchen wir den Terminus Texttyp als theoriebezogene Bezeichnung für eine Erscheinungsform von Texten, die im Rahmen einer Texttypologie beschrieben und definiert ist. (quoted from Gülich 1986:17).

Isenberg uses two terms, *Textsorte* and *Texttyp,* to refer to different realizations of the same phenomenon. In practical terms, one and the same phenomenon

---

38 See Adamzik 1995, Dimter 1981, Gülich 1986, Heinemann 2002, Sommerfeldt 2001.

39 See also Heinemann 2002, Adamzik 1995, Gülich 1986.

could be defined as a *Textsorte* (text variety, text type) if we are talking about each realization of a number of specific characteristics that distinguish it from other *Textsorten* (text varieties, text type) and, on the other hand, could be called a *Texttyp* (text type) if the aim is to define and describe a generalized realization of it with the means of text typology.

The difference between the two terms lies not only in the subject for analysis but also in the way analysis is carried out. *Textsorten* (text varieties, text type) are described as a collection of distinctive features while the analysis of a *Texttyp* (text type) is more complicated.[40]

As far as purely differentiating between the terms is concerned, a speaker's everyday knowledge could be said to comprise a number of text types that are represented in reality by a number of specific examples while in the text typology a generalized form of the text types is relevant for the purposes of text or speech analysis. This differentiation is clearly shown in the table below.

Figure 4: Differentiation of terms: text variety and text type

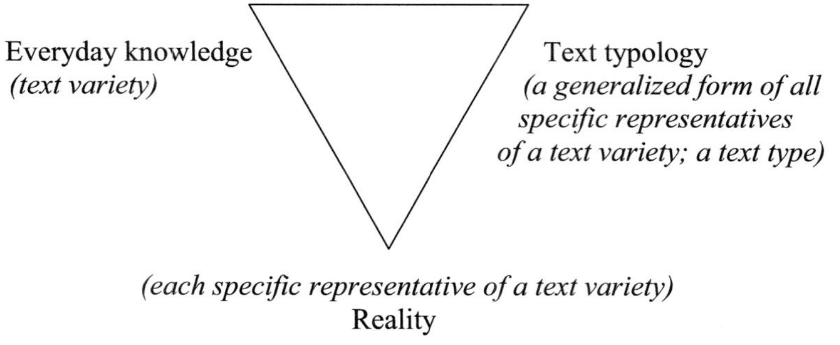

For the present research, any further distinction between the variety of texts or text types will not be made as, according to the diagram above, the terms *text type* and *text variety* can be used synonymously as different realizations of the same phenomenon. To support this, the following example could be provided.

Weather forecast

Everyday knowledge: a weather forecast is usually shown on TV after the news and is also reported on the radio. The forecast includes an update on the weather over the coming days and is usually two or three minutes long.

Reality: a weather forecast was broadcast at 9.15am on 9 August 2006 on BBC.

40 In this paper blogs will be analysed as a Texttyp (text type). See 1.7.2–1.7.3.

Text typology: a weather forecast on TV.

No matter how different the approaches are, the subject is the same in all three cases. In this work, the term *text type* will be used in relation to everyday knowledge, reality and text typology.

This paper deals with the text type *blog* with respect to text typology and text analysis, which is why an attempt will be made here to conduct the analysis based on the generalized form of specific representatives of the text type '*blog*' using a corpus made up of a number of specific representatives existing in reality. Although the *blog* is a relatively new phenomenon, it can hardly be traced back to traditional text types generally familiar to all speakers (e.g. prescription, letter, recipe, news, advertisement, etc). Blogs are becoming more popular day by day and gaining more and more attention.

1.7.2 Approaches to Analysis

As mentioned above, a text type in the sense of text typology cannot be described just as a group of distinctive features. A number of attempts have been made to establish a unified approach to the analysis of text types. Here are some examples.

Dimter (1981) distinguished four differentiating criteria: *form, situation of communication, function, and content.*

Regarding *form*, vocabulary, syntax and layout are referred to.

Situation of communication refers to the identity and number of producers, recipients, channel, time and place reference, correlation between the producer and the recipient, etc.

Function – "Die Funktion eines Textes ist dabei die einem Sprecher zu einem bestimmten Zweck, d.h. zur Erreichung eines bestimmtes Zieles zu dienen." (Dimter 1981:52)

Content – not just the subject but also the relationship between the content on the one hand, and the time and place of production on the other.

The approach of Gülich/Raible (1975), who differentiate between *textexterne* (text-external) and *textinterne* (text-internal) characteristics seems to be more detailed.

> Die textinternen Merkmale eines Textvorkommens ergeben sich durch eine Auswahl aus den Regeln des Sprachsystems und deren Anwendung durch den Textproduzenten. (quoted from Dimter 1981:15)

while

> Textexterne Merkmale sind solche, die sich auf die Faktoren " Sprecher", "Hörer"- und mit ihnen " Intention" und "Reaktion" sowie "Bereich der Gegenstände und Sachverhalte" bzw. "Kommunikationssituation" im Modell sprachlicher Kommunikation beziehen. (quoted from Sulter 1993:38)

This concept includes speech function, type of communication process, subject and circumstances of communication, common situation of communication between the producer and recipient, and the direction of communication.

The existing points of view were supplemented by Olaf Kron (2002:20), whose contribution is shown in the table below.

Table 4: Text internal and external characteristics

Text internal characteristics	*Text external characteristics*
Text structure, layout (formal visual characteristics of the text)	Type of communication process
Complexity of the text	Channel
Sentence types (what sentence types prevail)	Intention of producer and text function, illocution
Lexis (the register used: formal, informal, colloquial words, terms, use of Anglicisms, clippings, acronyms, etc)	Recipient behaviour
Deixis	Situation (circumstances) of communication (number of participants, how many times the speaker changes, the type of relationship between the partners, local and temporal orientation, theme fixation)
Greeting and parting formula	
Tense (the choice of tense due to the aims of communication)	

Basically, four criteria for text analysis exist,[41] namely:

- Structural (grammatical) criteria (concentrated on text-internal features) (Harweg 1979; Werlich 1975);
- Situational criteria (sociolinguistic perspective; Malinowski 1923; Firth 1957; Halliday 1964,1981);
- Functional criteria (the emphasis is on text external characteristics, with pragmatic text functions at the heart; Oomen 1971);

41 See also Kron 2002, Suter 1993.

- Integrative approach (de Beaugrande 1981; Dressler 1981; Dijk 1977).

Traditional text types are seen as institutionalised, internalised text strategies: conventional text patterns the study of which requires an interdisciplinary fusion of methods and insights from text and discourse linguistics, psycholinguistics, pragmatics, sociolinguistics, and artificial intelligence. (Sulter 1993:40)

The analysis of *blogs* as a new text type requires a combination of different criteria. In order to show the versatile nature of *blogs*, both text-internal features and text-external ones will be emphasized. Nevertheless, for the analysis and description of *blogs*, the above-mentioned criteria do not seem sufficient as we should also take into consideration the fact that *blogs* are part of Internet culture with its own peculiarities. Hence some additional criteria for analysis and description should be introduced, namely *hypertextual characteristics, orality vs. literacy* and *spelling.*

- Hypertextual layout

As already mentioned above, *blogs* have gained their popularity partly due to the transition from linear to hypertextual layout. The possibility of acquiring all the information one needs from one place can be realized by users of the WWW by just following the appropriate links.

"Mr. Nelson introduces the concept of the hypertext, which is a more flexible, more generalized, non-linear representation of material on a particular subject". (Wedeles 1965; quoted from Huber 2003:15) He considered that thoughts do not move in a linear way but form swirls. Hypertexts are made to support thoughts in moving in their natural way. To disclose the nature of hypertext, definitions by Oliver Huber (2003:45) can be presented: "Allgemein formal besteht ein Hypertext aus Knoten und per Mausklick direkt ausführbaren Links" and "Hypertexte sind im elektronischen Medium realisierte, tendenziell nichtlineare und potentiell multimedial ausgerichtete Texte".

The following hypertextual elements can be identified: *links, comments, search options, polls, guest books, possibility to change the layout, external contents, counter, calendar,* etc. Accordingly, each web page is an example of a hypertext as each page contains at least a number of links if not all possible elements.

Furthermore, it will be shown what hypertextual elements are typical of *blogs.*[42]

42 See Item 1.7.3.

- Orality vs. literacy

The terms konzeptionelle Schriftlichkeit (conceptual literacy) and konzeptionelle Mündlichkeit (conceptual orality) were introduced by Koch/Oesterreicher (1990). Konzeptionelle Schriftlichkeit means communication from a distance while konzeptionelle Mündlichkeit refers to communication in close proximity. The following table lists the main points of both phenomena and contrasts them according to conditions of communication and speech realizations.

Table 5: Conceptual literacy vs. conceptual orality

Koch/Oesterreicher 1990

Nähe		Distanz
Kommunikationsbedingungen		*Kommunikationsbedingungen*
- Privatheit		- Öffentlichkeit
- Vertrautheit		- Fremdheit
- Emotionalität		- keine Emotionalität
- Situations-und Handlungseinbindung		Situations-und Handlungentbindung
- physische Nähe		- physische Distanz
- Dialogizität		- Monologizität
- Spontaneität	**graphish**	- Reflektiertheit
	⟺	
Versprachlichungsstrategien	**phonisch**	*Versprachlichungsstrategien*
- Präferenz für nichtspachliche Kontexte		- Präferenz für spachliche Kontexte
- geringer Planungsaufwand		- hoher Planungsaufwand
- Vorläufigkeit		- Endgültigkeit
- Aggregation		- Integration

If we look at the characteristics of *conceptual orality* and *conceptual literacy,* it is clearly apparent that in the case of *blogs* they overlap with each other. Regarding *private vs. public* or *intimacy vs. estrangement*, there is no doubt that according to these categories *blogs* are definitely representatives of *communicative distance*. But if we consider the opposition *emotionalism vs. unemotionalism, blogs* tend towards an expression of emotionalism that is typical of orality (communicative proximity). Because in *blogs* communication is distant and is performed in writing to express emotions, grapho-stylistic means are applied (emoticons and smileys); in order to show emotions, the producer often uses interjections, onomatopoeic means, capital letters, etc. These means can sometimes be as emotional as mimics or gesticulation in face-to-face communication.

Situations und Handlungseinbindung vs. Situations und Handlungsentbindung (situation-and-activity involvement vs. situation-and-activity isolation). In the case of face-to-face oral communication, the participants tend to take an active part in conversation in order to become part of the situation and action surrounding it. On the other hand, the main aim of the producer of the written text is to pour out what they wish to say while that of the recipient is to accept it, with no situation or activity being involved. As far as *blogs* are concerned, the author can create a feeling of personal presence similar to in face-to-face conversation by using direct addresses and describing each detail of the setting, although this is rather rare. This makes overlapping between orality and literacy possible at this point.

The next point is *physische Nähe vs. physische Distanz (physical proximity vs. physical distance)*. This point poses no questions since in the case of *blogs* we are dealing with communication where partners are located at a physical distance from each other. A dubious point is, on the other hand, the question concerning *Dialogizität vs. Monologizität (dialogue-vs.-monologue form)*. It seems quite clear using the example of *blogs* that they should be classified under the monologue form. On the other hand, if we consider the possibility of the reader to leave comments on entries (implying feedback by the author and an additional reaction on their behalf), a kind of a dialogue may appear on the Internet stemming from a pure monologue genre, a diary.

Moreover, the question of *Spontaneität vs. Reflektiertheit (spontaneity vs. consideration)* is relevant for discussing the problem of orality and literacy. It is evident that some *bloggers* write their entries spontaneously without any preparations, mental or otherwise. An entry consisting of just one smiley is evidently spontaneous. If an entry is written immediately after some event has happened in order to describe and capture it, it can also be regarded as spontaneous. On the other hand, a long detailed story is an instance of careful planning when the story has been thought over. Therefore, in *blogs* these two characteristics, namely spontaneity and consideration, overlap each other.

Talking about *Versprachlichungsstrategien*, overlapping can also be observed here. It is evident that *Präferenz für spachliche Kontexte (preference for language contexts)* and *Endgültigkeit (finality)* are typical of the text type *blog,* while *hoher Planungsaufwand (high planning effort),* as in the case of *Spontaneität vs. Reflektiertheit (spontaneity vs. consideration)*, is not an obligatory feature, and instances of *Aggregation (aggregation)* can be found in *blogs* along with *Integration (integration).*

The qualities of *blogs* in respect to the uncertain points of overlapping orality and literacy are shown in the following table:[43]

Table 6: Orality and literacy in blogs

BLOGS	
orality	*literacy*
emotionalism	strange
situation and activity involvement	public
dialogue form	physical distance
spontaneity	
little planning effort	preference for language contexts
aggregation	finality

- Spelling

A relaxed attitude tends to be taken to language on the Internet, sometimes ignoring the basic rules. Typing means saving time. And in order to maximise people's spare time, tools have been invented that make typing not only faster but more productive as well. One example is clippings, along with other varieties of shortening such as acronyms and the ellipsis. Furthermore, greater tolerance of spelling mistakes is to be observed. For example, ignoring the rules of capitalizing nouns in German seems to have become a norm, as has a lack of commas and other syntactic signs.

If someone makes a bad spelling mistake on the WWW, it is simply accepted and not construed as indicating that the person is unintelligent or uneducated – as would have happened had the same mistakes been made on paper.[44] To sum up, therefore, having examined all the peculiarities of *blogs*, the representation and analysis of them as a new text type will be based on the following characteristics.[45]

43 The realization of the characteristics will be shown in the next part of this chapter.

44 Examples will be given in the next part of this chapter.

45 See Gülich, Raible 1975.

Figure 5: Main characteristics of blogs

Text-internal features	*Text external features*
- Form (visual characteristics)	- Situation of communication:
- Hypertextual peculiarities	- Function
- Language (lexis, syntax, spelling)	- Number of participants
- Oral and literal features	- Exchange of the roles between participants
- Text-picture relations	- Type of relation between partners
- Content	- Time relation
	- Local relation
	- Channel
	- Form of communication

1.7.3 Text-internal Features[46]

It is evident that there is a great difference between *personal blogs* and *news blogs* or some other types of *blogs*.[47] Peter Schlobinski (2005:126ff) singles out the following linguistic differences and peculiarities concerning *personal blogs:*[48]

- Conversationality (on a graphical, lexical. and syntactic level);
- A rather large number of errors (mostly typing mistakes);
- Expressivity (new words, metaphors, inverted word order);
- Ironical character (word play, style mix).

All these features belong to text-internal features and will be discussed below along with corresponding examples.

a. Form/layout

"Hinter der Fassade eines Weblogs liegen grundsätzlich so genannte Templates, in welche Datenbankwerte an vorher definierte Orte automatisch eingefügt werden". (Schlobinski/ Siever 2005:58)

46 See the classification by Gülich, Raible (1975) in Item 1.7.2.

47 See Item 1.1.

48 Only personal blogs are relevant for the present analysis.

The software produced especially for the creation of *blogs* has given each user the opportunity to easily create their own *blogs*. Based on this software, all *blogs* look practically the same.

There is a header at the top of the page, followed by one, two or three columns. It may look like this, 2 and 3 being the most popular layouts.[49]

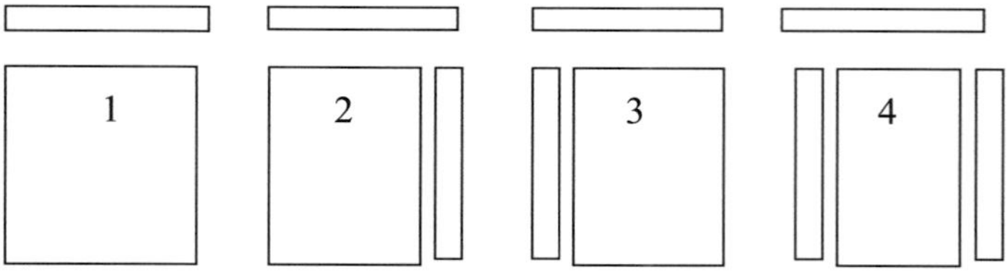

The header contains the name of the *weblog*. Naming the journal is essential.

The following features are also normally preserved in the diary and can be seen in the layout:

- Personal info;
- Calendar;
- Archive;
- Friends;
- Search;
- Guest book;
- Comments;
- Links;
- External content;

etc.

Most of them belong to the hypertextual characteristics and will be discussed later in this chapter. Here it is relevant to point out that all the categories mentioned are placed either in the header, as the case of layout 1, in the side columns, as in layouts 2 and 3, or separated between side columns, as in layout 4. The background is normally coloured or consists of pictures.

---

49 100 blogs were examined – and 78 blogs out of 100 were found to correspond to layouts 2 or 3.

Basically, what a user can do to customize their *weblog* is to choose a layout (layouts 1–4), state personal features from info to external content, choose the background colour and style, and finally lay out their content until the site is done.

b. Hypertextual characteristics

Hypertextual characteristics constitute an important part of each diary. Their function is to introduce the author (*personal info)*, including demonstrating their productivity by naming and listing the entries written with the help of a *calendar* and *archive.* The features *friends* and *guest book* contribute to increasing the popularity of the journal. As each *blog* is a part of either a *community* or *blogosphere links* and *external content,* it is also relevant for the layout. The feature *comments* enables the author to receive feedback from the audience and to establish a kind of a dialogue form of communication.[50]

Generally speaking, the above-mentioned hypertextual characteristics aim to connect and link up not only the users of a *blogosphere* but also all the available information they exchange in order to imitate the *swirls*[51] of information. Hypertextual features are normally placed in the side columns. The most popular and commonly used ones are *links* and *comments*, both of which can be also placed directly after the entry.

c. Language

- Layout

Before analysing the language peculiarities of *blogs*, it is relevant to dwell on the layout of an entry. As mentioned above, an entry in a *blog* may contain anything from a smiley to a novel, although there are still some features that are obligatory for each entry. First of all, the date on which the entry was written is essential. (As the entries are placed in reverse chronological order, the new ones appear at the top of the page.) Secondly, the name of the entry is important, too. The name normally hints at the content of the entry or is somehow connected to it (e.g. 'Wochenende war nicht der Knaller.........', 'Hitzetod', 'Steuererklärung', 'последние выходные праздной жизни..', 'про людей'). Then again, there are entries with no subject.

Furthermore, some bloggers address the readers directly, as if they were friends, or address the diary, e.g.:

---

50 See Item 1.7.2.

51 Wedeles 1965.

- Hey..
- so hallö meine freunde...
- Liebes Tagebuch!
- He guten Morgen Ihr lieben.
- Доброе утро!
- Дорогие мои...
- Привет всем

Then the body of the text is to be found followed by parting words such as 'So long...', 'Na denn, auf bald', 'Wir melden uns wieder, sobald es Neues aus Bergen gibt', 'не скучайте', 'пока', etc. After that, some hints at the current mood of the author may optionally be provided. They take the form of smileys, pictures or words.

e.g. Current Mood: good, Winks , i'm a NICE person, , traurig, настроение: Ликующее.

Sometimes, the template allows for the music the author is listening at the moment to be mentioned, e.g.: 'music: Moby.'

Here are examples of a typical *blog* entry:

«•133•»	[Monday August 8th, at 1:05pm]
[**mood**|] Hmh... ja. Die letzten Tage viel zu tun. Und morgen gehts wieder los. Auf,auf nach Berliiiin *freu* Werde heute Sachen packen und mich freuen wie ein Schneekönig. Auch wenn wir nur 2 Tage dort bleiben. :) Bis dann ^^	

Чемоданное настроение	**Jul. 20th, 2006 @ 01:20 am**

	Ну всё, мои дорогие, остался всего один день для сборов. Вещей, кажется, как всегда больше, чем чемоданов... %) Вылет аж в 6.45 утра, так что поспать вряд ли удастся вообще мне завтра. Старший немного приболел еще. :(Но надеюсь, что всё будет нормально. Всем хорошей погоды, веселого настроения и побольше отдыха - по возможности! Не скучайте! :) (6 comments | Leave a comment)

- *Lexis*

The first point is the register of lexis used in *blogs*. The language of *blogs* is determined by common tendencies of Internet language, namely the use of mainly *colloquial style* such as:

- "noch 2 Folgen und die erste Staffel ist durch…Wir waren teilweise völlig *platt…*"
- "auf den scheinbar Schwächeren *rumzuhacken*",
- "*Hocke* im Büro"
- «за 12 деревянных *кусков* в месяц»
- «Прямо перед закрытием *вломилась* в магазин»

Specific suffixes are added to create colloquial equivalents to neutral lexis: погод-ка (погода), дене-жк-и (деньги), размер-чик (размер).

It is also relevant to point out the numerous *subcolloquial (taboo)* words and expressions:

- "Wobei der Morgen echt besch..... ist!"
- "Was soll die scheisse?"
- «геоактивный день, блять?!»
- «что всем откровенно насрать»

Discourse particles, interjections are also very popular among *blog* authors, e.g. hm..., ahja , Mh…,мммммммммм!!!, йеее etc.

Excessive use of anglicisms is also to be observed in *blogs* – which is why *blogs* were chosen as the object of the present research. As mentioned above, they reflect the natural spontaneous speech which has its peculiarities as being part of Internet culture, with the excessive use of anglicisms being one of these peculiarities making *blogs* valuable for the research of anglicisms in general. This aspect is addressed in the following chapters.

- *Syntax*

The common tendency to be observed in the Internet is ignorance of the rules in order to optimize and expedite writing. Syntactical level is characterized with the use of elliptical constructions. The ignorance of punctuation marks is also typical.

- *Spelling*

"Spontanschreiben und virtuelle Kommunikation direkten Einfluss auf die Verwendung des orthographischen Systems haben." (Schlobinski/Siever 2005:72) The following features are characteristical of this influence.

Shortening in all its possible realizations is a characteristic of *blogs:*

- Omission of final vowels by German personal forms of the verbs, adverbs, etc. (*brauch, hab, heut*);
- Omission of initial vowels of articles (*ne Frage*);
- Shortening (*и* instead of *und; фотка – фотография;чел – человек);*
- Blending, syncope, ellipsis, assimilation (*denkste, inne kühlkiste, Ex, so isser halt, die andern warn, son* instead of *so ein; мобила – мобильный телефон);*
- Acronyms (*смс, НГ – новый год, МЧ – молодой человек, ДР – день рождения*);
- Ignoring the capitalization of initial letters of nouns in German and also failing to capitalize the first word at the beginning of a sentence;
- Hybrid writing in Russian.

This point should be addressed in more detail. As put by Larissa Shchipitsina (Schlobinski/Siever 2005:225): "The most striking peculiarity (of *Russian blogs*) – the use of hybrid Latin-Cyrillic writing in words and word-combinations".

Five ways of integrating Latin writing into Russian web language were determined by Guseinov (2000):[52]

- Insertion of a word or word-combination in a foreign language (in the original writing) in the Russian text: "В конце концов завтра все закончится. yo, baby", "PS-Happy birthday dear _alexandr_:)";

52 Quoted from Schobinski/ Siever (2005:238).

- Complete transliteration of Russian text "Nashli internet i zavisli v seti. %) Zdes zharko, more klassnoe. Ya podzharilas mestami. % (A v ostalnom, prekrasnaya markiza... :)))";[53]
- The use of corresponding Latin letters instead of Cyrillic ones on the keyboard. (З.Ы. Instead of P.S.);
- The formation of words using the combination of Latin and Cyrillic case: «Все покрылось плес Enew..» or attaching Russian suffixes to the foreign words in the original writing: «по дороге познакомилась с обалденным Lexus-ом...»;[54]
- Simulation of Cyrillic writing with the help of twelve letters from the Latin alphabet: "A Y BAC KAK?";

Generally speaking, hybrid writing is widespread, especially the types described in 1 and 4, which can be found in almost every *blog*.

On the other hand, the use of Cyrillic type instead of Latin when reproducing anglicisms is also typical of *blogs:* «сессия из овер..йеее», «ай эм мизерабль», «пЫсЫ»for P.S. Such insertions have emphatic aims; they have a higher grade of expressiveness (i.e. they attract attention).

Basically, a characteristic of *blogs'* language can be specified as follows: when writing, users take into consideration the phonetic image of the word more than its actual written form, which leads to a disregard for spelling norms. This is why one more point that merits discussion is spelling mistakes, which can be subdivided into *deliberate* and *accidental* ones.[55]

Mistakes that are made on purpose have emphatic aims, like attracting the attention of the reader or stressing the emotions the author wishes to express, etc. Examples of deliberate mistakes include *eigendlich, irgentwann, чо, Ужос, пропки, а я не знаю пачиму, Гермиону в прынцессы*.

Accidental mistakes can be further subdivided into

- Typing mistakes (made due to the confusion of letters close to each other on the keyboard, the omission of letters, the wrong combination of letters, double use of the same letter, etc): *"Lass mir Teit, lass ihm Zeit!", Porblem, irentwie, jednefalls, wweil, познаомился, Врочем, кончиах ,*

---

53 Complete transliteration is typical of the Russian speaking users who live abroad and normally use only Latin alphabet. Getting used to it they do not switch into Cyrillic.

54 In the next chapters it will be dwelt on this point in detail.

55 In some cases it is impossible to distinguish between mistakes made on purpose and accidental mistakes. That is why this subdivision can be assumed as rough.

будтно. On the other hand, repeated use of the same letter may also have emotional tinge: fury, irritation, sadness, etc.: *меня плюююющит, божжжже;*

"*Morgen fahren wir nach MÜÜÜÜÜÜÜÜÜÜÜÜÜÜÜNCHEN*";

- Words wrongly written together or separately*: magenschmerzen, nurnoch, wiede rhalb, непоможет , ооченьрано;*
- *Double* use of the same word.

One more point to mention here is striking out words and phrases that are later replaced with *others: ~~дробилка для костей~~ измельчитель для мойки, ~~бутылки выгребала~~ уборку делала.* They look original and at the same time very expressive.

All in all, a special language of *code* exists that can be characterized with the above-mentioned features. This *code* can be understood as a deviation from the norm with respect to written text, but seems to be a norm with respect to *blogs.*

d. Oral features

Oral features that place *blogs* somewhere between writing and speaking were discussed above in detail.[56] Here some examples are cited that support the hypothesis that *blogs* (in contrast to their prototype, the *diary*) have absorbed and acquired some specific features from Internet culture that place them a step closer to oral conversation.

> Das, was im Gespräch Gesprächspartikeln und Interjektionen, Prosodie, Mimik und Gestik funktional leisten, wird in bestimmten Kommunikationsformen durch Smileys und andere Mittel (Iterationen, Großschreibungen) ausgedrückt. (Schlobinski/Siever 2005:75)

- Grapho-stylistic features

During an oral conversation, the partners are able to use paralinguistic means to express their emotions. Although *bloggers* do not have this opportunity, various grapho-stylistic means are able to reflect the emotional side of the conversation almost as well as paralinguistic means.

The first way of expressing emotions is to use *smileys:*

"*hör ich jetzt mal lieber auf ;-)*", "*Er ist gestern durch die unmenschliche Hitze von uns gegangen*", "*(проехала все возможные повороты...))))*", *«как же я без книжжки.:(»*

---

56 See Item 1.7.2.

The next possibility is *emoticons*. Although they have the same aim as smileys, since they look like pictures, they can express a wider range of different emotions and feelings. There are static *emoticons* and animated ones (which unfortunately cannot be shown in print):

Winks  *, Und auch heute ist das wedder wieder bestens* *, АБАЖАЮ!!!и больше нет слов)))* 

Iterations are popular not only to express emotions but also to create the atmosphere of *live* conversation,[57] e.g. **haha*, *kotz*, *Heul*, *Schniff* ,*genervt bin*, "erst mal sollte ich hier vielleicht aufräumen…" *Putzlappen hol* ... Obwohl ... *Putzlappen wieder wegstell*", "ich kenne ihn nun seit... *rechen* ... 5 Jahren";*пошла макаться в ванную*, *Бубнит**

Interjections are also used to add to more emotionalism to entries:

"Mh…gleich müsste ich eigentlich mal in die Pause…", "Achja... Hab ne Frage an meine verehrten und hochgeschätzen Leser", «AAAAAAAAAAAa...Мамочки....я только что поняла, что подсела на tokio hotel...»

Onomatopoeic means have the same function as *iterations,* namely to create the effect of the reader's personal presence at the time of the conversation and to enhance an emotional effect:

«Ну и погодка тут, в вашей Москве... бррр..», «ich will nach hause....lalalalalalalalalalalalalalalala»

Moreover, literal means are used to help the author stress an idea to show its special significance in writing or, as Werry (1996) puts it:

> ... a complex set of orthographic strategies designed to compensate for the lack of intonation and paralinguistic cues that interactive written discourse imposes on its users. (Schlobinski/Siever 2005:75)

- The use of capital letters

"Und viele andere Dinger zu hause gehen auch zu bruch.... Mein PC mein HANDY mein TELEFON und vieles mehr."

«пока молнии сверкают и вот - вот (ВОТ ВОТ) пойдет дожжь.»

- Italics

"Es winkt eine Woche *mit* anschließendem Wochenende ohne Nachtdienst."

---

57 What is meant here is that iterations help to create the atmosphere of the conversation held in the real time mode as if it were a face-to-face conversation when all emotions can be detected in the body language that is involved in the conversation.

- Double or multiple letters

«я смирно стою, тока глаза на лоб вылезают от красотищщщи», «кууууллллл», "Morgen fahren wir nach MÜÜÜÜÜÜÜÜÜÜÜÜÜÜÜNCHEN"

Some syntactical means also have their specific function. Repeated punctuation marks like *question* or *exclamation marks* have an emphatic effect:

«подарил огромаднейший паззл с видом Коллизея!!!!!!!» (delight)

«что делать на НГ ума не приложу!!!!» (irritation/embarrassment)

"Warum vergesse ich das sooft????"(irritation)

As far as numerous uses of *ellipses* are concerned, they serve to create the impression that the author paused between sentences or thoughts. Alternatively, they can express doubts or the incompleteness of the thought:

«за весь день почти ничего не сделала... и что так уже противно стало... поняла.., что хочу работать!!!!»

"Mh...gleich müsste ich eigentlich mal in die Pause..."

Inverted word order, isolations and *rhetorical questions* also contribute to the oral nature of *blogs:*

«Ужос какой-то однако. Осень? », «Чудное утро. холодное. светлое.», «Вот и подарок будет мне.» ,"Heimweh..?", "achja und bleiben soll er", "das tut mir wirklich sehr leid. wirklich. sehr. und irgendwie is es auch total doof. und hässlich. ja. ich brauch ein neues design. egal».

e. Text–picture relations

Blogs can definitely be called a multimedia text type as they not only comprise textual characteristics but may also include pictures and sometimes videos. True, *blogs* are above all a diary on the Internet, which is why the textual part prevails. Nevertheless, in 60 per cent of *blogs* text is sustained by pictures. (Schlobinski/Siever 2005:237)

f. Content

Regarding content, there is no template to be followed. As far as personal *blogs* are concerned, the subjects that can be discussed are countless. Each user decides for themself what to write about. Anything can be discussed; there are no limits. The subjects dwelt on in *blogs* are only limited by the author's imagination.

Even so, Dimter (1981) points out some features of content, even if the subject cannot be defined. He proposed the following criteria: *Zeitbezug (tense relation), Fallbezug (case relation)* and *Wirklichkeitsbezug (reality relation).*

- *Zeitbezug*

The topic discussed in *blogs* can be regarded as happening before or at the same time as the entry is being written. The authors normally describe the events that have already happened in their life, although sometimes the events taking place at the time of writing are described, too.

- *Fallbezug*

The subject matter of *blogs* can be described as singular, as happening only once at a definite period of time, with definite persons in a definite place.

- *Wirklichkeitsbezug*

It is impossible to tell whether the events described in an entry are truthful as they are connected to the private life of the author. Of course, if the entry is read by someone closely connected to the author who is familiar with particular circumstances of their private life, they can probably tell whether the information is true. But generally speaking, it is assumed that the information given is truthful (although this can hardly be proved).[58]

One more point is the *relationship between producer/recipient and subject* (Brinker 2001:139). In the case of *blogs* there are two possibilities: subject = producer or subject = beyond communication partners. If the author of a *blog* describes the events which happened to them, the topic of the *blog* = the producer. If a *blog* deals with events which happened to someone else and did not concern the producer personally, then topic = beyond communication partners, as the communication partners have nothing to do with it directly.

The last point concerning content is *subject disclosure* in a *blog.* There are assumed to be four types of *subject disclosure:* descriptive, narrative, explicable and argumentative. (Ibid.)

Here, it is relevant to define a *subject:*

> ..definieren wir Thema als Kern des Textinhalts...Das Textthema (als Inhaltskern) ist entweder in einem bestimmten textsegment (etwa in der Überschrift oder einem bestimmten Satz) realisiert, oder wir müssen es aus dem Textinhalt abstrahieren, und zwar durch das Verfahren der zusammenfassenden (verkürzenden) Paraphrase. Das Textthema stellt dann die größtmögliche Kurzfassung des Textinhalts dar. (Brinker 2001:56)

---

58 See also Item 1.3.

In the case of *blogs* we usually deal with *narrative* subject disclosure. It consists of representation of the subject with one singular event in which the narrator somehow takes part.

1.7.4 Text-external Features

- *Communication situation*

The first point is that *a number of participants* are involved. *Blogs*, as already mentioned above, can be described using the formula *one writing for many.*[59] In the process of communication, we have one producer and an innumerable number of readers, some of them taking an active part in the process of communication and giving feedback in the form of comments. Overall, the number of participants is unknown.

As far as the *exchange of roles* during interaction is concerned, *blogs* tend to the form of a monologue more than a dialogue, although some features of a dialogue are preserved.[60] Roughly speaking, therefore, there is no exchange of roles during the conversation. The author produces a text, the recipient/reader accepts it, and in some cases provides feedback.

The *type of relationship between partners* is also important for the description of *blogs* as a text type. Generally speaking, the anonymity of the author is preserved. It can be *complete* if in the personal information the author does not disclose any details concerning their real life, or *partial* if, for example, they give their real name, place of residence and job. Even if the author gives full information about themself, the relationship between them and the readers can be called *strange/foreign/distant*. But there are rare cases when the readers know the author personally, which are defined as *close/personal* relations between the participants of communication.

The *channel* of communication in the case of *blogs* plays an important role. The participants do not communicate directly but instead via technical means. The formula *'producer – text – recipient'* should be expanded to *'producer – computer – blog software – blog (entry) – computer – recipient'*. These are the main stages of text production and reception. Generally speaking, the Internet can be defined as the main channel of communication with respect to *blogs*. Here we are dealing with computer-conditioned communication.

The *local orientation* of *blogs* is distant as the participants of communication remain at a physical distance from each other. The *temporal orientation* of *blogs* is asynchronous. There is a time gap between the production of the text, its reception and probable feedback, in contrast with for instance chats where, as in

59 Ibid.

60 See part Orality vs. Literacy of this chapter.

face-to-face communication, just a few seconds separate an entry written by an author from the feedback they receive.

- *Form of communication*

The variety of *Kommunikationsformen* proposed by Brinker (1997:138) needs to be considered. He states that there are five media: face-to-face communication, telephone, radio, television and writing. The peculiarities of each medium define different types and forms of communication.

If we describe a *blog* from the angle of the new medium the *Internet*, we obtain the following results:

Blog – way of communication: monologue with the features of a dialogue; channel – optical; asynchronous; distant; written but with the features of oral conversation.

- *Function*

The *function of a text* can be defined as the meaning that a text acquires during the process of communication, namely the purpose a text serves in the situation of communication. (Brinker 2001:83)

Moreover, the function can be considered a particular communicative intention of the producer which the recipient ought to recognize (Ibid.).

To indicate a text function, the following criteria should be applied (Ibid.):

- Language forms and structures, with the help of which the producer makes their intentions explicit;
- Language forms and structures, with the help of which the producer shows explicitly or implicitly their attitude to the content of the text and the subject in particular;
- Contextual indicators, such as situational context, public participation in the action, institutional restrictions of the text, the background.

Blog as a text type has an informative function.[61] It lies in the fact that the producer posts some information about or somehow connected to themself or about past or expected events in their life in a *blog*.

At this point it is relevant to present a typical *blog* entry with all the features mentioned and discussed above.

---

61 According to Dimter (1981), the following classes of texts can be distinguished by their function: Informationstexte, Appeltexte, Obligationstexte, Kontakttexte, Deklarationstexte.

User: Passwort: Login Passwort vergessen?

Start Anmeldung Tagebücher Mitglieder Forum Chat ? FAQ

Gedanken, Gefühle, Geheimnisse ... lesen und schreiben in der größten deutschen Tagebuch-Community!

Startseite » Tagebuch » User: adam_weishaupt [34 J.]

Online: Wähle aus

Mo	Di	Mi	Do	Fr	Sa	So
31	1	2	3	4	5	6
7	8	9	10	11	12	13
14	15	16	17	18	19	20
21	22	23	24	25	26	27
28	1	2	3	4	5	6

Februar 2011

Februar 1990 GO

Die letzten Einträge

- stimme
- dicke suppe
- was denn
- will nicht mehr
- das neue leben

alle Einträge

Einträge anderer Tagebücher

myTagebuch-Links

- Die neuesten Einträge
- Die neuesten Messages

Autor abonnieren

Möchtest Du immer über neue Einträge von adam_weishaupt informiert werden? Trage einfach Deine E-Mail-Adresse ein, an die Du die Abo-Mails erhalten möchtest.

eintragen

Du musst angemeldet und eingeloggt sein, um diesen Service nutzen zu können. Noch nicht registriert?

- Hier kostenlos anmelden!

Tagebucheintrag von adam_weishaupt [34 J.] vom 24.03.2006, 1:28 Uhr

stimme

ich muss in 4 h aufstehen um nach g. zu fahren. ich muss einige sachen erledigen. ich kann nicht schlafen. zuviele dinge gehen mir gleichzeitig durch den kopf. unser intro für unseren gig morgen. die ganzen sachen die ich in letzter zeit mit einigen besprochen hab zwecks bookings. alls stürtzt auf mich ein habe ich das gefühl. ich muss mir mal eine auszeit gönnen. ich habe zuviel probleme um sie jedesmal verdrängen zu können. es häuft sich alles an..wird immer mehr. ich bin noch eine woche hier..dann ziehe ich um...
wie wird das wohl in g. ich werde lebendig sein...und lebendig heisst ich werde meine probleme in den griff kriegen.

ich knall mich zusehr weg..ich muss bei mir bleiben..
ich suche die stille...das gleichgewicht mit mir...
ich habe das gefühl das in meinen kopf zuviel bereiche sind die ich nicht unter kontrolle habe.
ich möchte meine innnere stimme hören. ist das denken über diese zeilen meine innere stimme. wieso hör ich sie nicht. ich verstehe ich sie einfach nicht. ist sie zu leise oder bin ich zu laut?
geb ich ihr keine chance zur mir zu sprechen? ich will auf sie hören.....wo ist sie bloss???
sie ist irgendwo in mir.verschüttet?versteckt? verstecke ich sie vor mir?oder sie sich vor mir?
ich würde so gerne mehr auf mich hören. dann würde ich die dinge besser machen..mich besser machen..

Messages zu diesem Eintrag

Message senden

- Private Message
- Öffentliche Message

Um eine Mitteilung senden zu können, musst Du als Leser oder Autor registriert und eingeloggt sein.

- **hier kostenlos registrieren**

Deine Message, max. 2500 Zeichen

Zeichen insgesamt (von 2500)

senden

alle Einträge von adam_weishaupt

adam_weishaupt [34 J.]

Einträge: 21 | *alle Einträge*

Leser: 2717 | Ø 129 / Eintrag

Abonnenten: 1

Messages: 20

- Ausführliches Profil

[Home] [Mitglied werden] [FAQ] [Presse] [Impressum] [AGB]

Based on the example, the main characteristics of a *blog* as a text type are summed up in the table below:

Table 7: Text-internal and text-external features of a blog

Text-internal features		*Text-external features*	
Form	One- to three-column layout with a header. Navigational and hypertextual features in the side columns, entries in the centre	Function	Informative
Hypertext	Personal info, calendar, friends, guest book, comments, archive, links, external content, etc	Number of participants	Unknown
Language	Entry has a header (date, time, name of entry) followed by the body of the text; colloquial style of lexis used, dialects; simple syntax; a range of mistakes on different levels accepted as a new code in order to create emphatic effect; shortenings, hybrid writing	Exchange of roles	No exchange
Oral features	Grapho-stylistic means; use of orthographic, syntactic means to make speech emphatic	Type of relationship between partici-pants	In most cases foreign/stranger, although in some cases close relation is possible
Text-picture relation	Pictures support the text	Time relation between the recipient and producer	Asynchronous
Content	No restrictions on content; narrative subject disclosure; singular subject matter; time relation – before or during production; subject = producer or subject = beyond communication partners; information assumed to be truthful	Place relation between the recipient and producer	Distant
		Channel	Computer communicati-on
		Form of communication	Monologue with the fetu-res of a dialogue; channel – optical; asynchronous; distant; written, but with the features of oral con-versation

At the beginning of this chapter, the intention was expressed to not only describe a *blog* as a new text type but also specify the features that distinguish it from adjacent genres such as the *diary* or a *personal homepage*. In the table below, the three text types are compared and their distinctive features identified.

Table 8: Distinctive features of blogs

	Diary	*Blog*	*Personal homepage*
Hypertextual features	–	+	+
Grapho-stylistic means	–	+	+
Shortenings /acronyms	–	+	–
Number of spelling mistakes, some deliberate	–	+	–
Dated entries	+	+	–
Greeting/parting formula	–	±	±
Channel: computer	–	+	+
Monologue	+	±	±
Spontaneity	±	±	–
Finality	+	+	–
High planning effort	±	–	+

The main difference between a *blog* and a *diary* is the channel of communication, which is a computer. The form of both text types looks similar: dated entries, with their content also being comparable. But the peculiarities that a *blog* acquires by means of the Internet make it more versatile in terms of form, language and content etc compared to a typical written diary.

On the other hand, a *personal homepage* and a *blog,* which have the same function (giving information about the author and their life etc), differ in form. For a *blog*, dated entries in reverse chronological order is a must, while a personal homepage can be created and freely designed as the creator sees fit.

On the whole, criteria that are normally applied to the analysis of text types should be supplemented with some additional criteria in order to analyse a *blog*, i.e. *hypertextual characteristics, orality vs. literacy,* and *spelling* should also be taken into account as they reveal the nature of *blogs* and distinguish them from other adjacent text types.

Having applied the above-mentioned criteria, we can draw the following conclusions. Firstly, *blogs* have developed their own unique *code* which can be characterized through the greater tolerance of mistakes, the simplicity of syntactic constructions and hybrid spelling. Moreover, oral and literal features overlap with each other in *blogs*. Traditionally belonging to a written discourse, the text type of a diary, having occurred in new surroundings like the Internet, is now leaning more to orality than to literacy. Thirdly, although hypertextual characteristics can be found only on the Internet, not all the adjacent genres possess them.

Accordingly, having pointed out and analysed in detail the main features of a blog and having compared it with the related text types, a blog really can be defined as a new text type.

2. Borrowings

2.1 Languages in Contact

Nowadays a whole branch of linguistics, namely contact linguistics, explores the field of language contacts and language interaction. It is undeniable that the intensity of language contacts is growing from day to day due to various reasons. Contact between nations or languages is possible if they live near each other or if there are links in connection with trade, religion, etc. Language contacts may be subdivided into:

- External language contacts which arise when the interacting ethnolinguistic groups belong to different social and political formations (different statehood) (Rot 1992:18);
- Internal language interrelations which are formed when the interacting ethnolinguistic groups are members of one and the same social or political formation (common statehood) (Ibid.).

Here it is important to pay attention to external language contacts as a drastically developing process in modern society, especially contacts with the English language due to the significant position of the USA in the main spheres of life (politics, modern technology, economy, etc).

As contacts between nations are intensifying in the modern industrial world, it is inevitable that languages influence each other.

The system of every language is harmonious but not stable – it is constantly developing. On the other hand, an attempt to influence the system of one language by the system of another is regarded as interference (Weinreich 1953:1).

> Every enrichment or impoverishment of a system involves necessarily the reorganization of all the old distinctive oppositions of the system. To admit that a given element is simply added to the system which receives it without consequences for this system would ruin the very concept of system. (Vogt quoted from Weinreich 1953:1)

Writing about interference, Weinreich stresses that the term *interference* is only applicable when the changes in the system affect "the phonemic system, a large part of the morphology and syntax, and some areas of the vocabulary (kinship, colour, weather, etc)" (Weinreich 1953:1); otherwise the term *'borrowing'* might be applied. On the other hand, he admits that even in the case of borrowings, "the possibility of ensuing rearrangements in the patterns, or interference, cannot be excluded." (Ibid.)

Here, even though Weinreich differentiates between *'borrowing'* and *'interference'*, it is clear from the quotation above that the two phenomena are of the same nature. Borrowing could be treated like a particular kind of interference phenomenon which cannot produce any significant impact on the language system, while *interference*, according to Weinreich, affects the fundamentals of the system. In terms of degree it looks like this:

Figure 6: Borrowing vs. interference

Furthermore, the types of interference need to be defined:[62]

Phonological interference. The phonemes of language A are identified by the speaker with the phonemes of language B. During conversation, the phonemes of language A are substituted with phonemes of language B. Moreover, intonation, rhythm and stress transferred from system A to system B can be attributed to phonological interference.

Grammatical interference. "Grammatical interference is defined as the first language influencing the second in terms of word order, use of pronouns and determinants, tense and mood". (Skiba 2006:1) An example of such grammatical interference by English with Russian could be the use of compounds consisting of two nouns where the first is determined by the second (бизнес-ланч/business-lunch), whereas in Russian the opposite construction is typical, i.e. the first component determines the second (город-герой/ city-hero).

Lexical interference. This type of interference is the most significant and common, as lexis is an open system ready to welcome new 'members'. The result of lexical interference is manifested in the forms of borrowings of different kinds.[63]

Semantic interference. The influence of one language on the system of the other is not just reduced to the plane of expression, but also touches the plane of content. According to Weinreich, the results of the effect may be as follows (Weinreich 1953:54):

---

62 See Weinreich 1953, Skiba 2006.

63 See Item 1.3.

- Confusion in the usage of borrowings and native words;
- Old words being discarded;
- Content becoming specialised.

On the whole, in connection with language contacts, Weinreich was writing about bilinguals. Bilingualism in society could nowadays be subdivided into *artificial subordinative bilingualism* and *natural coordinative bilingualism* (Rot 1992:16). The former term refers to knowledge of the foreign language acquired during prolonged study of it at secondary school, university, etc; the latter applies to knowledge of the second language (not treated as foreign) acquired naturally during everyday use along with the first. For the present study, the former type of bilingualism is relevant, as the corpora analysed contain examples taken mostly from artificial bilinguals. The number of such artificial bilinguals is growing, especially those with English as their second language. But as the processes taking place in the speech of a natural bilingual differ from those of an artificial bilingual, the two phenomena 'interference' and 'borrowing' introduced by Weinreich cannot cover the needs of terminology concerning the processes of language alternations or changes in the speech of artificial bilinguals. Therefore, other terms that support the present research but which are nevertheless based on the interference phenomena introduced by Weinreich (1953: 73ff) need to be introduced.

The problem of differentiating between *borrowing*, *code-switching*, *code-mixing* and other phenomena has addressed in various papers. In this chapter, an attempt will be made to categorize them and point out their distinctive features.

First of all, it should be mentioned that confusion still exists between the three most significant terms: *code-switching, code-mixing and borrowing*. Let us consider the definition of code-switching first introduced by Uriel Weinreich (1953:73): "The ideal bilingual switches from one language to the other according to appropriate changes in the speech situation, and certainly not within a single sentence" and compare it to that given by Einer Haugen (1956:40): "Code-switching [...] occurs when a bilingual introduces a completely unassimilated word from another language into his speech." Here some differences in the opinions of the two linguists are to be found. Weinreich treats code-switching as an *intersentential* phenomen, whereas Haugen sees it as *intrasentential.*[64]

---

64 Intersentential (or inter-sentential) codeswitching refers to a type of code-switching: the alternation in a single discourse between two languages, where switching occurs after a sentence in the first language has been completed and the next sentence starts with a new language. (Appel & Muysken 1987:118) .

The definition given by Carol Myers-Scotton seems to convey the main idea of the phenomenon of 'code-switching': "Codeswitching is the term used to identify *alternations* of linguistic varieties within the same conversation." (1993:15) This definition seems to sustain the idea of Weinreich and his perception of code-switching, whereas Haugen's definition is more likely to be called 'insertion'.

Peter Auer introduced the classification of phenomena as differentiation between the alternation of the language and the insertion or transfer of lexical units. He developed the following typology: *alternational code-switching, alternational mixing, insertional code-switching, insertional mixing and fused lects*.[65] It is from this classification that the opposition between *'alternation'* and *'insertion'* arises, where *'alternation'* is a process of changing from language A to language B and vice versa within the same conversation and *'insertion'* an act of using individual lexical units from language A in conversation held in language B.

The insertion of individual lexical units (usually nouns) is the most frequent phenomenon found in the corpus analysed. This type of interference has been called 'borrowing', 'transfer', 'insertion', 'intra-sentential code-switching' (Poplack), 'code-mixinig' (Sridhar and Sridhar) and 'nonce-borrowing' (Poplack). Here we prefer the term *'borrowing'* referring to the use of individual lexical units of one language in a speech act carried out in the other language. This definition concerns only evident loans (Aüßeres Lehngut),[66] as hidden loans (inneres Lehngut)[67] are not treated by the speakers as part of the foreign language system but seen as part of native vocabulary.

It is also relevant to differentiate between *'borrowing'* and *'code-switching'* from the angle of monolingualism vs. bilingualism. Pfaff stated that:

> Borrowings are thought of as part of another language lexicon whereas code-switches are not. Borrowings therefore occur in the speech of a monolingual whereas code-switches appear only in bilingual speech. (Pfaff, 1979 quoted from Esma Gregor 2003:96)

Intrasentential codeswitching refers to a type of code-switching: the alternation in a single discourse between two languages where switching occurs within a sentence. (Quoted from Glottopedia. Discovering Linguisics)
URL: http://urts120.uni-trier.de/glottopedia/index.php/Codeswitching (17 June, 2004).

65 See Auer 1999.

66 See Carstensen 1965.

67 Ibid.

As for the bilinguals[68] whose first or second language of communication is English, among the few who live in Germany or Russia and keep a diary on the Internet in German or Russian, all lexical units of foreign origin found are treated by them as borrowings and not as code-switches, and can be considered part of their lexicon.

The term 'borrowing' could be further subdivided into *'nonce-borrowing'* or *'on-the-spot'* borrowing and *'long-term'* borrowing.[69] As Gillian Sankoff states:

> Various criteria were invoked in an attempt to separate the legitimate, or legitimated loan words, from nonce-borrowings or switches. These included phonological or morphological integration, as well as attestations of use by a wider community of speakers. (Sankoff 2002:650)

One more point of view, presented by Sándor Rot, is relevant for subdivision:

> When a speaker of language X uses a form of foreign origin not as on-the-spot borrowing from language Y, but because he has heard it used by others in X-utterances, then this borrowed element can be considered, from descriptive view point, to have become a part of language X. (Rot 1991:89)

All in all, the following conclusion can be drawn: if an element of language A has been used more than once by at least two different speakers in language B, this element can be considered a 'long-term' borrowing and therefore as belonging to the system of the recipient language. Practically speaking, such criteria are unreliable because it is impossible to state whether a borrowing has only been used once. Therefore, borrowings that have found their way into dictionaries or official lists of borrowings will be treated below as long-term borrowings and all others as on-the-spot borrowings.

On the other hand, the insertion of units on the syntactic level in monolingual speech cannot be ignored. It is evident that they cannot belong to the category of borrowings, because only individual lexical items refer to 'borrowings' as, stated above. A variety of opinions exist about syntactic loans.[70] As the term 'code-switching' is restricted to bilingual speech, here the term *'code-mixing'* needs to be introduced for insertions on the syntactic level. The idea that code-switching is treated as alternation and code-mixing as a phenomenon of insertion should be stressed. A monolingual inserts syntactic units such as phraseological units, greetings, emphatic phrases, etc. From their point of view, they insert units of the foreign language (foreign to them as monolingual). *Code-mixing*

---

68 Natural bilinguals are meant here.

69 See Weinreich 1953.

70 See Weinreich 1953, Heath 1989, Auer 1999, Thomason 2001.

is the use/insertion of foreign units "not restricted to word level"[71] *in monolingual speech.*[72] It should be mentioned that the instances of correct code-mixing are very rare, as properly mixing codes entails an advanced knowledge of the foreign language from which units are taken. A 'mixed code' as a result of such insertion could be defined as consisting of some (two or more) syntactic units belonging to different systems, where *different* is a synonym of 'foreign'. The inserted units are treated as if foreign by the monolingual speaker, whereas in the case of 'switching' all the languages in use are considered native.

On the whole, 'borrowing' is the term for lexical borrowings while 'code-mixing' represents syntactic borrowings in monolingual speech. Considering the classification proposed by Weinreich, who differentiated between 'on-the-spot' borrowing and 'long-term' borrowing, it could be stated that syntactic borrowings should be treated as 'on-the-spot' borrowings since their use in monolingual speech is spontaneous and they are not normally reflected in dictionaries or other official lists. On the other hand, 'long-term' borrowings among syntactic borrowings are very rare. They are deliberately inserted into monolingual speech for a number of different reasons, and they are normally reflected in dictionaries. The use of both phenomena in monolingual speech could be considered as interference "not threatening language of interaction" (Auer 1999:328).

The table below presents the terminology dwelt upon in this chapter.

Table 9: Terminology applied to language contact

Code-switching	*Code-mixing*		*Borrowing*	
Bilingual speech	Monolingual speech		Monolingual speech	
Alternation	Insertion		Insertion	
Lexical units as well as syntactical units	Syntactic units		Syntactic units	Lexical units
	'On-the-spot' borrowing	'Long term' borrowing	'On-the-spot' borrowing	'Long term' borrowing

If we consider 'borrowing' not as different elements of one language found in the other but as a process, the following differentiation of the elements with re-

71 Auer (1999:328).

72 Here only evident syntactic units are meant and not loan syntax.

spect to their capability of being independently transferred from one language to another can be established:[73]:

- Elements that are capable of independent transfer:
  - Lexical elements (words);
  - Semantic elements (the form of the foreign word that causes the new formations in the recipient language: loan translation, loan rendition, loan creation; the meaning of a foreign word that causes extension of meaning to the 'old' borrowing or the appearance of homonyms);
  - Syntactic elements (sentences, word combinations formed using the example of foreign structures);
  - Stylistic elements (figurative, euphemistic meaning, etc) that are added due to the influence of the foreign word.
- Elements that are incapable of independent transfer:
  - Phonetic, phonological and morphological elements are normally transferred only as part of higher structures (words, sentences, etc).

To draw a line, it should be stated that due to the development of contacts between the languages and the contact between the English language and other languages in particular encouraged by various factors such as the predominant position of the USA in different spheres of life, the number of borrowings is inevitably growing. The problem of terminology concerning the terms *code-switching, code-mixing, borrowing,* etc has been exhaustively discussed by researchers. Even so, confusion among the terms persists.

Having considered the terminology discussed in the present paper, the following conclusion can be drawn. For the purposes of the present research, the following subdivision should be applied: on the lexical level *borrowings* are distinguished to denote the use of individual lexical units of one language in a speech act carried out in the other language. Furthermore, *borrowings* can be subdivided into *long-term borrowings* that have found their way into dictionaries and other official lists, and *on-the-spot borrowings* inserted spontaneously into conversation, i.e. types of neologisms that are not reflected in any dictionaries of the recipient language but can still be considered part of the lexicon of the speaker using them.

On a syntactical level we speak about *code-mixing*, namely the use of word combinations, sentences, etc of one language in a conversation held in the other

73 See Aristova 1978.

language. Some instances of code-mixers were found in the corpus analysed and examples of them will be presented in the present paper.

2.2. Reasons for Borrowing

The problem of borrowings and their influence on the recipient languages arose a long time ago along with the question of why loans arise and why they are increasing in number.

Nowadays, as more and more borrowings are being accepted into languages, which sometimes seems to be a non-welcoming tendency, a deeper insight into the reasons for this process needs to be obtained. A number of different reasons have been pointed out by German, Russian and other linguists. In this chapter, the opinions of such researchers – Djakov (2003), Wolodarskaja (2001, 2002), Krisin (1965, 1968), Aristova (1978), Schelper (1995), Kupper (2003), Carstensen (1965, 1975), Weinreich (1953, 1976) – are summarised, and some modern tendencies concerning the borrowing of anglicisms in particular are highlighted.

First of all, it should be mentioned that the main reason that makes the exchange of lexical items between languages possible is to be found in language contacts.[74] It is incontrovertible that if there were absolutely no contact between languages, there would be no borrowings.

Wolodarskaja mentions three types of language contacts that encourage the growth of loanwords. (Wolodarskaja 2001:12) The first type is direct communication between nations living side by side, the second is through the exchange of goods and cultural values, and the third is through the translation of books and films etc.

Nowadays direct communication between nations is intensifying due to the rapid spread and influence of new media such as computers and the Internet, the possibility to watch TV programmes in the original language, etc. In fact the range of such possibilities is growing every day. On the Internet, users can communicate with each other not only by typing instant messages and e-mails but also by talking directly, the English language serving as the 'lingua franca' used by not only native speakers to communicate with each other but also most non-native speakers. Some users are eager to talk to others in English as it helps improve their own English skills. Taking into account computer jargon, primarily of English origin, there is a strong motivation among the educated part of society keen to obtain information from all over the world using all possible

74 See also Item 2.1.

means such as the Internet, television and newspapers to learn English in order to overcome the obstacles on the road to unfettered communication in a global context. The use of English, in non-excessive proportions, contributes to the growing number of loans in every sphere of life.

Furthermore, it is not just direct communication that plays an important role. Many English[75] borrowings have entered other languages through the names of products invented and manufactured in the USA. Marketing and advertising specialists use the original American names and labels as they are associated in people's minds with high quality. As a result, products with original American names sell well and their names are accumulated in the vocabulary of other languages. Typical examples in Russian and German include Jeans/ джинсы, CD, DVD, Bodylotion/ лосьон для тела, Whirlpool/ джакузи, Pringles (a brand of potato crisps) and памперсы (meaning nappies).

The last point concerning language contact is borrowing through translation. Compared to the other ways of language contact, it is the least significant nowadays in terms of the number of loans coming this way.

Having mentioned the most likely ways for loans to enter the recipient languages, we need to ask why other languages need borrowings. On the one hand, it is a process that is not easy to get under control due to the reasons mentioned above; on the other hand, in some cases the borrowings have some positive impact on the recipient language.

Two major groups of motives for borrowing anglicisms in particular have been pointed out, namely linguistic reasons and extralinguistic ones.[76]

Linguistic reasons:

- The need to name notions, things and ideas to fill lexical gaps. Lexical units are borrowed because no corresponding lexical item is to be found in the recipient language to denote the borrowed concept. For example, the names of various technical gadgets have been borrowed from English along with the introduction of the gadgets themselves, e.g.: toaster – Toaster – тостер; scanner – Scanner – сканер;
- Enrichment of vocabulary, broadening of stylistic, grammatical potential of the recipient language. Using loans, it is easy to create a certain atmosphere (humorous, annoying, etc) because the borrowings seem more emo-

75 This includes any kinds of borrowings from the English language, irrespective of their variety.

76 See also Wolodarskaja 2001, Fink 1997, Weinreich 1953, Kupper 2003, Djakov 2003.

tional than their native correspondents (in most cases they possess evident negative or positive connotations in the recipient language, even though such connotations are not typical of the source language. As an example we can take the borrowing 'Sorry!', which is frequently used in both Russian and German mainly by young people to express apology. In order to apologize it is easier to use the borrowing than the native 'Entschuldigung' or 'извините' as it sounds more neutral and, on the one hand, 'sorry' helps to augment the task – the person has apologized to the other person but, on the other hand, the anglicism does not make them feel that he has done anything wrong;

- As far as grammar is concerned, in Russian a growing number of analytical constructions has been observed due to the influence of English borrowings (топ-менеждер – top manager, бизнес-план – business plan);
- The need for synonyms. "Where synonyms are available from another language they are gladly accepted." (Weinreich 1953: 57) This tendency can be explained by a need to more precisely name an object which can only be satisfied by borrowing or a need for euphemisms. For example, 'One-Night-Stand' in German can be regarded as a kind of euphemism. Another example is 'loser': in Russian 'лузер' instead of 'неудачник', and in German 'Loser' instead of 'Verlierer'. In both cases the word has a negative connotation and sounds more offensive than the native units;
- Correction of polysemy. When a unit is borrowed which has a close lexical meaning to the native one, one of the polysemantic words is ousted, being replaced by the borrowed synonym;
- Economy of language means. In some cases the use of borrowings clearly saves effort and time compared to the use of the corresponding native phrase for both the speaker and the recipient. Examples include acronyms like смс, CD, DVD, as well as sale instead of Ausverkauf and распродажа, and юзер instead of пользователь;
- Low frequency of words (Ibid.). A rarely used native word can be easily replaced by a more active borrowing: мерчендайзер instead of распространитель.

Extralinguistic reasons

- Political, cultural and economical globalization. Globalization has definitely contributed to the more intensive use of the English language as nowadays English is considered to be the 'lingua franca'. The more different countries, nations and languages communicate with each other to tackle global problems and establish contact, the more intensely English is used;

- The predominant position of the USA in some spheres of life. It has been proved that the highest number of loans is to be found in such spheres as economy, politics, hi-tech, sport, etc,[77] in which the USA is among the world leaders;
- Growing interest in the English language. This is closely related to the other extralinguistic reasons. While watching English-language news on TV or reading newspapers, at least the basics of English are essential in order not to feel ill at ease;
- The use of borrowings is prestigious. The use of some borrowings may serve to demonstrate intelligence, versatility, the level of education of the speaker, their membership of the elite, or their expertise in some spheres of life;
- Development of scientific sublanguages. For example, programmers have developed their own sublanguage which consists mainly of anglicisms and in some cases it is impossible to understand what they are talking about without sufficient knowledge of the English language.

The interaction of extralinguistic and linguistic reasons in the process of borrowing and use of anglicisms cannot be denied.

> Außersprachliche Faktoren bestimmen das Angebot an sprachlichen Varianten zu einem gegebenen Zeitpunkt, während die innersprachlichen die Selektion einzelner Varianten aus diesem Angebot begünstigen oder verhindern. (Schütte 1996:26)

Nowadays the number of different reasons that influence the process of borrowing anglicisms, in particular in other languages, is growing and new ones constantly appear. It is very difficult to state what reason influences the process of borrowing most of all, but it is undeniable that together they sustain and motivate the rising number of anglicisms in other languages.

2.3. Classification of Loans

The problem of defining borrowings has been studied since the process of exchanging vocabulary items between languages began. Nowadays numerous definitions dealing with naming and renaming the terms and classification of loans exist side by side.[78]

---

77 See Item 4.2.

78 See also Carstensen, Zindler, Duckworth, Haugen, Katamba, etc.

To begin with, the term 'borrowing' or 'loan' needs to be generally defined.

> A loanword is a word belonging to one language which is imported or adopted by another. (Katamba 1994:193)

This is the general definition applicable to most types of loans that exist nowadays. But in order to specify and to conduct the analysis of the corpora used for the present research, a deeper insight into the nature of *borrowing* – namely classifying borrowings according to some parameters – is required.

A number of scholars have classified loans in their own way. The table below lists four classifications of loans given by Fink (1995, 1997, 2000), Duckworth (1979), Haugen (1956) and Carstensen (1979).[79]

Table 10: Classification of loans

Fink	***Duckworth***	***Carstensen***	***Haugen***
1. keine Substitution (complete importation) Such types of loans as foreign word, loanwords and pseudo loans belong to this group 2.Teilsubstitution (partial importation) Hybrids 3.Vollsubstitution (no importation) Semantic loans and other compounds or phrases created from means of the recipient language patterned on the English model	1. völlich fremde Exotica (exotisms) 2. Lehnwörter, die fremde Form und Aussprache behalten, sie werden morphologisch wie einheimische Wörter behandelt. (Loanwords that are not assimilated graphically and phonetically, but completely assimilated grammatically) 3.Entlehnungen aus Latein und Griechisch, die zum internationalem Wortschatz gehören (international words) 4.anerkannte Lehnwörter (completely assimilated loans)	1. evidentes (äußeres) Lehngut Foreign words, loanwords, pseudo loans and, hybrids. All these categories fully or partially consist of English morphemes. 2.latentes (inneres) Lehngut No English morphemes to be found here. Such loans are loan translation (Haugen), loan translation proper (Weinreich), loan rendition (Weinreich), loan creation, semantic loan, loan syntax.	1. Loanwords – show the importation of form and meaning with degrees of phonological integration (all, none or partial) 2.Loanblends – hybrids or combinations of foreign and native forms 3.Loanshifts in which a foreign concept is represented by a native form (loan translation/calques, semantic loans, semantic extensions)[80]

79 See Fink 1968, Carstensen 1979, Duckworth 1979, Haugen 1956.

80 See Field 2002.

Having summed up the above-mentioned classifications and also adding some more points for the needs of the present research, the following terms will be further used in this paper:

- *Loanwords* – borrowings that have preserved their foreign form but have been assimilated in at least one respect (phonetically, grammatically or semantically);
- *Foreign words* – are not assimilated at all;[81]
- *Exotisms* – words denoting phenomena that do not exist in the recipient language;
- *Pseudoloans* – made up of lexical material of the source language, although they do not exist as such in the system of the source language;
- *Hybrids* – consist partly of native material and partly of the material of the source language.

They all constitute a large group of evident loans (in analogy to Carstensen's "evidentes Lehngut") as they are easily recognizable as belonging to the system of the other language. The most widespread types of evident loans are loanwords, foreign words and hybrids.[82]

Another group includes hidden loans or semantic loans, which are all, to some extent, based on the process of translation:

- *Loan translation proper* – the exact (literal) translation from one language into another, e.g. *кредитная карта* in Russian from 'credit card', *Textbuch* in German from 'textbook';
- *Loan rendition* – some constituents are translated literally, some freely, e.g. *Wolkenkratzer* ('cloud scraper') from 'skyscraper', *сейф-ячейка* ('safe-cell') from 'safe-deposit box';
- *Loan creation* – free reproduction of meaning of the concept with the means of the recipient language, e.g. *Spitzenverkehr , час пик (rush hour)*;
- *Loan syntax* – borrowings on a syntactic level. As stated in the previous chapter, most cases of insertions on the level of syntax should be treated as *code-mixing*,. i.e. syntactic units that have been borrowed mostly

81 As examples of such foreign words we can probably take only borrowings which have preserved their original spelling in Russian. All other borrowings in Russian are assimilated graphically and along with the borrowings in German join the declension and conjugation paradigm of the recipient language.

82 This conclusion is based on the results of the present analysis.

through translation. In contrast to *mixers* they fully consist of the material of the recipient language and so are referred to as hidden loans, e.g. *'увидимся'* from *'see you'*.

Given the above mentioned classifications, the following criteria can be applied to the classification of loans:[83]

- Form

– Loans consisting only of foreign lexical material (keine Substitution, Duckworth (1), evidentes Lehngut)

loanwords;

foreign words;

pseudoloans;

exotisms.

– Loans consisting of foreign lexical material + native material/native affix

hybrids

– Loans consisting only of native material;

– Loan translation proper;

– Loan rendition;

– Loan creation;

– Loan syntax.

- Speaker's perception

Speaker's perception refers to the speaker's attitude to anglicisms. Some of the borrowings used in conversation can clearly lead to misunderstanding and the failure of communication if the recipient treats the loan as foreign and strange.[84] On the other hand, in some cases loans contribute to the success of a communicative act if they are understood and treated like native ones by the participants. Such loans treated as native are welcomed in conversation as they sometimes replace bulky native synonyms and save the speakers effort while sustaining the maxim of manner.

---

83 See also Muhr 2004, Nettman-Multanowska 2003.

84 Sometimes the speaker does not know the meaning of the lexical unit or realizes that they are dealing with a borrowing because of the form of the word. The speaker's perception of the anglicisms as foreign or native can also depend on the level of knowledge of English. In this case no common tendencies can be found, as whether an anglicism is treated as foreign or native depends only on the speaker.

Table 11: Speaker's perception of loanwords

Form	*Meaning*	*Examples*
Foreign	Strange	trading, merchandising, мерчандайзер
Foreign	Clear	jeans, handy, mixer, компьютер, навигатор, фанат
Half native, half foreign	Clear	Sicherheitstraining, сейф-ячейка
Native	Clear	Teilzeitarbeit, танцпол

On the whole, speakers perceive the anglicisms of the first category like foreign words due to both their form and their meaning. The meaning could be unclear because of the rare use of the borrowing, its relatively recent adoption, or the absence of the concept it denotes in the recipient language. This type includes foreign words and exotisms. The second category is represented by loanwords which, although they have a foreign form, are understood and perceived by the speakers as native words. Mixed in form but clear in meaning are hybrids, followed by semantic loans, loan translation proper, loan rendition, loan creation and loan syntax, which are treated like native words in form as well as meaning.

- Degree of integration

Sándor Rot (1991:42) suggested a rather complicated system of classification concerning the incorporation of lexical units into the system of the recipient language. He points out three stages of incorporation: accommodation, adaptation and assimilation. These stages could be described as follows:

- *Phonetic, phonological adjustment* to the system of the recipient language. The original phonemes are substituted by phonemes of the recipient system, while stress and intonation patterns are also adjusted;
- *Grammatical assimilation* (gender assignment, word order, adjustment to declination and conjugation system, etc[85]);
- *Lexico-semantic incorporation.* Loans are not perceived as intruders but as members of the lexico-semantic system of the recipient language, where they become established by ousting the native word, sharing their place

85 Grammatical integration will be discussed in detail in Chapter 6.

with a native unit due to the specialisation of meaning of both of them, etc;[86]

– Word-formational assimilation.

Loans take part in the process of word formation.

Here it would be also relevant to mention *graphical adaptation* as the initial stage the loans undergo. For example, in German all loan nouns are written with a capital letter.

Aristova (1978) suggests another classification. She singles out three stages, namely *penetration, borrowing* and *implantation.* At the stage of penetration, loans are normally associated with the reality of the source language, with most of the words preserving the original spelling. Borrowing is defined through the growth of semantic influence on the word and the broadening of its sphere of use in the recipient language. During implantation, a loan is subordinated to the norms of the recipient language.

The four stages mentioned above, namely *phonetic, phonological adjustment, grammatical assimilation, lexico-semantic incorporation* and *word-formational assimilation*, are obligatory for a borrowing to become a full member of the system, i.e. to stand on the same level with the native words as far as all parts of the language system (phonetics/phonology, grammar, syntax, semantics, stylistic, etc) are concerned. But unfortunately, not all loans undergo the above-mentioned stages of incorporation.

Due to the degree of integration and the accomplishment of the stages mentioned above, loans can be subdivided into:[87]

– *Completely assimilated loans*

These do not differ graphically, grammatically or phonetically from native words (hidden loans) and have passed all four stages of incorporation.

– *Partially assimilated loans*

Words which have not been assimilated in one at least respect: graphical, grammatical, phonetical or semantical (hybrids, foreign words, pseudo loans, exotisms, loanwords). In the case of foreign words, their 'assimilation' is inevitable in some cases, e.g. German nouns written with a capital letter. This is why the category of foreign words is mentioned here, which has missed at least one stage of incorporation.

---

86 See Chapter 7.

87 See also Fink 1997.

– *Non-assimilated loans*

Words that are not assimilated in any of the above respects. Here the loans mentioned above in partially assimilated loans could be also traced to non-assimilated ones, with the exception of pseudo loans (which have been created to fit the system of the target language) and loanwords (as they are meant to be assimilated in at least one of the respects, otherwise they are treated like foreign words).

- Relevance to communication

Here frequency of use is the decisive criterion. It is undeniable that there is a direct connection between frequency of use and importance for communication. On the other hand, it is almost impossible to subdivide all loans into those which are frequently used and therefore important, and those which are not frequently used and not important, because this is subjective and depends on each individual speaker's background. The borrowings that one speaker eagerly uses in their conversation may seem strange and not at all important to the other. It is also important to mention that the frequency of use and hence the degree of importance do not in any way depend on the form of the borrowing or its semantics; it is only the speaker's individual perception which contributes to the subdivision of loans into frequently used and therefore important ones and vice versa.

- Substitution/ supplementation

This criterion deals with the semantics of borrowings. There are two types of relationship between native words and 'newcomers': either a borrowing contributes to the enrichment of a semantic field, adopting its own position within it, or it replaces the native item.

In the former case, processes such as the necessity to distinguish two semantically related or almost identical phenomena and to delimit the tinges of meaning take place, e.g. *Einfuhr – Import, обслуживание – сервис*. In this case, a borrowing and a native item exist side by side.

There are some cases of substitution of native lexical items by borrowings. First of all, there is the process of complete substitution, when the native item is ousted by the loan. For example the Russian ЭВМ (электронно-вычислительная машина/ electro-calculating machine) has been replaced by ПК (PC) or компьютер (computer). Secondly, in some cases the adoption of a loan drastically restricts the use of the native word, resulting in the narrowing or degradation of its meaning. For instance the Russian '*магазин*' used to be the only word denoting a place where things are sold. Nowadays it has been restricted in meaning due to the anglicisms '*шоп*' (shop), '*супермаркет*' (supermarket) and '*молл*' (mall), and its meaning has also been degraded because now '*магазин*' means a place where inexpensive, low-quality or merely ordinary things are sold. In addition, processes such as the change of stylistic register, the acquisition of positive/negative connotation and the elevation of meaning are possible.

Those are the criteria that help to categorize borrowings. It is also relevant for the present paper to differentiate among borrowings by their origin. First of all, there are direct borrowings that are taken directly from the donor language. In some cases, however, loans do not come directly from the donor language but are taken from a mediating language, resulting in the chain *donor language – mediating language – recipient language*. As the present paper deals with borrowings from the English language, all the borrowings that originated in the English language or have been directly borrowed from it are considered. Such borrowings are referred to here as *anglicisms*.

As far as the definition of *anglicism* is concerned here, we cite Zindler's basic definition frequently used in different research papers:

> Ein Anglizismus ist ein Wort aus dem britischen oder amerikanischen Englisch im Deutschen oder eine nicht übliche Wortkomposition, jede Art der Veränderung einer deutschen Wortbedeutung oder Wortverwendung (Lehnbedeutung, Lehnübersetzung, Lehnübertragung, Lehnschöpfung, Frequenzsteigerung, Wiederbelebung) nach britischem oder amerikanischem Vorbild. (Quoted from Carstensen, 1965)

The problem of differentiation of the source of borrowing, namely British or American, and the problem of whether to name such borrowings 'anglicisms', 'americanisms', or 'angloamericanisms' have been exhaustively discussed.[88] As far as our research is concerned, it deals with borrowings belonging to American or British English which are imported and adopted by German and/or Russian. Such borrowings are denoted below as a*nglicisms* since they belong to the English language in general regardless of variety, especially as the exact source (American, British or some other variety of English) is sometimes impossible to determine.

As regards the definition given above, here it is necessary to introduce the definition to fit the aims and subject of our research.

An anglicism is a phenomenon found in German and Russian on the lexical or syntactic level whose form and/or meaning can be traced back to its English origin.

---

88 Carstensen 1965, 1975, Fink 1997, Nettman-Multanovska 2003, Schütte 1996, Viereck 1980 etc.

There are many different ways of classifying loans in general and anglicisms in particular. The criteria of classification affect form as well as meaning, relevance to communication, and the relationship of loans and native lexical units, and in addition some particular stages of incorporation are observed. Even so, as the number of loans is growing from day to day, adoption sometimes does not go the way it should, i.e. not all stages are accomplished while, on the other hand, as the general level of knowledge of the English language among non-native speakers is growing, sometimes it is also difficult to ascertain whether the form or content seem strange to the speaker or not. Moreover, this tendency concerns the relationship between loans and native vocabulary units, since the modern tendency is to supplement vocabulary as more and more notions appear that are named with the help of the English language due to progress (technical and otherwise). As far as the present paper is concerned, in the following chapters an attempt will be made to show the modern tendencies regarding the incorporation of lexical units into German and Russian.

3. The Blog Corpus

3.1 Corpora in Contrastive Linguistics

Any contrastive linguistic analysis is based on some corpus defined as "a collection of information or material to be studied."[89] Depending on the aims of research, the types of corpora may vary.

The languages involved in the research corpora can be monolingual or multilingual. Monolingual corpora consist of texts or other units of speech belonging to the same language, while multilingual corpora contain these items in different languages. Corpora comprising two languages are sometimes also called bilingual.[90] In the present paper, any corpora representing the texts in two different languages will be called multilingual as distinguishing bilingual corpora as a separate type appears irrelevant.

Although the two types of corpora mentioned above do not raise any queries, the terms *'parallel'* and *'comparable'* corpora should be discussed in more detail to avoid confusion. This subdivision is based on the methods involved in compiling the corpus.

'Parallel' corpora are sometimes also called *'translation'* corpora as they are based on the process of translation. "Translation corpora consist of original texts in one language and their translations into one or several other languages." (Altenberg, Granger 2002:8) They can be further subdivided into *unidirectional* corpora when texts in language A are translated into language B only and *bidirectional* corpora when translation goes from A to B and vice a versa (Ibid.).

A translation corpus has certain advantages. In contrastive studies it is necessary to compare like with like, and the main features of the original text such as function, meaning and stylistic features are preserved in all the constituent parts of translation corpora. On the other hand, translated texts undergo some changes due to various translation effects. Moreover, not all texts tend to be translated and consequently the compilation of translation corpora is restricted to particular genres and text types.

For the present research, comparable corpora were compiled. "[A comparable corpus] refers to one which is composed of non-translation data collected from different languages using the same sampling technique" (McEnery, Xiao, Tono 2006:47) or "consists of texts in each language, matched as far as possible

89 Dictionary of Contemporary English (1995:304).

90 See Altenberg, Granger 2002, McEnery 2006 etc.

in terms of text type, subject matter, and communicative function". (Altenberg, Granger 2002:8)

The definite advantage of any comparable corpus is that it represents natural language as it is free from any external influence, as in the case of translation corpora.

The problem with comparable corpora though is that they really must be comparable. This problem does not affect parallel corpora, as they consist of texts that are originally identically structured and changed only due to translation, without altering their similarity or comparability.

By contrast, the compilation of comparable corpora is more complicated. The constituents of any comparable corpora must match each other quantitatively and qualitatively, as is stated in the definition above. In other words, they must match each other in terms of "proportion, genre, domain, and sampling period"[91] (McEnery, Xiao, Tono 2006:48). Only in this case can one be sure that comparative study will be possible.

It should be also mentioned that translational corpora can only be multilingual while comparable corpora can be multilingual or monolingual. Furthermore, corpora can be specialized or general. Specialized corpora consist of texts belonging to some particular type (e.g. newspaper articles, weather forecasts, etc), while general corpora contain as many text types as possible.

All the types of corpora discussed above are shown in the following diagram.

Figure 7: Types of corpus

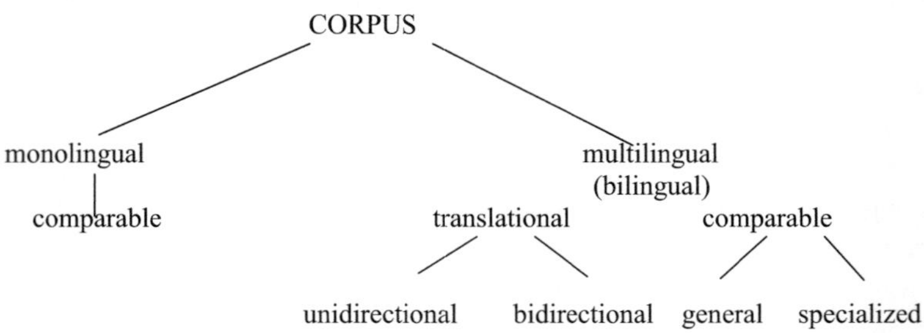

For the purpose of the present research, a specialized multilingual comparable corpus was compiled. It comprises texts – *blog entries* – in German and Rus-

91 These points in respect to the compiled corpus will be discussed in the next part of this chapter.

sian taken from the Internet. In the next part of this chapter, the process of compilation and restrictions will be discussed.

3.2. Compilation of Corpora: Limitations

As mentioned above, a specialized multilingual comparable corpus was compiled for the present research. The number of *blogs* existing in Russian and German is about 1,500,000, and every day this number is growing as new *blogs* appear. As considering all of them would be impossible, a definite number of *blogs* were taken to compile the corpus. The whole corpus consists of 216,860 words altogether, the Russian part (108,561 words) being almost the same size as the German section (108,299), making it *a quantitatively balanced corpus*. The number of words included in the corpus seems large enough to obtain reliable results as far as anglicisms (the subject of the present research) are concerned.

The constituent parts of the corpora are also quantitatively balanced, namely most constituent parts consist of about 10,000 words, with only the examples of *blogs* written by women under 25 being around 16,000 words in length. This deviation is due to the fact that *blogs* written by women under 25 exceed the number of other *blogs* by about 60%. The proportion that is presented in the number of blogs written by women under 25 to all other age categories and sex coincides with the real state of things, namely the proportion found on the Internet. Again it should be mentioned that the length of the constituent parts of 10,000 words seems to provide enough practical material for analysis and to obtain reliable results.

Going back to the similarity of both parts of the corpora, it should be mentioned that both parts are subdivided into two primary parts, namely into 'topic-oriented' and 'non-topic-oriented' *blogs*. It is well known from numerous works on anglicisms that frequency of use of anglicisms in some fields is definitely higher than in others. To confirm this, the following topics were chosen for analysis: computer, fashion, showbusiness/music and sport.

In a *topic-oriented blog*, the author writes about some definite subject – in our case computer, fashion, music or sport. The age and sex of the author do not matter in the case of *topic-oriented blogs*. The main criteria are that it should be an individually written note not belonging to some discussion among community members, and the author should not be a professional in the subject he is writing about. The number of words in each post varies from 100 to 1,000, although most *blogs* contain about 250–350 words.

Non-topic-oriented blogs are not restricted some particular subject matter but are more of a potpourri. Their content normally depends on what is going on in the author's life, how they feel at the time of writing, etc. *Non-topic-oriented blogs* reflect the chain of events happening and usually look like standard diary entries.[92]

One of the hypotheses of the present paper is that the frequency of the anglicisms used depends on the age and sex of the authors. To prove this hypothesis, *non-topic-oriented blogs* were further subdivided by the age and sex of their authors.

As far as age is concerned, three main groups were formed. Generally speaking, the age of *bloggers* is urestricted. We came across *blogs* written by people aged between twelve and seventy. However, the most represented group is aged between fifteen and thirty-five, and there seem to be more female than male *bloggers* – a finding confirmed by the results of other researchers.[93] People in this age range can be referred to as the 'computer generation', since computers were already commonplace when they were born or went to school. Accordingly, it is particularly younger people who enjoy surfing on the Internet and writing online diaries. The fact that there are more women among *bloggers* could be due to their more open nature (i.e. a greater willingness to share their emotions and feelings with others than men) and having more spare time for pastimes they regard as important, such as writing a diary.

It is well known that the most recent big wave of the adoption of anglicisms into German and Russian started in the 1990s and is still continuing. Consequently, under-twenty-fives are bound to use more anglicisms in their speech than older people. The second age group is between twenty-five and thirty-five years – young people who are also open to everything new but likely to use fewer anglicisms. The last group – the over-thirty-fives – seems to adopt older anglicisms from the 1960s and 1970s in their speech but does not use many of the 'newcomers'. These are the hypotheses concerning the age of the *bloggers* in relation to the frequency of the anglicisms used.

The entries of *non-topic-oriented blogs* were selected randomly. Each entry was taken from a different author living in Germany or Russia. The number of

92 See Chapter 2.

93 Susan C. Herring, Lois Ann Scheidt, Sabrina Bonus, Elijah Wright in their genre analysis of the weblogs state that, "While bloggers of both genders and all ages create personal journals, females and teens create them somewhat more than do males and adults."(Herring 2004:6).

words in entries varies, as it does in *topic-oriented blogs*, but is on average between 250 and 400 words.

The time when the entry was written is also considered. All the entries analysed were written between June 2005 and June 2006.

The quantitative and qualitative indices of the corpora are stated in the following table.

Table 12: Quantitative and qualitative indices (non-topic-oriented blogs)

Age	*Up to 25*	*25–35*	*Over 35*
Female Russian	16,073 words	10,683 words	10,180 words
Female German	16,057 words	10,529 words	10,202 words
Male Russian	10,092 words	10,094 words	10,066 words
Male German	10,020 words	10,095 words	10,107 words

Table 13: Quantitative and qualitative indices (topic-oriented blogs)

	Sport	*Computer*	*Fashion*	*Showbusiness*
Russian	10,151 words	10,317 words	10,515 words	10,390 words
German	10,189 words	10,316 words	10,436 words	10,248 words

For the present research, the analysis of the anglicisms found in both languages using the example of *blogs* is relevant. For each contrastive study, *tercium comparationis* is needed. In our case it is anglicisms found in Russian and German which could be traced to the same source in the English language:

Source

/ \

German Russian

Although some of the anglicisms have undergone different changes in structure, in a Russian list of anglicisms 410 original stems were used in the analysis compared to 391 original stems in German. The quantitative difference amounts to 4.6% and cannot be considered a falsification of the results.

The previous chapter[94] dwelt in detail on the types of anglicisms. Here it should be mentioned that in the present paper both evident and hidden loans are analysed. However, as far as hidden loans are concerned, quantitative analysis

94 See Item 2.3.

will be excluded since identifying all the hidden loans used is impossible due to their complete merger with native vocabulary.

The time of borrowing is also considered. Quantitative analysis will be applied to ascertain which anglicisms belong to older borrowings and which to the new ones.[95] Regarding qualitative analysis, old borrowings need to be distinguished from new ones due to the degree of adoption. Generally speaking, older borrowings have gone through all the stages of adoption and are treated by ordinary native speakers as native units. On the other hand, new borrowings are still undergoing the process of integration into the system of the recipient language at various degrees due to the time of adoption. As far as graphical and morphological adoption is concerned, it seems relevant to concentrate our attention on new borrowings as they suggest different variations and possibilities in connection with quantitative analysis. The same could be said of semantics – and the stylistics of the older borrowings which having been accumulated in the bulk of the native vocabulary belong in most cases to neutral lexis with zero connotation.

Another factor, which is also important to mention, is the manner of transition. Two main categories can be pointed out, namely '*donor language*' and '*mediating language*'. In the present paper, all anglicisms directly borrowed from the English language, regardless of their origin, will be taken into consideration alongside those adopted from some other language but originally stemming from English.

95 By old borrowings we mean those loans that were adopted before the 80ies-90ies of the 20th century.

4. Anglicisms in Blogs

4.1 Non-topic-oriented *Blogs*

4.1.1 Statistics

General principles concerning how the corpus was compiled were discussed in detail in 3.2. Here we will dwell on the results and determine whether the hypotheses proposed above are true or false.

As already mentioned, all *non-topic-oriented blogs* were classified by the age and sex of the authors, with three age categories and two sexes being singled out for the present analysis.

The following hypotheses are to be tested in this chapter:

- *The number of anglicisms in topic-oriented blogs exceeds the number of anglicisms in non-topic-oriented blogs;*
- *The age of the 'producer' is related to the number of anglicisms used, i.e. the younger the producer, the more anglicisms are used;*
- *The age of the producer influences the anglicisms used;*
- *The sex of the producer may influence the number of anglicisms used;*
- *Men and women use more anglicisms in specific topics, which vary between the sexes.*

Moreover, it is relevant to determine whether the general number of anglicisms in German is larger than in Russian – or to ascertain the age/ sex categories in which this is the case.

Let's start by considering the results in the table below showing statistical data of three age groups. The users are also subdivided by their sex and native language (female Russian, male German, etc). In each category, the number of words analysed is shown first, then the number of anglicisms found, followed by the number of unique anglicisms (we need to differentiate between the total number of anglicisms found and the number of unique anglicisms as some frequently used units are found more than once). After that the anglicisms found are subdivided by the part of speech they belong to (nouns, adjectives, verbs and adverbs).

Table 14: Number of anglicisms found in non-topic-oriented blogs

	Users < 25	*Users aged 25–35*	*Users > 35*
Female users (Russian)	16,073 words/ 89 anglicisms/ 51 unique anglicisms nouns – 50 verb – 1 adjectives – 0	10,683 w/ 60a/ 49ua nouns – 43 verbs – 3 adjectives – 3	10,180w/ 75a/ 46ua nouns – 40 verb – 1 adjectives – 5
Female users (German)	16,057w/ 150a/ 88ua nouns – 66 verbs – 13 adjectives – 9	10,529w/ 97a/ 57ua nouns – 44 verbs – 5 adjectives – 8	10,202w/ 62a/ 53ua nouns – 45 verbs – 5 adjectives – 3
Male users (Russian)	10,092w/ 75a/ 47ua nouns – 42 verbs – 2 adjectives – 3	10,094w/ 107a/ 63ua nouns – 54 verbs – 5 adjectives – 4	10,066w/ 107a/ 72ua nouns – 68 verbs – 3 adjectives – 1
Male users (German)	10,020w/ 72a/ 52ua nouns – 46 verbs – 2 adjectives – 4	10,195w/ 106a/ 61ua nouns – 54 verbs – 4 adjectives – 3	10,107w/ 49a/ 41ua nouns – 32 verbs – 3 adjectives – 6

The number of anglicisms and the number of unique anglicisms found differ, while the number of nouns found exceeds the numbers of adjectives and verbs.

In the table below, how many anglicisms and unique anglicisms were used by different age and sex categories are calculated.

Table15: Anglicisms by age and sex

	< 25	25–35	> 35
Female Russian	0.554% /0.317%	0.562%/0.459%	0.737%/0.452%
Female German	0.934%/0.548%	0.921%/0.541%	0.608 %/0.52%
Male Russian	0.743%/0.466%	1.06%/0.624%	1.063%/0.715%
Male German	0.719%/0.519%	1.04%/0.598%	0.485%/0.406%

As is clear from the table, in most cases the number of anglicisms used does not even exceed 1% of the total lexis. Only Russian male authors aged 25–35 use anglicisms exceeding 1% of their speech.

On the whole, the number of anglicisms used in German does not differ drastically from those used in Russian. Generally speaking, the number of anglicisms used depends on factors such as sex, the age of the producer and the topic concerned rather than the language the conversation is held in.

A similar table was drawn up showing the results concerning topic-oriented blogs to test the first hypothesis, i.e. *The number of anglicisms in topic-oriented blogs exceeds the number of anglicisms in non-topic-oriented blogs.*

Table16: Anglicisms in topic-oriented blogs

	Russian	German
Computer	5.64%/1.49%	4.39%/1.54%
Fashion	2.14%/0.608%	2.71%/0.843%
Music/showbusiness	3.71%/1.36%	4.06%/1.22%
Sport	3.507%/0.807%	2.62%/0.873%

Having compared the results in the two tables, *the number of anglicisms in topic-oriented blogs exceeds the number of those in non-topic-oriented blogs in nearly all cases* with just one exception (the number of unique anglicisms in the Russian topic 'Fashion' is lower than in some categories of non-topic-oriented *blogs*). Accordingly, the hypothesis is true.

4.1.2 Age Groups and Anglicisms

The following statistical data should be mentioned in connection with the hypothesis *the age of the 'producer' is related to the number of anglicisms used, i.e. the younger the 'producer', the more anglicisms are used.*

Table 17: Minimum and maximum number of anglicisms used

	Minimum number of anglicisms used	Maximum number of anglicisms used
Russian	Female users aged < 25	Male users > 35
German	Male users > 35	Male users aged 25–35

As is apparent from the table above, the hypothesis *The younger the producer, the more anglicisms are used* is not true. Furthermore, the number of anglicisms used does not depend on the age of the speaker. This is additionally proved by the following diagram.

Figure 8: Age of producer and anglicisms

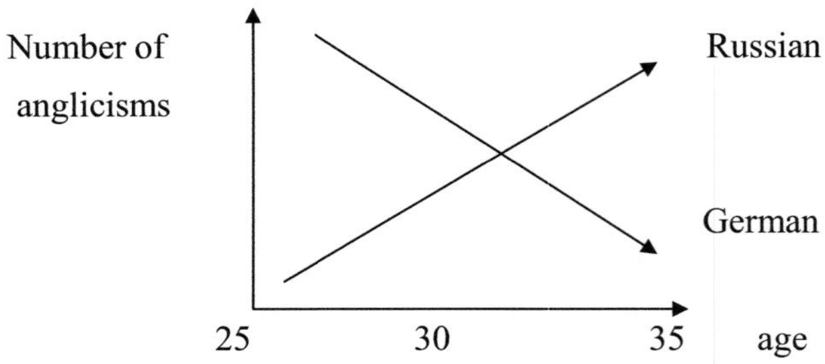

As mentioned above, younger producers might be assumed to use more recent borrowings in their speech than older ones. However, this is contradicted by the following table based on the results of the present research.

Table 18: Time of borrowing and age of producers

	Russian		German	
	Old borrowings	New borrowings	Old borrowings	New borrowings
Aged < 25	57%	43%	63%	37%
Aged 25–35	54%	46%	62.5%	37.5%
Aged > 35	52%	48%	80%	20%
General tendency	↘	↗	↗	↘

When non-topic-oriented *blogs* were analysed, 1,049 anglicisms and 680 unique anglicisms were found in the corpus. To make the analysis clearer and to state whether *the age of the producer influences the anglicisms used*, all the anglicisms found were further subdivided into 15 topics: *general vocabulary (everyday use), business/finance/work, the Internet, computers, technical gadgets/technology, music/showbusiness, fashion/beauty, hobbies and leisure, TV, sports, food, films, education, names of professions/people* and *building*.

Some of these topics coincide with those discussed further in topic-oriented *blogs*. This choice was made since traditionally the majority of anglicisms used can be found in the topics *computers, fashion, music* and *sport*. That is why it is clear that such topics are also discussed or mentioned in non-topic-oriented *blogs*.

The total number of unique anglicisms found is shown in the following table broken down by authors' age and nationality. The columns indicate the number of unique anglicisms and their percentage of all unique anglicisms in this age group in these particular topic overviews.

Table 19: Total number of anglicisms found in particular topics

	< 25 Rus (100)	*< 25 Ger (140)*	*25–35 Rus (112)*	*25–35 Ger (118)*	*> 35 Rus (118)*	*> 35 Ger (94)*
General	23/23%	45/32.1%	24/21.4%	52/44%	25/21.1%	42/44.6%
Business/ finance/work	7/7%	3/2.1%	11/9.8%	6/5%	7/5.9%	4/4.25%
The Internet	13/13%	19/13.5%	19/16.9%	18/15.2%	19/16.1%	9/9.5%
Computers	10/10 %	3/2.1%	10/8.9%	3/2.54%	9/7.6%	4/4.25%
Technical gadgets/ technology	6/6%	10/7.1%	10/8.9%	10/8.47%	12/10.1%	6/6.38%
Music/ showbusiness	4/4%	10/7.1%	2/1.78%	3/2.54%	3/2.54%	3/3.2%
Fashion/ beauty	4/4%	5/3.5%	11/9.8%	3/2.54%	2/1.7%	1/1.06%
Hobbies/ leisure	5/5%	3/2.1%	–	3/2.54%	3/2.54%	3/3.2%
TV	1/1%	1/0.71%	–	1/0.84%	–	1/1.06%
Sports	8/8%	14/10%	7/6.25%	4/3.38%	6/5.08%	6/6.38%
Food	3/3%	6/4.2%	1/0.89%	–	2/1.7%	4/4.25%
Films	1/1%	3/2.1%	5/4.4%	1/0.84%	2/1.7%	1/1.06%
Education	2/2%	–	–	–	–	–
Names of professions/people	3/3%	5/3.5%	2/1.78%	6/5.08%	2/1.7%	2/2.13%
Building	1/1%	–	1/0.89%	–	1/0.84%	–

To sum up the statistical data presented above and to state whether the hypothesis *The age of the speaker influences the anglicisms used* is true, the following table was compiled. The ten topics used most (in order of use) are presented:

Table 20: The most frequently used topics

<table>
<tr><th colspan="2">< 25</th><th colspan="2">25–35</th><th colspan="2">> 35</th></tr>
<tr><th>Rus</th><th>Ger</th><th>Rus</th><th>Ger</th><th>Rus</th><th>Ger</th></tr>
<tr><td>1. General</td><td>1. General</td><td>1. General</td><td>1. General</td><td>1. General</td><td>1. General</td></tr>
<tr><td>2. Internet</td><td>2. Internet</td><td>2. Internet</td><td>2. Internet</td><td>2. Internet</td><td>2. Internet</td></tr>
<tr><td>3. Computer</td><td>3. Sports</td><td>3. Fashion and work</td><td>3. Techn. gadgets</td><td>3. Techn. gadgets</td><td>3. Techn. gadgets</td></tr>
<tr><td>4. Sports</td><td rowspan="3">4. Techn. gadgets and music</td><td rowspan="3">4. Compters and techn. gadgets</td><td rowspan="2">4. Business and work.</td><td rowspan="2">4. Computers</td><td rowspan="2">4.Sports</td></tr>
<tr><td rowspan="2">5. Business</td></tr>
<tr><td>5. Sports</td><td>5. Business</td><td>5. Business</td></tr>
<tr><td>6. Technical gadgets</td><td>5. Food</td><td>5. Sports</td><td>6. Computers</td><td>6. Sports</td><td rowspan="2">6. Computer and food</td></tr>
<tr><td>7. Hobbies</td><td>6. Work and fashion</td><td>6. Film</td><td>7. Music</td><td>7. Music and hobbies</td></tr>
<tr><td>8. Music and fashion</td><td rowspan="2">7. Films, hobbies, computers, business</td><td rowspan="2">7. Music, work, building, food</td><td>8. Fashion</td><td rowspan="2">8. Fashion, food, films and work</td><td>7. Music and hobbies</td></tr>
<tr><td>9. Food and work</td><td>9. Hobbies</td><td>8. Work</td></tr>
</table>

Irrespective of age, two main topics prevail, namely *general* and *the Internet.* Together they constitute 36–54.1% of all the anglicisms used. *General* vocabulary covers lexical items that do not really belong to some particular topic while as far as *the Internet* is concerned, it is natural that people who use this medium to create their journals cannot avoid using lexical items belonging to this field. Accordingly, it seems logical to exclude both topics, namely *general and the Internet,* from the quantitative analysis. Regarding the categories *business/finance/work, music, fashion* and *sport*, some definite tendencies can be identified. Users between 25 and 35 years old use more anglicisms from the topic *busines/finances/work* than younger or older users. This could be attributed to career achievements. The topics *music, fashion* and *sport* are more popular among the younger generation under 25, which can also be easily explained. The quantitative differences among other topics are rather insignificant – mainly because they reflect the interests of all generations such as *food, computer, technical gadgets, film, TV,* etc.

On the whole, the hypothesis *The age of the speaker influences the anglicisms used* is partly borne out by the present research. Some topics were identified that are used by certain age groups more than by the others.

4.1.3 Sex of the Producer and Anglicisms

The following hypothesis is to be tested in this section: *The sex of the producer may influence the number of anglicisms used.* This entails considering the above table again:

	< 25	25–35	> 35
Female Rus	0.554%/ 0.317%	0.562%/ 0.459%	0.737%/ 0.452%
Female Ger	0.934%/ 0.548%	0.921%/ 0.541%	0.608 %/ 0.52%
Male Rus	0.743%/ 0.466%	1.06%/ 0.624%	1.063%/ 0.715%
Male Ger	0.719%/ 0.519%	1.04%/ 0.598%	0.485%/ 0.406%

In all three age groups in Russian, men use more anglicisms than women, while in German in two cases out of three women use more anglicisms than men. Therefore it does not hold that the sex of the speaker influences the number of anglicisms used.

The next hypothesis to be tested is *men and women use more anglicisms in specific topics, which vary between the sexes.*

As earlier in this chapter, the total number of unique anglicisms found is presented in the table below by authors' sex and nationality. The columns show the number of unique anglicisms and their percentage of all the unique anglicisms in this age group accounted for by this particular topic.

Table 21: Total number of anglicisms found in particular age groups

	Female Russian (146)	*Female German (198)*	*Male Russian (182)*	*Male German (154)*
General	24.6%	44.4%	23.6%	46.7%
The Internet	17.1%	14.1%	23.07%	14.2%
Business/ finance/ work	6.8%	3.5%	8.24%	5.19%
Computers	4.8%	3.03%	12.6%	2.6%
Music/ showbusiness	2.7%	4.5%	3.29%	5.2%
Fashion/ beauty/ clothes	6.8%	2.02%	3.84%	3.9%
Hobbies/ leisure	4.8%	3.03%	1.64%	4.5%

	Female Russian (146)	*Female German (198)*	*Male Russian (182)*	*Male German (154)*
Technical gadgets/ technology	10.2%	9.09%	10.4%	7.14%
Sport	8.2%	8.6%	5.49%	5.2%
Food	3.4%	5.05%	0.54%	1.3%
TV	-	1.01%	0.54%	0.64%
Film	4.8%	1.5%	1.09%	1.94%
Building	1.36%	-	1.09%	-
Education	1.36%	-	-	-
Names of professions/ people	0.68%	1.01%	3.29%	4.54%

To show the subjects in which the most anglicisms are used by men and women, the following table was compiled. It lists the topics by decreasing quantities of anglicisms.

Table 22: Female and male topics

Female Russian	*Male Russian*	*Female German*	*Male German*
General	General	General	General
Internet	Internet	Internet	Internet
Technical gadgets	Computers	Technical gadgets	Technical gadgets
Sport	Technical gadgets	Sport	Music
Business	Business	Food	Sport
Fashion	Sport	Music	Business
Computer	Fashion	Business	Work
Hobbies	Music and work	Computers	Hobbies
Films		Hobbies	Fashion
Food	Hobbies	Fashion	Computer
Music	Films and building	Films	Films
Building and education	Food and TV	TV and work	Food
			TV
Work			

As in the case of age and anglicisms, three topics occupy the top positions in all sex groups, namely *general, the Internet* and *technical gadgets* (with the exception of *technical gadgets* being in fourth place among male Russian users). The complete coincidence of the first four categories is to be observed among female users in Russian and German.

Food is a typically 'female' topic while *work* can be described as a 'male' theme. In the case of *computers*, which could be traditionally assigned to 'male' topics, male users in German did not pay them much attention. Similarly, *fashion*, which might be assumed to be a 'female' topic, is at the bottom of the list among German females.

On the whole, after analysing statistical data, it can be stated that there are no 'female' or 'male' topics. The use of anglicisms in a particular subject is usually not influenced by the sex of the producer.

4.2 Topic-oriented *Blogs:* General Description

As mentioned above, the process of globalization and the leading role of the USA in most economic and political spheres has enabled the English language to acquire the status of *lingua franca*, which has inevitably led to the growing number of English loans in other languages. In fact there are certain semantic fields where the number of loans sometimes even exceeds the number of native units. This primarily concerns the terminology used in modern technology, high-tech, computing, sport, showbusiness and fashion.[96]

In the present paper the following topics have been chosen for analysis: computers, fashion, sport, music/showbusiness. This choice is based on the fact already dealt with that these topics definitely comprise a larger number of anglicisms than the other ones. On the other hand, the topics mentioned above are popular for discussion in *blogs*.

We will attempt to determine whether the number of loans in German exceeds the number of loans in Russian or vice a versa and in which topics.

Having analysed the corpus, the following statistical data can be shown here.[97]

96 See also Görlach 2002, Gester 2001.

97 Detailed statistical data are contained in the appendix.

Table 23: Anglicisms in topic-oriented blogs

		No. of words	*No. of anglicisms*	*No. of unique anglicisms*	*Nouns*	*Verbs*	*Adjectives*	*Adverbs*
Computer	Russian	10,317	582	154	127	15	12	0
	German	10,316	453	159	145	12	2	0
Fashion	Russian	10,515	226	64	53	1	8	2
	German	10,436	283	88	77	7	4	0
Music/ showbusiness	Russian	10,390	386	142	129	1	12	0
	German	10,248	416	125	114	6	5	0
Sport	Russian	10,151	356	82	75	1	6	0
	German	10,189	267	89	78	7	3	0

As can be seen from the table above, the total number of anglicisms found and the number of unique anglicisms differ drastically.[98] If we analyse the statistical data of each topic, we can state that the topic *computers* contains the greatest number of anglicisms, followed by *music/showbusiness*, *sport* and *fashion*. As far as the quantitative ratio between the number of anglicisms found in the German and Russian parts of the corpus is concerned, the following conclusions can be drawn. First of all, the number of all anglicisms in the Russian part exceeds that in the German part in the topics *computers* and *sport*, while the number of unique anglicisms found in *blogs* devoted to these topics is higher in the German part. On the other hand, in the topic *music/showbusiness*, the total number of anglicisms is larger in the German part, while the number of unique anglicisms is higher in the Russian one. As far as *fashion* is concerned, there are more anglicisms and unique anglicisms in the German part of the corpus.

On the whole, the hypothesis *the number of loans in one language definitely exceeds the number of loans in the other one* is not true. The number of loans depends on the topic, and if the number of all loans found is higher in one language, this does not mean that the number of unique loans will be also larger in this particular language.

The general tendencies concerning the subdivision of loans into parts of speech can be also clearly seen from the table. Most of the loans are nouns. As far as verbs are concerned, in all topics with the exception of *computers* the German part of the corpus proved to be richer in verbs than the Russian one,

98 Complete lists of unique anglicisms are contained in the appendix.

where in all other topics only one verb per topic was found. This can be explained by the conversion possibilities and peculiarities of the grammatical systems of the languages under consideration. Nouns converted into verbs are more typical of German, while in Russian in the same cases the verb is used to form a verb phrase, e.g. *Bowling → bowlen; боулинг→ играть в боулинг; Snowboard → snowboarden; сноуборд→ кататься на сноуборде; Shopping→ shoppen; шоппинг→ делать шоппинг*. The opposite tendency, though, applies to adjectives, the number of which prevails in the Russian part of the corpus. Almost any noun in Russian can be converted into an adjective, which is not possible in German, where the tendency to build compounds prevails, e.g. Designerfälschung – дизайнерская подделка, Demoaufnahme – демовая запись, Studioalbum – студийный альбом.

Only two adverbs were found in the Russian part of the topic *fashion*.

The following table shows the minimum and maximum number of anglicisms found in topic-oriented *blogs* in the two languages.

Table 24: Topics with minimum and maximum number of anglicisms

	Min	*Max*
Russian	*Fashion*	*Computer*
German	*Fashion*	*Computer*

As the table shows, general tendencies emerge concerning the number of anglicisms used in different topics in Russian and German.

Since the present paper is devoted to a comparative analysis of the anglicisms found in the German and Russian parts of the corpus, it makes sense to examine the anglicisms that have the same source in the English language with the approximate time of borrowing[99] and compounds found in the analysed corpus.

99 The first date of borrowing (in German) was taken from "A dictionary of European anglicisms: a usage dictionary of anglicisms in 16 European languages" ed. by Manfred Görlach (2001) and the second one (where there is no agreement concerning the German part of the corpus) from "Anglizismen-Wörterbuch: der Einfluß des Englischen auf den deutschen Wortschatz nach 1945" begr. von Broder Carstensen. Fortgef. von Ulrich Busse (1993, 1994, 1996).
The first date of borrowing (in Russian) was taken from "A dictionary of European anglicisms: a usage dictionary of anglicisms in 16 European languages" ed. by Manfred Görlach (2001) and the second one (where there is no agreement concerning the Russian part of the corpus) from «Современный словарь иностранных слов: толкование,

Table 25: Anglicisms of the same origin found in topic-oriented Russian and German blogs

- Sport

English	*German*	*Russian*
bowling	Bowling 1960s/1963	боулинг mid-20c
fitness	Fitness 1960s/1969 Fitness-Check Fitness club Fitnesstudio Fitness Studio Fitnesscenter	фитнес 1990s фитнес-фанатка фитнес-клуб фитнес-центр фитнесс-центр
training	Training mid-19c/early 20c Gerätetraining Trainingseinheiten Trainingsplan	тренинг end 20c/late 19c
trainer	Trainer mid-19c/early 20c Hometrainer	тренер mid 19c/first half of 20c тренерша тётка-тренер баба-тренер
snowboard	Snowboard 1980s/1983–89	сноуборд 1980s
sport	Sport 1820s	спорт early 20c
	sportlich	спортивный

- Fashion

English	*German*	*Russian*
designer	Designer 1960s/1961–66 Designerfälschung Designer Outlet Modedesigner Mode-Designer	дизайнер mid–late 20c
glamour	Glamour 1950s/1953–60	гламур 21c
jeans	Jeans 1960s/1959–69	джинсы mid-20c джинса джинсики
model	Model 1970s/1966–74	модель late 20c via Fr
sale	Sale	сейл late 20c

словоупотребление, словообразование, этимология» Л.М. Баш, А.В. Боброва и др. (2005).

English	*German*	*Russian*
shopping	Shopping 1970s/1963–69 Samstagvormittashopping Shopping-Rausch Shopping tour Shopping-Tour Shoppingtour Shoppingqueen Shoppen	шоппинг 1990s гранд шоппинг
top	Top 1970s/1968–69	топ late 20c
trend	Trend early 20c/1960s	тренд late 20c
to shop	Shoppen	шоппить
trendy	Trendy/1977 trendig	трендовый

- Music

English	*German*	*Russian*
beat	Beat 1960s–70s/1953–60	бит mid-20c/post 1950
CD	CD 1980s/1981–86 Doppel-CD CD-Inlet	CD 1980s
chart	Chart 1980s	чарт late 20c
clip	Clip 1980s/1977–90	клип mid–late 20c
demo	Demo-Tape 1980s Demoaufnahme Demoversion	демка рок-дэмка
DVD	DVD	DVD
folk music	Folk song 1960s Folkpop	фолк late 20c фолк-метал фолк-рок фольк
funk	Funk 1980s/1973–82	фанк 1980s фанки-диско-коммершиал хаус
hit	Hit 1960/1956–66	хит mid–late 20c
label	Label 1980s/1966–70	лейбл late 20c
live	Live 1954–70	лайв
mix	Mix 1970s/1963	микс late 20c
player	Player 1980s/1982	плейер 1980s
playlist	Playlist	плейлист

English	*German*	*Russian*
		плей-лист
pop music	Pop 1950s/1964–70	попса mid-20c поп-группа поп-музыка
producer	Producer 1960s/1961–66	продюсер mid-20
project	Projekt	проект
punk	Punk 1977–80	панк 1980s
remix	Remix 1990s	ремикс 1990s
rock music	Rock 1960s/1974–80 Rock-Legende Rockfestival	рок late 20c рок-барабанщик рок-гимн рок-группа рок-драйв рок-дэмка рок-музыка рок-обработка рок-опера рок-студия рок-театр рок-хитмейкер
sampler	Sampler 1970s/1973–82	сэмплер
show	Show end 19c/mid 20c	шоу early 20c реалити шоу
single	Single 1970s/1963–69 Maxi-Single	сингл late 20c
sound	Sound 1960s/1975 Sound Qualität	саунд 1990s саунд-продюсер
track	Track 1970s/1973–77	трек трек-лист трек лист
video	Videoclip 1980s	видеоклип late 20c

- Computers

English	*German*	*Russian*
backup	Backup 1980s	бэкап 1990s
boot	Boot 1980s Bootvorgang Bootmenü	бутсектор

English	*German*	*Russian*
browser	Browser	браузер late 20c
computer	Computer 1960s/1963–66 Computerspiel Computeranschluss Computerchaos Computer-Expert Computer-Gehäuse Computerkenntnisse Computerladen Computerschaden Computershop Computerspiel	компьютер mid-20c комп
driver	Driver 1980s	драйвер late 20c
e-mail	E-mail 1980s	e-mail 1990s
hacker	Hacker 1980s/1984	хакер late 20c
Internet	Internet 1990s Internetaktivität Internet-Installations-CD Internetleitung Internetgebühren	инет 1990s интернет, нет
laptop	Laptop 1980s/1988–89 Lappi	лэптоп 1990s лаптоп
log in	Login	логин
monitor	Monitor early 20c	монитор post 1950 (2)
notebook	Notebook 1990s	ноутбук 1990s ноут
PC	PC 1980s/1983–86	ПК late 20c
screenshot	Screenshot	скриншот
server	Server 1990s	сервер late 20c сервак
site	Site	сайт
upgrade	Upgrade Clamupgrade	апгрейд
Windows	Windows	винд винда виндоус
to install	installieren	инсталировать,инсталяться
to test	Testen 1950s	тестировать 20c

As can be seen from the tables above, the categories where the most identical anglicisms were found in both Russian and German are *computers*, *music/ showbusiness*, followed by *fashion* and *sport*. This tendency can be explained by the fact that both the categories *computers* and *music/ showbusiness* comprise a great number of late borrowings. In the category *computers*, the oldest loan is *computer*, whose date of borrowing can be traced to the 1960s, while most of the other loans were borrowed in the late 20th century. One more point to mention here is that there is no drastic difference between the time of borrowing of the majority of the same loans into German and Russian, the anglicisms mentioned being borrowed at approximately the same time. In the category *music /showbusiness*, the time of borrowing varies between the mid and late 20th century. Nevertheless, there are a few loans, which were borrowed into Russian and German at very different times. For example, the anglicism *hit* was borrowed into German in the 1960s but into Russian only in the late 20th century. The same goes for the anglicisms *rock* and *sound.* The anglicisms in the category *fashion* are older, being borrowed into German between the 1950s and 1970s. Here the difference between the time of borrowing into both the languages is clearly seen. The time of borrowing only coincides in the case of *jeans,* which was borrowed into German in the 1960s and into Russian in the mid-20th century. The time of borrowing of all other loans in Russian can be traced to the late 20th or even the early 21st century. This can be attributed to the historical background. Until perestroika, there was no *fashion* in the Soviet Union. Everybody wore the same clothes that were produced inside the country. And everything connected with the 'West', including clothes, was frowned-upon. This is why such borrowings as *designer, top, glamour, model, etc* only came into use at the end of the 20th century after the disintegration of the Soviet system.

Loans in the category *sport* are the oldest compared to the others. As new sports and related activities appear (traditionally emerging in the USA or at least pursued there), the vocabulary is enriched with the new loans, as in the case of *snowboard* or *fitness.* The oldest loan *sport* was borrowed into German in the early 19th century and into Russian only a century later.

To draw a line, the following conclusions can be drawn:

- On the whole, the number of anglicisms used in German does not really exceed that in Russian as far as *blogs* are concerned. According to the results, the use of anglicisms depends more on factors such as the sex and age of producers and the topics discussed;
- The number of anglicisms used depends on the subject matter of the text. More anglicisms are to be found in certain topic-oriented texts. The statis-

tics show that while in non-topic-oriented *blogs* anglicisms constitute around 1% of all lexemes used, in topic-oriented *blogs* this level is around 5%;

- The age and sex of producers do not influence the number of anglicisms used. Here completely contrasting tendencies can be observed in German and Russian. According to the statistical data, more anglicisms are used by young women in German but by older men in Russian. Even so, the hypothesis concerning the interdependence of anglicisms and the sex and age of producers was partly borne out. As different age groups have different interests, it is natural that they use anglicisms belonging to different topics. The same can be said about women and men, who also have different interests, and in some cases male and female topics can be distinguished.

In the case of *blogs*, the new medium *the Internet* influences not only the lexis of the producer but also their interests. That is why sex, age and language distinctions do not really work in the case of *blogs* as far as the number of anglicisms is concerned. The main factor influencing the use of anglicisms is the subject matter. As can be seen from the results of the present research, anglicisms that are directly related to Internet culture, computers, progress, etc are to be found in *blog* entries by all users regardless of their age, sex or nationality.

5. Graphical Integration

As far as adoption into the graphical systems of Russian and German is concerned, we ought to dwell on each system separately since, as is widely known, Russian employs the Cyrillic alphabet while the Latin one is used in German.

The most interesting examples from the analysed corpus will be examined in this chapter. Note that subdivision into topic-oriented and non-topic-oriented *blogs* is irrelevant to the graphical analysis of the anglicisms in the languages under consideration as the process of graphical integration takes place irrespective of the topics in which they are used.

5.1 Russian

The process of the adoption of anglicisms into the graphical system of the Russian language is complicated by the fact that the adopted anglicisms are originally rendered in the Latin alphabet, whereas Russian uses Cyrillic. Clearly, most anglicisms (ideally all of them) ought to be transferred from Latin to Cyrillic in order to become full members of the recipient language system.

The process of transfer can take place in different ways. Timofeeva suggests three ways in which anglicisms are adapted to the graphical system of the Russian language: *transplantation, transliteration* and *transcription.* (Timofeeva, 2005) But since these three ways of integration do not cover all the examples of the anglicisms found in the analysed corpus, *hybrid spelling* and *the mixed type* (including both transliteration and transcription) need to be added.

5.1.1 Transplantation[100]

Transplantation means that the anglicisms are transferred into Russian in their original form preserving their Latin spelling.

This type of adoption is primarily typical of proper and geographical names. But, on the other hand, it can be regarded as the first stage of integration. When a word occurs in the recipient language for the first time or can be traced to the new borrowings, the use of *transplantation* is common.

One example of transplantation is the abbreviation *sms*. Not long ago, it was difficult to imagine its Cyrillic variant. Nowadays both versions, *sms* and *смс,* are frequently used, e.g.:

100 Timofeeva 2005, Fink 2000.

«Одной из таких форм я и хочу посвятить свой пост, а именно письменной, а точнее выражение своей любви через *СМС*. Ведь нужно очень постараться уместить в одно *СМС* все те чувства, которые ты хочешь высказать своему самому дорогому».

«Он пробрался в мою телефонную книжку, выбрал там самого красивого, доброго и умного человечка и отослал ему эту любовную *sms*».

The abbreviations DVD and CD have also preserved their original form. In the case of CD, a loan translation is used along with the original form, namely компакт диск, whereas DVD remains unchanged.

5.1.2 Hybrid Spelling

The next stage of adoption is *hybrid spelling*. It should be pointed out that loan words found in their original spelling in Russian are not normally integrated into the grammatical system. However, when the need arises, cases of *hybrid spelling* are to be found. The most typical case is when an anglicism preserves its original spelling, namely its stem, but in order to function normally in the grammatical system, Cyrillic inflexions are added with the help of an apostrophe or hyphen:

Abbreviations: CD-Rom'ы, UPS'ы , XP-шка;

Full forms: user'ов, firewall-ы.

In addition, the combination of two stems, one of which preserves the spelling of the source language while the second adopts that of the recipient, is widespread. In such cases the stems are separated by a hyphen or written separately:

IP-адрес, USB-привод, VIP-карта;

DVD диск, CD компиляция, DVD плеер.

It is worth mentioning that English always seems to come first and Russian second and it should be also stressed that in all the examples given above, the anglicisms fulfil an attributive function in the noun phrase.

One more point to mention here is that no mixed instances of Latin and Cyrillic stems or inflexions written in the same word were found in the analysed corpus. There is always a clear separation between the two types of writing, with the help of either an apostrophe, a hyphen or just a space.

The instances of anglicisms that have preserved their original spelling or hybrid-spelling are not to be found in dictionaries of the Russian language. Although such spellings are not standard, enough examples can be found in *blogs*, where users write in a way that is convenient to them and the norms of the language are often ignored:

«Сколько раз я сталкивался с тем что *хр'шка* не дружит с 1с».

«Сижу и плачу. был запланирован большой переезд – серверы, активное сетевое оборудование, *Firewall'ы* и т.д.»

«Во-первых, Windows машины находятся за *Linux-овским NAT-ом*, то есть *firewall-ы* можно, в принципе, отключать».

«Один, казалось бы недостаток, связанный с дисковым пространством, необходимым для такого количества виртуальных машин, решается отчасти при использовании *linked-clone-ов*».

«А дело было так: ехала *BMW-шка* по ул. Красного курсанта, точнее не ехала, а летела…»

5.1.3 Transliteration

Transliteration can be also called 'letter-by-letter' transfer. This method of representing anglicisms in Russian is based on the graphical principle and the phonological peculiarities of the transferred word are not taken into consideration. Here each letter of the source word is reproduced with the corresponding letter in Cyrillic. The Cyrillic–Latin transliteration standard is shown below.[101]

Table 26: Cyrillic-Latin transliteration standard

Letters		Examples	
Cyrillic	*Latin*	*Cyrillic*	*Latin*
а А	a A	адрес	adres
б Б	b B	баба	baba
в В	v V	вы	vy
г Г	g G	голова	golova
д Д	d D	да	da
е Е	e E	еда	eda

101 ГОСТ 7.79:2000 «Система стандартов по информации, библиотечному и издательскому делу. Правила транслитерации кирилловского письма латинским алфавитом». URL: http://www.linginfo.it/rus/support/translit/gost/ (12 September, 2007).

Letters		Examples	
ё Ё	jo Jo	ёлка	jolka
ж Ж	zh Zh	журнал	zhurnal
з З	z Z	звезда	zvezda
и И	i I	книга	kniga
й Й	jj Jj	первый	pervyj
к К	k K	как	kak
л Л	l L	липа	lipa
м М	m M	муж	muzh
н Н	n N	нижний	nizhnijj
о О	o O	общество	obshhestvo
п П	p P	пара	para
р Р	r R	рыба	ryba
с С	s S	сестра	sestra
т Т	t T	товарищ	tovarishh
у У	u U	утро	utro
ф Ф	f F	физика	fizika
х Х	kh Kh	химический	khimicheskijj
ц Ц	c C	центральный	central'nyjj
ч Ч	ch Ch	часы	chasy
ш Ш	sh Sh	школа	shkola
щ Щ	shh Shh	щит	shhit
ъ Ъ	"	объявление	ob"javlenie
ы Ы	y Y	был	byl
ь Ь	'	альбом	al'bom
э Э	eh Eh	это	ehto
ю Ю	ju Ju	южный	juzhnyjj
я Я	ja Ja	яма	jama

As can be seen, in some cases one Russian grapheme requires more than one Latin grapheme. Even so, there are 20 monographs.[102] In the next table, the correspondence between Russian and English graphemes (monographs) is enumerated.[103]

Table 27: Correspondence between Russian and English monographs

English monograph	*Russian grapheme*
A	А
E	Е
I	И
O	О
U	У
B	Б
C	К/ С
D	Д
F	Ф
G	Г
K	К
L	Л
M	М
N	Н
P	П
R	Р
S	С

102 A monograph refers to a correspondence between one Russian grapheme and one Latin grapheme or vice versa.

103 See also Timofeeva 1995.

English monograph	*Russian grapheme*
T	Т
V	В
Z	З

Transliteration is based on the principle of equivalence. Accordingly, if there is no equivalence between an English monograph and a Russian grapheme, transliteration fails in this case.

The following English monographs do not have Russian equivalents, which is why they are not involved in the process of transliteration: y, h, q, w, x, j. Nevertheless, reverse transliteration from Russian into English is possible, as can be seen from the table above. These letters are transferred into Russian according to the rules of transcription. It should, however, be noted that the English *h* in the initial position corresponds to the Russian *x* as in *Hard rock → хард рок* and can be transliterated.

Examples of *transliteration* include:

- fitness→фитнес

Although the process of transliteration takes place here, judging by the examples found in the corpus ,there is no conensus concerning spelling. In some cases it is spelled with one '*c*' at the end of the word (the dictionary norm), in some cases double '*c*' is found. Note that there are few examples of borrowings with double consonants at the end of the word.[104] The double-*c* spelling is

104 «В исконно русских словах удвоенные буквы, как правило, стоят на месте долгих согласных: вожжи, можжевельник, ссора (в корнях); главветврач, госсектор (в сложносокращенных словах). На стыке приставки и корня - долгий согласный звук также сохраняется (поддать, раззадорить), на стыке корня и суффикса – необязательно, ср. двойное НН по разным основаниям. Аналогичная ситуация и с заимствованными словами. Во второй половине слова двойной согласный исчезает легче, чем в начале - на стыке приставки и корня". (Виталия Павлова "Правописание заимствованных слов". URL: http://forum.lingvo.Rus/actualthread.aspx?-tid=28172 (29 June, 2005) (In Russian words, double letters occur in the place of long consonants, such as вожжи, можжевельник, ссора (in the root), as well as главветврач, госсектор (in compound abbreviations). At the junction of a prefix and the root a long consonant is preserved.(поддать, раззадорить), but not always at the junction of the root and the suffix. Compare the double H in different circumstances. Loans are

probably used more often by people with a good knowledge of English as they transliterate the original English spelling into Cyrillic.

«На *фитнес* чтоли записаться или бодибилдинг....»

«Сегодня после доооолгого перерыва сходили с другом в *фитнесс*».[105]

- model→модель

Note the soft 'l' at the end of the word.[106]

«Там все на другом уровне, к тому же *модель* получает проценты с каждого билборда».

- demo→ демо

«Поверь на слово человеку, отслушавшему на своем веку сотни *демо*».

- server→ сервер

«На работе полетел *сервер*. Причем, это был не простой *сервер*».

The following examples are interesting due to their incomplete transliteration:

- glamour→ гламур

---

treated in a similar way. At the word-ending, the consonant is more likely to disappear than in the beginning on a prefix and root joint).
On the other hand, Timofeeva (1995:51) makes the following suggestions: in anglicisms that do not have long consonants but are still written with double consonants, the frequency of use influences the spelling or the realization of the sound image of the word in writing: «Именно частотность употребления и тенденция к передаче произношения заимствований на письме, «готовность» русского языка отказаться от удвоения букв в иноязычных словах приводит к упрощению звуков в произношении и удвоенных звуков на письме [...] В целом транскрипционные формы - без удвоения - представляются нам перспективными, поэтому мы рекомендуем писать новые англицизмы в соответствии с произношением: киднепинг, хэви-метал и под». (Frequency of use, a tendency to reflect the pronunciation in writing and the readiness of the Russian language to abolish double consonants in loans lead to the simplification of pronunciation as well as spelling [...] On the whole, transcriptional forms without doubling seem really far-sighted, so we advise spelling loans based on pronunciation киднепинг, хэви-метал etc.).

105 As far as syntactic peculiarities are concerned, they will not be discussed in the present paper.

106 There are two allophones of [l] in Russian. In the final position English middle [l] is changed into soft [l'].

In the cluster -ou, -o is omitted, probably because such vowel clusters do not normally occur in Russian.

«*Гламур*, как много в этом слове для сердца русского... ну и так далее».

- discount→ дисконт, дисконтный.

In the cluster *-ou*, *-u* is omitted in both cases and as in the case of *glamour* incomplete transliteration takes place.

«Решили мы поиграть в игру с *дисконтом*».

«Третий тариф – если я не ошибаюсь, *дисконтный*, сумму я не назову».

5.1.4 Transcription

The sound image of the anglicisms is reproduced with the letters which can express these sounds in writing more precisely. The pronunciation of the word is achieved in writing.

Transcription is a complicated process as the phonetic systems of Russian and English differ drastically. Such English phonemes and diphthongs as [æ], [ə:], [uə], [əu], [θ], [ð], [w], etc have no equivalents in the system of Russian phonemes that could be realized in writing.

The process of *transcription* theoretically has the following stages:

- The graphic image of the word is transcribed: upgrade→[ʌpgreɪd].
- An attempt is made to imitate the sound image of the English word by means of Russian phonemes: [ʌpgreɪd]→ [апгрэjд].
- The sound image, changed or at least adapted to the system of Russian phonemes, is again realized in writing, albeit with the help of another alphabet, namely Russian: [апгрэjд]→апгрейд.

The process is hence as follows: upgrade→[ʌpgreɪd]→ [апгрэjд]→ апгрейд.

Based on the examples from the analysed corpus and the research by Timofeeva (1995), the following table was compiled charting the most typical correspondences between English phonemes and Russian graphemes.[107]

---

107 The cases of pure transcription are relatively rare, which is why a number of examples in the table illustrate the mixed type.

Table 28: Correspondences between English phonemes and Russian graphemes

Vowels		
English phoneme	Russian grapheme	Anglicisms[108]
i:	И	*Ридер* (reader ['ri:də])
ɪ	И,Е	*Чип* (chip [ʧɪp]), *девайс* (device[dɪ'vaɪs])
e	Е,Э	*Чек* (check [ʧek]), *хеппи энд* (happy end['hæpɪ end])
æ	А,Е,Э	*Матч* match [mæʧ], *бренд* brand[brænd], *бэкап* back up['bækʌp]
ə:	Ё	*Бёздей* birthday['bə:ədeɪ]
ə	А,Е,Ø	*Аккаунт* account [ə'kaunt] *фермер* farmer['fa:mə]партишн *partition*[pər'tɪʃən]
ʌ	А,Е,О,У	*Апгрейд* upgrade[ʌp'greɪd], *регби* rugby['rʌgbl], *ром* rum[rʌm], *клумба* clump[klʌmp]
ɔ :	О	*Бейсбол* baseball['beɪsbɔ:l]
ɔ	О	*Хот-спот* hot spot['hɔt spɔt]
ɑ :	А,Е	*Чарт* chart [ʧɑ:rt], *фермер* farmer['fɑ:mə]
u:	У,Ю	*Бутсектор* boot sector[bu:t 'sektə], *блюминг* blooming['blu:mɪŋ]
ʊ	У	*Футбол* football['fʊtbɔ:l]
eɪ	ЕЙ,ЭЙ,Е,Э	*Апгрейд* upgrade[ʌp'greɪd], *нью-эйдж* new age[nju:'eɪʤ], *бэби* baby['beɪbɪ], *тренер* trainer['treɪnə]
aɪ	АЙ,ЯЙ	*Девайс* device[dɪ'vaɪs], *батерфляй* butterfly['bʌtəflaɪ]
aʊ	АУ,ОВ,О	*Аккаунт* account[ə'kaʊnt], *ковбой* cowboy['kaʊbɔɪ]

108 Although the time of borrowing is not taken into consideration here, it should be pointed out that the time of borrowing influences the way of transcription, as in the case of уикенд (earlier borrowing) and Виндоус (later borrowing). Transcription is taken from Longman Dictionary of Contemporary English, 3rd Edition, 1995.

ɔ ɪ	ОЙ	*Джойнт* joint[ʤɔɪnt]
oʊ	ОУ,О	*Виндоус* windows['wɪndoʊz], *профайл* profile['proʊfaɪl]
iə	И	*Пирсинг* piercing['pɪərsɪŋ]
eə	Е	*Софтвер* software['sɒftweə]
uə	УЭ	*Спиричуэлс* spirituals['spɪrɪʧuəlz]
Consonants		
p	П	*Клинап* clean-up['klɪnʌp]
b	Б	*Браузер* browser['braʊzə]
t	Т	*Трек* track[træk]
d	Д	*Драйвер* driver['draɪvə]
k	К	*Клипмейкер* clip maker[klɪp meɪkə]
g	Г	*Гольф* golf[gɒlf]
s	С,З	*Скейт* skate[skeɪt], *стипльчез* steeplechase['stɪplʧeɪs]
z	З	*Дизайнер* designer[dɪ'zaɪnə], *бизнес* business['bɪznəs]
m	М	*Матч* match[mæʧ]
n	Н	*Ноутбук* notebook['nəʊtbʊk]
l	Л	*Лейбл* label['leɪbəl]
r	Р	*Апгрейд* upgrade[ˌʌp'greɪd]]
ʃ	Ш	*Партишн* partition[pa:'tɪʃən]
f	Ф	*Флэш* flash[flæʃ]
h	Х,Г	*Хай-кат* high cut[haɪ kʌt], *Гандбол* handball['hændbɔ:l]
ʤ	ДЖ,Ж	*Джойс* joys[ʤɒɪs], *диск-жокей* disk-jockey['dɪskʤɒkɪ]
ʧ	Ч,ТЧ	*Чек* cheque [ʧek], *скотч* scotch[skoʧ]

θ	З	*Бёздей* birthday['bɜ:θdeɪ]
ð	З	*Бразерз* brothers['brʌðəz]
v	В	*Девайс* device[dɪ'vaɪs]
w	В,У	*Виндоус* windows['wɪndəʊz], *уикенд* weekend['wɪkend]
j	Й,Ь	*Йогурт* yogurt['jɒgət], *компьютер* computer[kɒm'pju:tə]
ʒ	Ж	*Фьюжн* fusion['fju:ʒən]
ŋ	НГ	*Пирсинг* piercing['pɪərsɪŋ]

Therefore, as Timofeeva puts it:

> ...фонетический принцип предполагает фиксацию произношения в письменном облике заимствования. (Timofeeva 1995:23) ("the phonetic principle suggests the fixation of pronunciation in the written form of the loan")

Here in most cases we are dealing not just with original pronunciation but with adopted forms of it. Long vowels typical of the English language cannot be achieved in Russian, and the same can be said about diphthongs and triphthongs. The word *player*, which has a triphthong in the middle *[eɪə]*, is realized in writing as *плейер [пл'ejep]* or *плэер [плэjep]:*

- player→ плейер, плеэр, плеер

Although the process of transcription takes place, this results in the appearance of a number of different versions of the same word.

«*Плеер* успешно читает с этих винтов».

«Музыку слушаю, загружая небольшими порциями в МП3 *плеэр*, а кино не смотрю уже неделю».

«*Плейер* не мог диск найти».

- track→трек[109], трэк

109 «Раньше в русском языке действовала закономерность: перед /э/ могли быть только мягкие согласные. Поэтому в заимствованных словах перед /э/ твёрдые согласные заменялись парными мягкими. Сейчас эта закономерность утрачена; во многих заимствованных словах произносятся только твёрдые согласные». (Earlier in Russian the following rule was applied: before /э/ only soft consonants were used. This is why in borrowings hard consonants were substituted by soft ones. Nowadays

«А ещё есть такая тема, как обязательно прослушать *трек* хотя бы до того момента, когда он засчитается на ласт фм=))».

«...тут система не как у обычного радио, а отдельные *трэки*, которые есть у них на сайте с похожим тэгом проигрываются в плейлисте...»

- backup→ бэкап, бекап

«Установил недавно Висту и теперь не могу с помощью Акрониса сделать *бэкап* ФФ».

«Любопытная статья про *бекап* и различие между системами архивирования и резервного копирования».

- e-mail→ е-мейл, е-мэйл

«Получить божественный е-*мейл* можно следующими способами».

«Соответственно, если с кем-то из этих у вас намечается конфликт, прячьте пароли и не светите е-*мэйл*, тем более ..»

5.1.5 A mixed Type

Most of the anglicisms introduced into the graphical system of the Russian language are transferred using both *transliteration* and *transcription.*

Typical examples include the words with the suffixes *-ing* and *-er.* These suffixes are always transliterated as *-инг* and *-ер*, while the stem of the word can be transferred according to the rules of *transcription:*

- bowling → боулинг

The lexeme is adopted due to the mixed type. The diphthong [əʊ] is transferred according to the rules of transcription as [оу], while the rest of the word is transliterated.[110]

«После двух партий мне это занятие смертельно надоело, о чем я и сказала финдиру, сопроводив свое высказывание робким девичьим намеком, что *боулинг* – не мой вид спорта и отдыха».

---

this rule is not always applicable and therefore in many borrowings hard consonants before /э/ are used.) (Современный русский язык 2002:137). This rule can be applied here to fitness, player, backup, track, e-mail etc.

110 In Russian there is a back nasal phoneme [нг] that can be regarded as an analogue to the English nasal [ŋ]. This is why it is a moot point whether the suffix -ing should be transliterated or transcribed in Russian. In this paper it is viewed as transliteration as this back nasal sound does not occur at the end of the word in Russian.

- training → тренинг

The diphthong [eɪ] is transcribed and then converted into the monophthong [e] while the rest of the word is transliterated.[111]

«*Тренинг* по улучшению навыков общения от самого великого и ужасного манкубуса (кстати его сегодня должны показывать по ТНТ в правилах съёма)».

- snowboard → сноуборд

In Russian the diphthong [əʊ] is transferred according to the rules of transcription as [оу] as in the case of bowling. Then, the cluster oa is realized through transcription as [о] while the rest of the word is transliterated.

«*Сноуборд* крутая вещь, но он нас погубит !))».

- designer→дизайнер

The stem is transferred according to the rules of transcription, while the suffix is transferred using the rules of transliteration.

«Когда мне было 17, какие-то знакомые, узнав, что я *дизайнер*, рассказали, что есть компания, которая занимается воздушными шарами».

- shopping→шоппинг

The cluster [sh] is transcribed into [ш] while the rest of the word is transliterated.[112.]

«В этом году *шоппинг* оказался удачным и каждый купил то, что хотел :)))»

- compilation→ компиляция

The native suffix is attached to the stem in Russian. As far as the stem is concerned, the initial c is transcribed and realized as the Russian k in writing while the rest of the stem is transliterated.

«*Компиляция* самых удачных, на мой взгляд, ремиксов на песни Ladytron и ремиксов Ladytron на песни других «популярных композиторов», типа мистера Гэхэна или Felix da Housecat».

Sometimes, different ways of transition are applied to one and the same word. In this case, different varieties appear that exist side by side. For example: лаптоп – лэптоп – лептоп. The first version is a case of transliteration while the second and the third ones are cases of transcription:

111 Ibid.
112 Ibid.

«Думаю мало какая женщина устоит перед таким изящно оформленным *лэптопом*. А это именно *лэптоп*!) ...»

«В пятницу нашел *лаптоп* себе. Реально нашел».

«таскаю сегодня за собой *лептоп*, потому что а) все на работе, поэтому со всеми можно пообщаться, б) потому что всегда есть ощущение, что для работы необходим интернет, что есть абсолютная ложь!»

In the case of the English phonemes [m, n, r, l, p, b, k, g], etc, there is a coincidence of both transliteration and transcription.

- hacker→хакер

Here it is difficult to distinguish transliteration from transcription. The cluster ck is transcribed while the rest of the word leaves no doubt about the use of transliteration.

«Путем подбора и изменения пароля *хакер* получил несанкционированный доступ к информации, содержащейся в анкете потерпевшей на одном из сайтов знакомств».

- monitor→монитор

«Первое впечатление было, что почти ничего не изменилось, так, на эпсилон (*монитор* не самый поганый)».

- single→ сингл

«*Сингл* записывается собственноручно, мы пытаемся выжать как можно больше качества».

- hit→хит

«Это не бросается в глаза, но становится заметно, когда на «Русском радио» начинают звучать песни, которые на этот усредненный *хит* не похожи».

In this case the results of both transliteration and transcription coincide.

- top→топ

«За юбкой последовал шёлковый *топ* на бретельках».

On the whole, taking into consideration the examples analysed, it can be stated that transcription is an alternative method used when there are more sound-letter correspondences in a word than letter-letter ones, i.e. when transliteration fails due to absence of equivalences.

5.1.6. Spelling of Compounds

As far as the spelling of borrowed compounds in Russian is concerned, there are some definite rules:

> Примечание 1. При колебаниях между дефисным и слитным написанием слов иноязычного происхождения предпочитается второе, если в русском языке в слове не выделяются составные части с присущим им значением, например: *блиц-криг – блицкриг, ватер-машина – ватермашина, ватер-поло – ватерполо, гумми-арабик – гуммиарабик, метрд'отель – метрдотель, табльд'от – табльдот.* Ср. также: *крепдешин, файдешин, фильдекос, фильдеперс.* ("When there is no unity concerning the spelling of compounds, namely whether they should be written with a hyphen or in one word, the former way is preferred if it is impossible to distinguish the parts of compounds with distinctive meaning, for example: *блиц-криг – блицкриг, ватер-машина – ватермашина, ватер-поло – ватерполо, гумми-арабик – гуммиарабик, метрд'отель – метрдотель, табльд'от – табльдот.* Ср. также: *крепдешин, файдешин, фильдекос, фильдеперс.)* (Розенталь 1999: Chapter IX)

If a word is not perceived like a unity or compound but more as a noun phrase, separate spelling is applied.

Timofeeva (1995:59), however, suggests in her research some other rules concerning the spelling of borrowed compounds in Russian, namely:

- Spelling in one word is typical of compounds where the first component ends in a vowel and the second begins with a vowel or a consonant. For example: пром*ок*ассета, дикс*ил*енд, сно*уб*орд, скиборд, etc.;
- Spelling with a hyphen is typical of those borrowed compounds where one constituent ends and the other begins with the vowel. Even so, Timofeeva notes a tendency to spell such anglicisms in one word,[113] and this is borne out by the results of the present research: саун*дт*рек, кли*пм*ейкер, бло*кб*астер, брен*д-м*енеджер, ро*к-д*райв, саун*д-п*родюсер;
- Separate spelling is not typical of borrowed compounds. They are written separately only when the loan is translated as a word group: луз фит – свободный покрой, хеппи энд – счастливый конец.

5.2 German

As German and English both use the Latin alphabet, the process of integrating anglicisms into the graphical system of German is not as complicated as in Rus-

---

113 See Item 5.1.1.

sian since most of the anglicisms preserve their original spelling. Even so, there are a number of rules that all loanwords follow in the system of German.

The most striking peculiarity that German spelling has is that all nouns are written with a capital letter. This rule is also true for loans:[114] Fan, Baby, Song.

5.2.1 Spelling of Compounds

In Duden, the following rules are stated concerning compound nouns (DUDEN 2006:183ff.):

Großschreibung gilt

- für Substantive aus anderen Sprachen wenn sie nicht als Zitatwörter gemeint sind. Sind sie mehrteilig wird der erste Teil großgeschrieben;
- substantivische Bestandteile werden auch im Innern mehrteiliger Fügungen großgeschrieben, die als ganzes die Funktion eines Substantivs haben.

Given these rules, each constituent of a compound is capitalized if they are written with a hyphen and so function as a single noun, e.g. *Shopping-Tour, Fitness-Center, Firmware-Update.* If the constituents are written separately and do not constitute a whole functioning as a single noun, the first word is capitalized and the second is not, e.g. *Shopping tour.*

If there are more than two constituents, different ways of spelling are possible, such as all constituents capitalized, the first and the last, or just the first one, e.g.: *Afterwork-Chillout-Abend, One-Night-Stand,* or *Duty-free-Shop, Break-event-point.* The examples where all the constituents are capitalized were found in the analysed corpus while the others are taken from the research by Ilse Sörensen (1994) based mainly on DUDEN studies. Judging by the examples given above, it can be stated that in the case of compounds all types of capitalization are possible, although at any rate the first noun is always capitalized.[115]

One more problem concerning the spelling of compounds in German is the use of a hyphen or separate or joined spelling. Duden states the following rules (DUDEN 2006:1176 ff.):

---

114 In this paper, the anglicisms taken from computer language are analysed. In this case, ignoring this rule is typical. In most cases, users do not spell nouns with capital letters, but as this is a peculiarity of computer language, this cannot be considered a norm – which is why one of the ways anglicisms are incorporated into the system of German on the graphical level is the capitalization of nouns.

115 Though this statement is not always true for Internet language.

- Substantive, Adjektive, Verbstämme, Pronomen oder Partikel können mit Substantiven Zusammensetzungen bilden. Man schreibt sie ebenso wie mehrteilige Substantivierungen zusammen;
- Dieser Regel folgen auch lexikalisierte, ursprünglich aus dem Englischen stammende bzw. aus Englischen Einheiten gebildete Zusammensetzungen;
- Aus dem Englischen stammende Bildungen aus Adjektiv+ Substantiv können zusammengeschrieben werden, wenn der Hauptakzent auf dem ersten Bestandteil liegt, also Hotdog oder Hot Dog, aber nur High Society und Electronic Banking.

The above rules concern direct loans, consisting of foreign material and pseudoloans. It can also be assumed that hybrids are treated as native compounds and also follow the above-mentioned rules.

As far as spelling with a hyphen is concerned, Duden suggests the following rules (Ibid.):

- Aus anderen Sprachen stammende Verbindungen aus Substantiv + Substantiv, die sich im Deutschen grammatisch wie Zusammensetzungen verhalten, werden zusammengeschrieben; ebenso ist die verdeutlichende Schreibung mit Bindestrich möglich;
- Aus dem Englischen stammende Substantivierungen aus Verb + Adverb schreibt man mit Bindestrich; das Adverb wird dann kleingeschrieben. Daneben ist auch Zusammenschreibung möglich sofern die Lesbarkeit nicht beeinträchtigt ist.

Basically, the following rules are to be applied: a compound in which one of the components is stressed and which can be easily understood is written together. If there may be difficulties in understanding, the hyphen is used. And if both components are stressed, separate spelling is applied (Gester 2001:74). The use of a hyphen in German is a means for better understanding compound names, as noted by Stephanie Bohmann (1996:59).

Regarding the use of apostrophes, Silke Gester (2001:69) points out that the use of the apostrophe, especially in the genitive singular, was widespread in the early 1990s. Its use was based on a trend. Nowadays there are fewer examples of the apostrophe in German. Indeed, no instances were found in the analysed corpus.

5.2.2 Spelling of Particular Letter Combinations

In respect of letters or combinations of letters in the particular positions that are not typical of German, there is a number of possible ways for the anglicisms to be accepted into the system, namely: substitution with the close native combination of letters, coexistence of variants and the retention of the original spelling.[116] Even so, Duden suggests the following rules in connection with borrowings (DUDEN 2006:1171-1172):[117]

Fremdsprachige Laut-Buchstaben-Zuordnungen:

Laute	Buchstaben	Beispiele
[k]	C ch qu	Clown, crew Chaos, character Mannequin
[s]	C, ce	Chance, city
[ʃ]	Ch sh	Chance, chef Shop, shorts
[ʒ]	G,j	Genie, ingenieur
[t]	th	Theater
[v]	v	Virus
[ʤ]	G j	Manager, teenager Jeans, jeep, job
[lj]/[j]	ll	Billard
[ts]	C t (vor [i]+vokal)	Aceton Funktion, nation
[ʧ]	Ch ge dge	Chip, coach, College, Bridge

116 See also Görlach 2002.

117 Here the combinations of letters/ sounds typical of anglicisms are shown.

Im Prozess der Integration entlehnter Wörter können fremdsprachige und integrierte Schreibung nebeneinander stehen. Manche fremdsprachige Schreibungen sind nur noch fachsprachlich üblich:

[f]	ph-f	Photographie-Fotografie
[g]	gh-g	Joghurt-Jogurt
[j]	y-j	Yoga-Joga
[k]	c-k	Code-Kode
[s]	C-ss,ß	Sauce-Soße
[ʃ]	ch-sch	Sketch-Sketsch
[t]	th-t	Thunfisch-Tunfisch

Here are the rules introduced in *English in Europe*, ed. by Görlach, Carstensen et al. that supplement Duden rules and examples taken from *blogs*:[118]

- English <c> in the initial position or German <k>:
  - *substitution:* Keks < cakes, Kamera < camera;
  - *coexistence:* Cord/ Kord, Club/ Klub;
  - *retention:* Cash, coachen, Cover, Computer.
- English <sh> or <ch> in the initial position or German <sch>
  - *retention:* Shirt, Show, Shopping.
- Double consonants in the final position coexist with original spelling:
  - Tip/ Tipp, Spam/ Spam.

On the whole the following conclusions can be drawn:

As far as the spelling of compounds is concerned, in German a better understanding of compounds plays the decisive role in the choice between different spelling possibilities while in Russian it depends on how meaningful the constituents of a compound are.

118 See also Görlach 2002.

Using the examples taken from the analysed corpus, the following tendencies in spelling compounds in German and Russian can be stated:

Compound nouns (noun+noun, noun+adjective) in German tend to be written in one word while in Russian separate spelling prevails. In the case of compound nouns (noun+Acronym (abbreviation)) in both languages, the majority of the examples are written with a hyphen as are compounds consisting of more than two components.[119] In her research concerning compounds in German, Stephanie Bohmann (1996:59) arrives at the following results: "Unter den rein englischen Komposita sind fast 90% mit Bindestrich geschrieben." The results of our research differ drastically. Only 23.8% of compounds consisting only of English material found in German and 49.1% in Russian are spelled with a hyphen.

Regarding compound anglicisms written in one word (hybrids), the use of a linking element can be found in some cases. In German it is *-e, -(e)n* or *-s* (Pferd*e*sport, Training*s*plan, Kassete*n*rekorder); in Russian *-o* (френд*о*лента). These are the only compounds written with the linking element in the whole corpus. Hence whereas linking elements are used in some cases (13.13%) to create compounds with the help of loaned material in German, in Russian such a phenomenon is not at all typical.

As far as the spelling of particular letter combinations is concerned, the tendency of adjusting the original spelling to the native one takes place in both Russian and German: in Russian by transferring the original Latin spelling to Cyrillic, and in German through the adjustment of the original letter combinations to the closest native ones.

Once again it should be stressed that as far as the graphical adoption of anglicisms in the text type *blog* is concerned, the term 'norm' as presented in dictionaries in most cases ceases to exist. When adopting words, users choose the way of spelling which seems the most convenient to them at the time (in terms of saving time, user-friendliness, etc). Moreover, the background of each user influences the way the anglicisms are spelled. Users with a good knowledge of English may not change the original at all, or transfer Latin spelling into Cyrillic (in Russian), preserving the sound-letter combinations (the use of double letters). On the other hand, users with a poor background knowledge of English transfer units based on the sound image of the word. For the above-mentioned reasons, the ways in which the adoption of anglicisms takes place on the graphi-

119 The spelling of compounds was examined in detail in Item 5.2.

cal level vary from *blog* to *blog* and cannot really be standardized – and therefore can only partly bear out the norms provided in dictionaries.

6. Morphological Integration

6.1 Word Formation

6.1.1 Composition

The creation of new words and word clusters is frequently used means of composition in both German and Russian. Having analysed the corpus of both languages, we found 58.6% of all nouns in the German part of the corpus and 37.59% of the Russian nouns to be compounds representing various types of formation and origin.

Compounds can first of all be differentiated by the number of members they consist of (Chang 2003:116). In the corpus, two-member (by far the most common), three-member and four-member compounds were found. Interestingly, although German is famous for its tendency to create long, multi-member compounds,94.2% of all compounds found in the Russian part of the corpus were two-member compounds compared to just 90.2% in the German part.[120]

In addition, the form of compounds should be also taken into consideration. Applying this criterion, all compounds can be divided into:

- Compounds consisting only of foreign material, including both direct borrowings and pseudo-loans;
- Hybrids consisting either of borrowings from the English language and native material or borrowings from English and some other constituents of Greek or Latin origin which are used internationally but perceived as native.

In the German part of the corpus, the number of hybrids is similar to the number of compounds consisting only of foreign material (127 foreign-material compounds and 155 hybrids) while in the Russian part the difference between these two categories is far more pronounced, compounds consisting only of borrowed units outnumbering hybrids by nearly two to one (114 compared to 59). This is probably because in Russian the means of composition are not as frequently used as in German; compounds that are borrowed are integrated into the system whereas new compounds formed with the help of borrowed lexemes are less typical, although loan translations are more typical as compounds.

120 See the table below for examples.

Another important aspect of hybrids is that the foreign member can be either the first, second or last member of a compound, e.g. *саунд-драма, баба-тренер, Babybild, Bodentraining.*

Some of the hybrids found in the Russian part of the corpus are formed in a way that is completely alien to the system of the Russian language. It is a norm that the second member of a compound determines the first, as in the above-mentioned example баба-тренер. Yet most of the hybrids are built in a different way, namely with the first member determining the second. This form is gradually being accepted into the system of the language as more and more compounds like this appear: саунд-драма, борд-кросс, бренд-менеджер, интернет-карта, etc. As far as German is concerned, such constructions where the first member determines the second are a norm.

The part of speech the members of a compound belong to also varies. , As regards the material analysed, the patterns used most often are noun+noun, noun+adj and verb+noun.

Regarding *'loans consisting only of foreign material'* in Russian, here not only the anglicisms that have preserved their original spelling are taken into consideration but also compounds consisting of foreign lexical elements that have been assimilated into the system of the Russian language in writing and grammar.

The following table shows the most typical types of compounds along with examples found in the corpus:

Table 29: List of compounds

	Russian	German
Loans consisting only of foreign material		
Noun+Noun	nickname job offer ipod-video арт-рок блокбастер боди-бар бодибилдинг бодикомбат	American Football Baby-Shop Blog Editor Bodylotion Bodyshop Bootmenü Bootloader Boyband

	Russian	German
	бодипамп борд-кросс бренд-менеджер бум-бокс голкипер интернет-карта интернет-клип кард-ридер клипмейкер лаптоп/лэптоп пауэрлифтинг пиджак продакт плейсмент рок-группа рок-драйв рок-дэмка саунд-продюсер саундсистема саундтрек сервис центр/сервис-центр скейтборд скиборд скриншот сноуборд сноубординг сноубордист спортклуб степ-аэробика степ-платформа трек-лист/трек лист	Boygroup Browser game Cable guy Chatroom Citybus Club-Mate Cocktailbar Computer Band Computer-Expert Computershop Coverversion Crosstrainer Dancefloor Designer Outlet Downloadlink Downloadserver Entertainment-Product Fashiongirl Fashiontipp Fashion-Victims Firewall Firewire Fitnesscenter/Fitness-Center Fitness-Check fitness club Fitness-Studio /Fitnesstudio Framework Hardliner Hardware Headset

	Russian	German
	фанарт фитнес клуб фитнес- центр/фитнесс-центр фитнес-фанатка флэш-диск флеш-карта. флешмоб фолк-метал фолк-рок хит парад чекдиск чоппер-круизер шоу-бизнес юзеринфо юзернейм юзерпик	HipHop Homepage Shop Internet Community Jogging-Sessions Keyboard Keyboarderin Laptop Layers Look Mail-Account Mail-Software Mailbox Mountainbike Musicplayer Musikvideo Notebook Pingpong Playlist Powerbook Product-Key Programmcode Screenshot Server-Update Shopping tour/ Shopping-Tour/ Shoppingtour Shoppingqueen Snowboard Snowboarden Snowbombing Skitour Soundblaster Support-Team

	Russian	German
		Tray-Icon Clamupgrade Kernelupdates Videoclip Voice-Funktion Wakeboarden Webbrowser Weblog Weight Watchers Windows-Desktop Windows-Setup Windowsuser Wintersport
Noun+Adjective		Feedback Popup Showdown
Adjective+Noun	диксиленд дисконтная карта диско-клуб инди-лейбл компакт-диск кроссовер-кабель луз фит нью-метал нью-эйдж панк-рок попкорн пресс-конференция пресс-релиз реалити шоу системный хард	Backstage Bluescreen Clean install Cut Copy Down Phase Fairplay Fastfood/ Fast Food Flatrate Freelancejob High Heels Highlight Hotline Hot Pants Inline-Skater Liveperformance

	Russian	German
	софтвер софт-джойс топ-менеджер хай-кат харддрайв хардрок хеппи энд хеппи бёздей хот-спот дресс шорты этно-шоу bluetooth minimal techno	Light Version Live Video Longdrink Mighty Mouse Mainboard Newcomer New look Open air Onlinebanking Pole-Position Private Party Reallife Shortcut Special Edition Special Guest Surround-Sound Walking Programm
Verb+Noun	плейлист плей-лист страйкбол	Prepaykarte Swim-Suit
Abbreviation+Noun	пиар-компания CD компиляция CDROM DVD диск DVD плеер USB-дивайс USB-драйв USB-кабель USB-модем USB-порт VIP-карта	CD-Image CD-Inlet Mp3-Player PC-Pool PDF-Creator TV-Team USB-Stick VIP-Tour

	Russian	German
Abbreviation +	DVD-Audio	
Shortening+Shortening	вай-фай/ Wi-Fi	
Shortening+Noun	поп-группа ска-саунд течхаус стрип-бар wintalk	
Noun+Preposition	пикчерофф флэш-бек/ Flashback	
Verb+Preposition	плей-офф	
Participle II+Noun	релаксед фит	
Participle II+Acronym	mixed CD	
	post-production	
Preposition+Noun		In-Fashion
Hybrids		
Noun+Noun	бизнес-семинар блогосфера бутсектор бонус-трек веб-камера допинг-препарат интернет-газета интернет- соединение интернет торговля панк-группа панк-формация пресс-служба регги-звук	Alltagsbusiness Ausdauer-Training Babybild Babymassage Babyratte Babyszene Badmintonturnier Bandkollege Bandmädchen Bandmitglieder Barfrau Bergtour Blog-Eintrag

	Russian	German
	регги-тематика	Bodentraining
	рок-барабанщик	Bodybutter
	рок-гимн	Bootvorgang
	рок-музыка	Cashmerepulli
	рок-обработка	Chatverhalten
	рок-опера	Charterfolg
	рок-студия	Cocktailsoße
	рок-театр	Comicladen
	рэп-культура	Computeranschluss
	саунд-драма	Computerchaos
	сейф-ячейка	Computer-Gehäuse
	спамоборона	Computerkenntnisse
	техно-корни	Computerladen
	тётка-тренер	Comuterschaden
	баба-тренер	Computerspiel
	дама-тренер	Computertüftler
	флеш-память	Datenrate
	френд-лента/ френдолента	Designerfälschung
	cd-болванка	Fanhysterie
		Filmverweiß
		Fitnesshalle
		Gedankensplitter
		Gerätetraining
		Gildenhomepage
		Hammersong
		Hause-Track
		Heimtrainer
		hobbyfotograf
		Hometrainer
		Horrortag
		Intervalltraining

	Russian	German
		Internetadresse Internetaktivität Internetleitung Internetgebühren Internetseite Jammerstories Jobsuche Jobwechsel Joggingschuhe Joggingweg Kassetenrekorder Kraftsport Krafttraining Lichtshow Lautsprecherboxen Seematrosen Look Mailadresse Mailkontakt Marken-Shops Masterkeyboard Modedesigner/Mode- Designer Modulupdates Partyanimateure partygemeinde Party-Übermonster Pferdesport Pflegeset Plattendeal Playmobil Pophymn

	Russian	German
		Poplieder Probetraining Punk-Mode Return-Taste Rezepttips Rock-Legende Rockfestival Sachsen-Ticket Salzpeeling Schmuddelreporter Schockzustand Service Bereich Shopping-Fieber Shopping-Rausch Bühnenshow Sicherheitstraining Sicherheits-Update Single-Dasein Single-Veröffentlichung Snooze-Taste Softwarekonzern Sommertops Songschreiber Songtexte Sound Qualität Sportart Sporthosen Sportkurs Sport-Monster Sportsachen Sportsblick

	Russian	German
		Sportsgeist Sportunfähigkeit Sprintstrecke Startnummer Startseite Streikzeit Ärztestreik Strechmaterial Strongmen-Sport Studentenjob Tanzsport Teamkameradin teenagerzeiten Teeniemode Tennishalle Testballons Testphase Testag Tipp-Runde Trainerassistent Trainingseinheiten Trainingsimpuls Trainingsplan Trainingsprogramm Trekkingtour Unterhosendesigner Waldtour Webadresse Webseite Windowsfreunde Wochenendtrip

	Russian	German
		Word Format
Prefix+Noun	аквааэробика велоспорт велотренажёр видеокассета видеокарта видеоклип гипермаркет мегамолл метросексуал микро-шорты мультитрек постпанк супермаркет фотомодель гранд шоппинг	Bonus Track Demoaufnahme Demoversion Maxi-Single
Adjective+Noun	медиа-бизнес ночной клуб онлайн-дневник онлайн-магазин тренажёрный зал установочный диск файловая система	Groß-Event Onlinebestellung Spezialsoftware
Adjective+Acronym		Doppel-CD Top-DJ
Shortening+Noun	поп-звезда промо версия промокассета	
Numeral+Noun	секондхенд	

	Russian	German
Abbreviation +Noun	смс-викторина ТВ-канал CD-привод fm-радиостанция IP адрес/ IP-адрес USB-устройство	CD-Qualität CD-Regal DVD-Regal DVD-Spieler PC-Spiel
Noun+Acronym		Treiber CD
Verb stem+Noun		Buchtipps Einkaufstour Fernsehshow Sterberate
Three member compounds		
Noun+Noun+Noun	рок-хитмейкер сноуборд парк сноуборд-слалом	Folkpopstück Frickelfrackel-Sample-Elektro Miss-America-Look Punkrockversion Samstagvormittagshopping Wassersport-Saison Websitecreator Weltcuprennen Weltklasse-Entertainer Windows Update Patch
Noun+Preposition+Noun	Rock'n'roll	
Noun+Noun+Acronym		Internet-Installations-CD
Adjective+Noun+Noun	Opensource-can	Bluetooth-Modul Bluetooth-Tastatur Cheerleader-Team

	Russian	German
		Creolenohrclips Firmware-Update Mainstream-Pop Midlife-Crisis
Adjective+Adjective+Noun		Duty-free shop
Adjective+Acronym+Noun		Extrem-SSV-Shopping
Pronoun+Adjective+Noun	all-inclusive-tickets	
Pronoun+Participle II+Noun		Self-made-Genie
Numeral+Noun+Noun		One-Night-Stand
...+Noun+Noun	антиспам-движок	
...+Acronym+Noun		Demo-mp3-Dateien
Verb+Article+Adjective		Look-a-likes
Noun+Verb stem+Noun		Männerfindetip Mode-Einkaufs-Freaks
Acronym+Noun+Noun		PC-Tastatur-Layout TV-Computer-Kompatibilität
Four member compounds		
Prefix+Noun+Adjective+Noun	мини-бикини-купальный-сезон	
Adjective+Noun+Adjective+Noun	фанки-диско-коммершиал хаус	

The spelling of compounds, namely joined spelling, with a hyphen or separately, has already been dwelt upon in the previous chapter.[121]

121 See Chapter 5.

Having discussed the typical features of compounds found in the German and Russian parts of the corpus, the most interesting examples can now be presented. Examples need to be compared in order to obtain a clearer idea about the processes by which anglicisms are integrated into the systems of the two languages. Distinguishing between lexemes taken from topic-oriented and non-topic-oriented *blogs* is irrelevant for morphological analysis and is not always considered in the present chapter.

- *Bowling*

A number of compounds have been adopted into the system of the languages analysed along with the lexeme itself, and a number of hybrids and pseudo-loans have been created. Here are some examples:

"Eine *Bowlingbahn*, ist eine *Bowlingbahn*. Daran gibt's nix zu rütteln."

"Trotz all dem, herrscht hier eine riesige Nachfrage und man bekommt nur sehr schwer eine freie Bahn. Vor allem dann, wenn *Discobowling* angesagt ist."

"Die musikalische Untermalung in der *Bowlinghalle* darf getrost als Frechheit bezeichnet werden."

"Zu den interessantesten Beobachtungen gehörte sicherlich die slukesche *Bowlingtechnik* mit der er die Massen verzückte."

As far as Russian is concerned, just one instance of a compound was found in the corpus. Instead, noun phrases are normally used:

«Стало скучно и тут решили пойти в *боулинг-клуб*».

«Финдир сосредоточенно копошился в редикюле, своими размерами приближавшимся где-то к половине финдировского объема, а потом по одному вытащил оттуда свои персональные *боты для боулинга*. Из расстегнутой молнии ридикюля выглядывало что-то яркое и блестящее округлой формы, инстинктивно идентифицированное мной как *шар для боулинга*».

«Все это приводит к образованию довольно продолжительных отрезков времени, в течение которых *дорожки боулинга* остаются не занятыми».

Here are some German compounds and their equivalents in Russian:

Bowlingbahn – дорожка боулинга

Bowlingkugel – шар для боулинга

Bowlingschuhe – боты/ботинки для боулинга/ для игры в боулинг

- *Trainer*

The main difference between Russian and German constructions using the borrowing 'trainer' lies in the preferred use of compounds in German and noun phrases in Russian. Numerous different compounds can be formed in German depending on, for example, the sport a trainer works in: Fußballtrainer, Handballtrainer, Fitnesstrainer, etc.

"Der hat irgendwie was. Also 'unser' *Handball-Trainer*."

"So früh zu Hause bin ich schon, weil ich heute morgen nach 6h Schlaf aus dem Bett musste und mit einem *Fitnesstrainer* den Sportuni-Kraftraum austesten durfte, ich freu mich schon aufs morgige Aufstehen, aah Muskelkater…"

In Russian noun phrases are used: тренер по футболу, тренер по фитнесу, тренер по баскетболу.

«Сначала в понедельник меня похвалил *тренер по мини-футболу* за то, как я веду мяч. А в среду меня похвалил *тренер по футболу* в ЦСКА, сказал, что у меня есть прогресс».

This difference in constructions is attributable not to the borrowings themselves but rather the peculiarities of the grammar of the languages used, as already mentioned above.

- *Designer*

Compounds are very frequent in German as already mentioned above, while in Russian genitive noun phrases are more typical, e.g.:

дизайнер одежды = Modedesigner

«с треском провалившийся *дизайнер одежды*»

"Mein Name ist Jim McVlat, bin 25 und ein sehr junger *Modedesigner*."

дизайнерская сумка = Designerhandtaschen

«Моя *дизайнерская сумка* готова, пойду забирать».

"Aber bekanntlich ist es ja fahrlässig, sich beim Autofahren von Gedanken oder anderem ablenken zu lassen, und so passiert es dann, dass die eine oder andere Kiste mit Designerhandtaschen beim Fahren vom Lastwagen fällt."

- *Shopping/to shop*

In the case of *shopping*, the German language proves to be more productive than Russian.

Shopping is used in both languages by itself or as a part of compounds. In German compounds, *shopping* can be in the first or second place and therefore be either a determiner or a determined member of a compound. In Russian, however, the lexeme is normally determined by the other member of the compound:

"Nach der großen *Shopping-Tour* sind wir dann zu mir und haben gefrühstückt uns ein paar Sachen im Net angeguckt und anschließend eine ganze Kassette Kickers geguckt."

"Anschließend sind wir ins *Shoppingviertel* der Mittelklasse gefahren, wo wir leider ebenfalls nichts gefunden hatten."

"Danach konnte ich es mir nicht verkneifen, noch ein bisschen *Weihnachts-Shopping* in einem unserer Berliner Einkaufszentren zu betreiben."

"Ich habe mich gestern in die Stadt gewagt, um ein bisschen *Geschenke-Shopping* zu machen."

«Концентрированное *шоппинг-счастье*».

«всю пятницу я проработала не вылазя ~~из оффиса~~ из *шоппинг-центроф*...»

«Такие *шоппинг-моллы*, как сейчас, тоже имеют право на существование, многие ведь заходят сначала в свои любимые бутики».

- *Chart*

A number of compounds were found in German:

"Von 0 auf 6: das bedeutet für U2 die beste deutsche *Single-Chart-Position* seit gut 15 Jahren und damit der zweitbeste *Chart-Entry* in der langjährigen Karriere der irischen Über-Band ("The Fly" schaffte es 1991 auf Platz 5)!"

"Dann bin ich bei der *Chartshow* auf RTL hängen geblieben: 70iger Jahre."

"Die DJ's dieser Welt (ich nehme mich da nicht aus) kommen aber leider einfach nicht drum herum, den ein oder anderen grässlichen Komerz- oder *Charthit* in Ihr Set einzustreuen, da das Gros der Gäste nunmal auf Komerz voll abfährt."

"In Sachen *Album-Charts* hat sich Norah Jones mit ihrem Album "Not Too Late" den ersten Rang gesichert."

"Sah sie neulich zufällig in der Glotze, bei einer dieser doofen, aber irgendwie doch unterhaltsamen *Chart-Shows*, und dachte bei mir: "Das wird ne schöne Scheiße sein!"

“Kurzfristig begünstigt wird in nächster Zeit das Wiedereinsteigen von Singles, die bereits seit längerer Zeit in den regulären Charts nicht mehr gelistet wurden, jedoch noch weiter in den *Download-Charts* vertreten waren.”

“*Chart-Einstieg* ohne Plattenfirma prinzipiell möglich”

No instances of compounds in Russian were found. Instead, noun phrases are widespread:

«А уж про обноваление *недельных чартов* вообще отдельный разгвор».

«Ещё можно сказать про *итоговые чарты* – когда группу, которую вы любите больше догоняет группа,которую вы любите меньше,то нужно обязательно помочь той,что вы любите больше и погонять её альбомчики=)».

«Решение: переложить обсчитывание хотя бы *персональных чартов* на клиента».

- *Hit*

“Als Gründungsmitglied der "Say-No-to-Komerz Bewegung" entsage ich in der Regel jeglichen *Chart-Hits* (sowas kommt einfach nicht auf meinen Plattenteller)”

“Wundert sich wirklich jemand darüber, dass vor allem aktuelle *Pop-Chart-Hits* mit sehr häufig sehr kurzem Verfallsdatum schnell mal geladen und nach wenigen Wochen gelöscht werden?”

“Jeder Band kann es so gelingen alleine durch das Online zum Verkauf stellen ihres Songs in die *Hitparade* zu gelangen.”

“Der Uraltschinken kann doch nicht genauso viel kosten wie der aktuelle *Top-Hit*.”

«Теперь я стал переслушивать эту пластинку и обнаружил, что хит, который у них «стрельнул», попал в кино и *хит-парады*, был на этой демозаписи аж десятым номером».

«У нас был своеобразный *хитлист* самых-самых “уносящих” трэков».

In conclusion it can be stated again that more compounds formed with anglicisms were found in German, while in Russian noun phrases are pervasive. This tendency is probably due to the grammatical peculiarities of the specific languages: while German tends to form compounds, Russian prefers less bulky noun phrases.

6.1.2 Shortening

Apocopé (final clipping)

Examples of apocopé can be found more frequently in the Russian than the German part of the corpus. In Russian native suffixes are sometimes attached:

- Админ (administrator)/Admin (administrator)

«Только после этого ты можешь просто и беззаботно воткнуть свою рабочую машину в настенную панель, а *админ* – сидеть за клавиатурой и настраивать почту, базу данных или что-нибудь еще».

"*Das gesamte Admin*-Team der fc arbeitet schon seit gestern Abend emsig hier mitten im Wald in Nastätten mit dem Ziel, die fotocommunity besser zu machen."

- Винд/Винда (Windows)

«Благодаря тому, что вокруг есть такие замечательные вы – мой *винд* ожил. но с нуля.»

«Накрылась *винда*. Востанавливаю».

- Коммент (commentary)

«В ответ на *коммент* Левы скажу следующее: С одной стороны, трудно не согласиться, что «Копуша», «непутевый» – действительно более уместны на турнирах в России».

- Комп/компик (computer)

«Забить на *комп* и прикупить списаную "Су"шку».

«А я завтра продаю свой *компик*. Именно за ту цену, которую и хотела!»

- Моник (monitor)

«искали седня товарищу *моник* нормальный, нашли легендарный 959нф бушный, человек уезжал срочно, поэтому годами и кровушкой накопленые железки продавал в два-три раза дешевле их реальной стоимости...»

- Прога (programme)

«Для виндоуса есть подобная *прога*, но у нее не очень удобный интерфес».

- Pulli (pullover)

"mmhh habe einen scharfen *pulli* an mit löcher"

- Disco/диско (discotheque)

"In Frankfurt gibt es eine *Disco* wie es sie wahrscheinlich in jeder Stadt gibt."

«Завтра в институт, тяжелый день, зато потом иду к другу курить кальян(хыхы) а потом гоу гоу на *диско*!!!»

- Teeny (teenager)

"ich weiß... ach so ein *teeny* bin ich gar nicht mehr ...mmhhmm da könntest du recht haben..."

Ellipsis

The examples of ellipsis found in the analysed corpus are also numerous:

- Демка ← demo-tape / Demo← demo-tape

«Начал с этим богатством писать новый трек. Уже есть *демка*».

"Mir ist klar dass die Qualität nich irgendwie toll sein wird, aber wir brauchen dieses *Demo* schnell (2 wochen) und haben nicht sehr viel Geld."

- Компашка ← compact disc

«и еще прикидочка: 691200Kb – это даже меньше, чем *компашка*. т.е. если в нормальной домашней сетке я фильм в нормальном качестве из двух частей выкачиваю за полчаса, то тут на это уйдет больше двух суток!»

- Локалка ←local net

«Болт вам, а не *локалка*. Ее, считай, нет. Вся сеть поделена по районам, прямого роутинга между ними нет».

- Мобильник/мобила ← mobile phone

«И вот, после того, как автор этих строк, т.е. я, – потерял очередной *мобильник*, и проблема выбора вновь встала со всей очевидностью, было решено суммировать свой богатый опыт, и провести наконец-то системный анализ того, как всё же нужно их выбирать – наших маленьких и подчас надоедливых друзей?»

«*Мобила* Должна Умереть! Да, я не люблю мобильные телефоны и не боюсь в этом признаться всему миру в целом и району Шабаны в частности».

- Ноут ← notebook

«[info]acekievua как-то жаловался на свой *ноут*... Женя, сделай с ним то же, что и в ролике – вдруг твой *ноут* поймет, что негоже огорчать хозяина?»

- Попса ← pop music

«Интеллигентская *попса* вообще по существу мало отличается от двух других видов *попсы* – мещанской и пролетарской».

- Клип ← video clip / Clip← video clip

«Хороший *клип*! Как мужик играет с 4 красавицами в покер на раздевание, и он выигрывает из-за того что у него в вухе наушник, Песня супер и *Клип* супер, качаем, залил специально для вас!».

"Das die japaner keine Scrupel haben, beweist wieder mal dieser *Clip*"

- Секонд ← second hand

«Поход сегодня на *секонд* не принес никакого удовольствия! Такое впечатление, что наши зимние группы скупили весь запас прикольных шапок и перчаток!!!».

- Хард ← hard disc drive

«Всё работало тип топ но после переустановки виндов *хард* определяется как юсб. не знаю с этим связано или нет но пара прог в принципе не хочет устанавливаться в частности пинакль студио 9».

- Lappi ← laptop

"inzwischen habe ich meinen *Lappi* zurückbekommen.Gestern zwischen 15 Uhr und 15:30 Uhr hat UPS geklingelt und mir das Packet gebracht."

- Nick ← nickname / ник ← nickname

"So das keine Endungen in dem *Nick* erlaubt sind!"

«Пыталась редактировать профиль – меняется все, а *ник* остается!»

Syncope

An example of a syncope was found in the Russian part of the corpus:

- Инет ← Internet

«Статус загорелся, но входить в *инет* всё равно не могу((»

Aphaeresis

- Нет ← Internet;

«никак не могу отыскать *в нете* хорошую фотку... и вот вхожу сегодня в кабинет к одному из сотрудников... а на столе большущий портрет....»

- Studio ← Fitnesstudio

“Meistens gehe ich zwei-bis dreimal pro Woche ins *Studio* und mache meine Übungen am Rückenstrecker, auf dem Wackelbrett, mit der Beinpresse, dem Crosstrainer usw.”

Abbreviation

The examples of acronyms found in the Russian and German corpus are almost identical. The peculiarity of some acronyms in Russian lies in the fact that the native Latin spelling is transferred into Cyrillic.

Дос←DOS, пиар←PR, ПК←PC, смс← sms, аська←ICQ, ТВ←TV, fm, IP, XP

DJ, HDD, HP, ICQ, PC, RAM, SMS, TV, WWW

The following abbreviations have identical forms in Russian and German: CD, DVD, USB, VIP.

6.1.3. Derivation

Derivation in German is not as common as in Russian, where the attachment of native suffixes to anglicisms is widespread.

The following derivative suffixes attached to the borrowed lexemes were found in the German part of the corpus:

- *in* – to form the feminine gender of nouns that denote professions: *Managerin, Stylistin;*

-chen – as a diminutive suffix: *Schöpchen;*

-ler: *Sportler;*

-y/-i by shortenings: *Pulli, Lappi, Teeny;*

-isch, -lich, -ig by adjectives: *chat-technisch, sportlich, rockig.*

In Russian the process of derivation is rather complicated, as some anglicisms acquire two or sometimes even three native suffixes at a time. Here are examples taken from the corpus:

-ер: модельер;

-ик: клуб-еш-н-ик, айпи-ш-н-ик;

-ка: демка, видюшка, бейсболка, татушка;

-ик/-ок (diminutives): компик;

-ист: баскетбол-ист, программ- ист, сноуборд-ист;

-ак : серв-ак, лейб-ак.

Furthermore, a number of examples were found in the corpus when verbs were formed from nouns:

фанат→ фанатеть, смс → смсить; coach→ coachen, chat→ chatten

and adjectives formed from nouns:

баннерный, дефолтный; sportlich, rockig.

Here are some interesting examples taken from the Russian and German parts of the corpus:

- *Snowboard*

A parallelism of constructions is to be observed in German and Russian. Along with the noun, with the help of derivation a verb is created together with a synonymous verb phrase, although in German a substantivized infinitive is also in use.

Das Snowboard	*Сноуборд*
Snowboarden "Auf den Bergen bin ich im Winter weiterhin *gesnowboardet*."	Сноубордить «А если я не умею *сноубордить*, то и лыж мне не видать, как своих ушей».
Snowboard fahren "Eigentlich wollen wir ja *Snowboard fahren*, aber laut Wetterbericht liegt da bisher kein Schnee."	Кататься на сноуборде «Вчера, наконец то поехали с Максом на покататься на *сноубордах*».
Das Snowboarden "*Snowboarden* ist wirklich eine feine Sache (ich habe es selbst erst letzten Winter gelernt) – und von den (anfangs) vielen blauen Flecken mal abgesehen, macht es um einiges mehr Spaß als Ski- oder Schlittenfahren"	

- *Design/designer*

Similar to English, a directly derived verb *designen* is used in German:

"Aber aus irgend einem Grund hatte ich nie daran gedacht selbst welche zu *designen*. Also habe ich mich darauf eingelassen."

"Ich gebe auch zu Bedenken, dass dieses Paar *designed wurde*, als Puma wieder zur führende Trendmarke aufstieg und das Geschäft wieder zu brummen anfing."

The interesting peculiarity in Russian is the absence of the verb with different verb phrases being used instead. For example:

«Обязательно возникнут дизайнеры, которые захотят *делать дизайн* только для того, чтобы улучшить свою карму, а не ради денег».

«Будем *создавать* такой *дизайн*, который повысит прибыли Леши».

On the other hand, in German the absence of the directly derived adjective is to be observed. The noun Designer functions as an attributive in compounds:

"Der neueste Trend in Shanghai sind *Designerkopien* oder T-Shirts mit englischer Aufschrift, die lustige Druck – oder andere Fehler haben."

"Aber bekanntlich ist es ja fahrlässig, sich beim Autofahren von Gedanken oder anderem ablenken zu lassen, und so passiert es dann, dass die eine oder andere Kiste mit *Designerhandtaschen* beim Fahren vom Lastwagen fällt."

In Russian, though, a direct adjective is to be found: дизайнерский

«Для тех, кто желает соединить свою любовь к спорту и *дизайнерским* вещам».

- *Glamour*

In Russian a number of different derivatives[122] are to be found. Here are some examples:

Nouns:

«За эффективное сопротивление *гламуризаторам* культуры?»

«Так что *антигламурщики* трубят о надуманной проблеме».

Adjectives:

«Он сказал, что речь у меня *гламурная*».

---

122 Most of them are not contained in any dictionaries of the Russian language and are created by users on the spot.

«Справедливости ради, слово ‘гламур’ в разы чаще других употребляют ‘*негламурные*’, или ‘*антигламурные*’ люди».

Verbs:

«лауреаты прикладывают много усилий, чтобы оказать эффективное сопротивление некоторым силам, пытающимся *гламуризировать* часть российской культуры».

Adverb:

«Прозрачные лямочки – *гламурно*».

In German, though, no variety of forms can be observed. The only form that can be found in the dictionary is the adjective *glamorous*, although it should be mentioned that no instances of it were found in corpus.

- *Shopping*

As far as the expression of action is concerned, in German structures analogous to native ones are used, namely:

Einkaufen gehen = Shoppen gehen

einkaufen = shoppen

Einkaufen gewesen sein = Shoppen gewesen sein

“Gestern war ich zum ersten Mal *Shoppen*.”

“aber dafür gehen wir ja wieder am nächsten Samstag *Shoppen*.”

“Ich war im Kino, habe ein wunderbares Candlelight-Dinner hinter mir… *hab* ein bißchen Accessoires *geshoppt* und heute hatte ich ein wunderbares Fotoshooting, mit zwei tollen Outfits.”

Instances of the verb derived from a noun were found in the Russian part of the corpus, although the users themselves were not keen on their use in Russian:

«Днем со стилистом ходили по Меге, *шоппились* :) (ужасное слово по моему, лучше наверно «закупались»)». (...a horrible word, it is better to say ‘zakupalis’)

6.1.4 Prefixation

Prefixation plays an important role for German verbs. The following examples were found in the corpus: *an-testen, ein-loggen, ein-tippen, herum-klicken, weg-klicken, mit-streiken, raus-picken.*

In Russian the prefixation of verbs also seems to be common judging by the examples found in the corpus: *за-коннектиться, по-пиарить, про-апгрейдить, рас-френдить.*

The same could be also said about adjectives in Russian, but not German: *бес-кулерный, за-паркованный, не-хайтековский, полу-попсовый.*

On the whole, the following conclusions can be drawn. German and Russian are both synthetic languages, which is why as far as the processes of word formation are concerned, some common tendencies are to be found. Shortening occurs in both languages in the same way, while abbreviations for example can also be found in both languages. As far as composition is concerned, although the structure of English compounds is alien to Russian (unlike German), this structure has found its way into the system of the Russian language and is used more often nowadays. The structure of German and English compounds is identical, which is why no problems arise. One more thing to mention here is that German uses more compounds, while in Russian less bulky noun phrases are preferred. In respect of derivation, it should be mentioned that the means used are not as widespread in German as in Russian. Prefixation, on the other hand, is popularly used in both languages with verbs and in Russian also with adjectives.

6.2 Noun

6.2.1 Gender Assignment

The grammatical category of *gender* plays an important role in Russian and German. Each noun borrowed into the system of these two languages is automatically assigned to one of the three genders *masculine, feminine,* or *neuter*. The absence of grammatical gender in English, the source language of anglicisms, greatly complicates the process of gender assignment.

The question of gender assignment has been exhaustively discussed by linguists[123] and diverse criteria for it have been suggested.

There are several criteria that influence gender assignment in Russian and German, namely *formal (morphological) criteria* and *semantic criteria.*[124] Arndt (1970) proposed the following factors for gender assignment (Quoted from Carstensen (1980:54)):

---

123 Zindler 1959; Carstensen 1965; K. Viereck 1980; Bohmann 1996; Gester 2001; Fischer 2005; Nettman-Multanowska 2003; Schulte- Beckhausen 2002, etc.

124 See also Fischer 2005.

1. Sex;
2. Form of the word;
3. Semantic association with a displaced native equivalent;
4. Suffix analogy;
5. Graphic analogy;
6. Homonymity;
7. Semantic categories;
8. Syllabicity.

where 2, 4, 5, 6, and 8 are formal criteria and 1, 3, and 7 semantic ones. Although the criteria mentioned are applied in both languages, it should be stated that for Russian *formal criteria* are of the highest priority, while in German *semantic criteria* seem to be readily applied for gender distinction.[125]

Here an attempt will be made to describe all the above-mentioned criteria in detail using examples taken from both parts of the corpus analysed.

- Formal (morphological) criteria[126]

  - Suffix analogy

If there is an analogy between the suffix/inflexion of a borrowing and a native suffix, the borrowing is assigned to the gender normally associated with this suffix/inflexion in the native language.

The gender assignment of nouns with the following suffixes is based on suffix analogy in Russian (Pyo 1997: 167ff.).:

-tion *-cija (-ция)*, -teraphy, *-terapija (-терапия)* -graphy, *-grafija (-графия)* -logy, *-logija (-логия)* -metry, *-metrija (-метрия)* -cracy, *-kratija (-кратия)* - ic(s), *-ika (-ика).* Nouns with these suffixes take the feminine: аэробика (aerobics), мотивация (motivation), джоггинг-терапия.

Nouns with the suffixes –изм (*-izm)* -ист (*-ist)* are of masculine gender: конформист (conformist), джингоизм (jingoism).

Nouns with the following suffixes are assigned to the system of gender in German according to the principle of suffix analogy:[127]

---

125 Carstensen (1980:55) points out that "Die wesentlichsten Faktoren für das Deutsche sind natürliches Geschlecht, semantische Kriterien und suffixale Analogie, d.h. morphologische Kriterien."

126 According to the classification of Arndt (1970).

127 See also Zürn 2001, Nettman-Multanowska 2003.

Masculine gender:

-all, -er, -ster, -or, -ant, -ismus/-ist, -us

der Basketball, der Browser, der Horror, der Warrant, der Behaviorism, der Campus

There are several exceptions, such as das Monster and das Deodorant. In these cases some other rules for gender assignment are applied, namely semantic ones.[128]

Feminine gender:

The English suffix *-ity* corresponds in German to *-ität, -ship* to *-schaft,* and *-ence/-ense* to *-enz.* The following suffixes have the same form in both languages: *-ness, -ion, -ation, -y (-ie):*

die Bodylotion, die Comedy, die Connection, die Version, die Fitness, die Championship, die Community.

Here again a couple of exceptions should be pointed out, namely das Business and der Champion.

Neuter gender:

English nouns ending in *-ing* are based on the form of participle I. The same process is to be observed in German when by conversion the infinitive is substantivized. Due to this analogy, nouns ending in *-ing*, formed from the verbs take the neuter in German:[129]

das Shopping – shoppen; das Training – trainieren; das Jogging – joggen.

The exceptions are der Looping and der Smoking, both of which are pseudo-loans.

The suffixes *-ment, -ge* and *-al* are also markers of the neuter gender:

das Entertainment, das Management, das Serial, das Revival, das College.

One more point to mention here is that in the process of borrowing, the original suffixes can sometimes either be substituted by native ones or preserved. In Russian, most of them are changed due to the graphic and phonetic peculiarities, and so suffix analogy is observed only in the case of suffixes of Greek or Latin origin that have become international. The other suffixes are substituted by native ones, which is why gender assignment based on the suffix analogy cannot be described as a really decisive factor in Russian, in contrast to

---

128 See p. 161.

129 See also Nettman-Multanowska 2003.

German, where a large number of suffixes have correspondences in English and therefore exert a direct influence on the processes of gender assignment. The following table contains an overview of the suffixes of both languages with their English correspondents subdivided into three genders with their markers.

Table 30: Gender assignment based on suffix analogy

	English suffixes	*German correspondents*	*English suffixes*	*Russian correspondents*
Masculine	-all -er -ster -or -ant -ism/-ist -us	-all -er -ster -or -ant -ismus/-ist -us	-ism -ist	-izm(-изм) -ist(-ист)
Feminine	-ity, -ship -ence/-ense -ness -ion -ation -y (-ie)	-ität/-ity -shaft/ship -enz/-ence/-ense -ness -ion -ation -y (-ie)	-tion -sion -teraphy -graphy, -logy -metry -cracy -ic(s)	-cija (-ция) -sija (-сия) -terapija(-терапия) -grafija(-графия) -logija (-логия) -metrija (-метрия) -kratija (-кратия) -ika (-ика)
Neuter	-ing, -ment -ge	-ung/-ing -ment -ge		

– Sound and rhyme analogy

There are some cases when borrowed English items are similar to the native ones from the angle of sound image and/or rhyme analogy. Although such examples are rare and by no means predominant in gender assignment criteria, when such an analogy (sound or rhyme) is to be observed, the gender of the anglicism is influenced by its native counterpart.

der Oven < der Ofen

der Dish < der Tisch

der Pool < der Pfuhl[130]

die Show < die Schau

der Drink < der Trunk

In Russian this criterion for gender assignment does not apply.

– Graphic analogy

This criterion is based on the same principle as *sound and rhyme analogy.* If two words, the anglicism and the native one, look graphically almost the same, the anglicism acquires the same gender as the native noun.

Der Trouble < der Trubel

It often happens that the words, a loan and a native one, display both *sound and rhyme* and *graphic analogy* simultaneously. Accordingly, it is often difficult to distinguish between these two criteria.

This criterion is not applied in Russian at all.

– Syllabicity

It has been proved[131] that the number of syllables is directly related to the gender the noun is assigned to. It was stated that most monosyllabic English borrowings in German are *masculine,* and despite some exceptions this tendency is definitely to be observed:

Der Bug, der Club, der Crash, der Film, der Funk, der Grill, der Hit.

Among monosyllabic nouns in the German part of the corpus, 44 belong are masculine, 13 neuter, and 7 feminine.

Although the same tendency is to be observed among Russian monosyllabic nouns, in this case gender assignment is motivated not by only the number of syllables but also the form of the word, i.e. most borrowed monosyllabic nouns in Russian end in a hard consonant, which is why they are automatically assigned to the masculine gender.

– Form of the word

In Russian the most numerous and important group of criteria concerning the gender assignment of borrowings is connected to the form of the word. The

---

130 After Nettman-Multanowska (2003:107).

131 See Zürn 2001; Carstensen 1965; Gester 2001.

following principles are used to divide loans into the masculine, feminine and neuter[132] gender:[133]

a. Loanwords with a final hard consonant are *masculine:*

аккаунт, бан, банкомат, матч, респект, слоган;

b. Loanwords ending in -a (-а) , -ja (-я) are *feminine:*[134]

аэробика, татуировка, тренировка, компания, шопоголия;

c. Loanwords ending in -i (-и), -u (-у), -ju (-ю), -e (-е), -o (-о) are *neuter:*

джакузи, кантри, бикини, шоу, авеню;

d. Most nouns that end in -e (like 'tape') are masculine in Russian, as when the ending *-e* disappears the noun ends in a hard consonant serving as a mark of the masculine gender.

Драйв < drive, имидж < image, перформанс < performance.

The opposite tendency takes place in German. Here the ending *-e* is pronounced like [ə], which is the mark of the feminine gender.

e. Nouns ending in *-l* in English become *-l'* in Russian[135] and behave like native nouns ending in *-l'*, which means that they can be assigned to either the masculine or the feminine gender.

коктейль (*cocktail*), *мотель* (*motel*) – masculine gender;

панель (*panel*) – feminine gender.

- Indeclinable nouns

In Russian there is a group of nouns that do not fit into a declension paradigm. Formally, they do not have any markers of case or number. By assignment into the grammatical category of gender, such nouns follow some specific rules, namely:[136]

- Nouns denoting persons by their profession are masculine:

атташе, буржуа

---

132 The following rules concern only declinable nouns denoting inanimate objects. The case of indeclinable nouns and nouns denoting persons and animate objects will be discussed separately.

133 See also Pyo 1997; Aristova 1978.

134 Here the native suffixes are attached to the original stems.

135 There are two allophones of [l] in Russian. In the end position the English middle [l] after a soft vowel is taken for [l'].

136 See Современный русский язык 2002.

- Nouns denoting animals are masculine:

буффало, кенгуру

- Nouns denoting inanimate objects are neuter:[137]

интервью, кафе, метро

As far as German is concerned, besides the criterion of suffix analogy already mentioned above, the so-called G*enuszuweisung nach dem Wortausgang*[138] *(gender assignment due to word ending)* can be applied here. The following table shows examples of interdependence of suffixes and gender, and sums up the criteria mentioned as *suffix analogy* and *word ending*.

Table 31: Gender assignment (suffix analogy and word ending)

Gender	*Suffix*	*Example*
Masculine	-er -or -ster -ismus	der Computer der Monitor
Feminine	-ade -ance -anz -e -enz -erie -ery/-ry -erei -ness -ia -ie -y -ity -ship	die Hardware die Fitness die Party die Connection die Session

137 Although there are some exceptions such as кофе – м.р., due to the general ignorance of the rule among native speakers, the noun кофе is treated as neuter.

138 See also Schulte- Beckhausen (2002:56).

Gender	*Suffix*	*Example*
	-(t)ion -tude -ure -ur	
Neuter	-al -et -ing -let -ment	Das Musical Das Internet Das Bowling Das Management

Here it is relevant to present some examples of anglicicms found in the corpus whose gender is defined by formal criteria in German as well as in Russian:

Bowling, n	*Боулинг, m*
Suffix analogy. The anglicism in this case is treated like a substantivized infinitive, which normally ends in -ing and takes the neuter in German. "Übrigens noch Dank an Andi, der *das Bowling* organisierte." "Und zum Schluß dachten wir, weil die Musik so schön war, gönnen wir uns nochmal *das Bowling*..."	The form of the word/ending. Loanwords with a final hard consonant are assigned to the masculine gender in Russian. «В результате *боулинг*[139] нам ставил пиво-соки-чай за счет заведения». «финдир повернул руль и мы оказались перед трехэтажным зданием *боулинг-а*, освещенным со всех сторон и обвешанным вывесками, что восточная женщина – цацками». «Каждый раз, несмотря на сказанное мне по телефону, я приезжал в *боулинг* и благополучно играл несколько часов…».

139 Semantic differences and peculiarities are not taken into consideration here.

Fitness, f	*Фитнес, m*
Suffix analogy. Nouns ending in -ness are normally feminine in German. “Ich habe heute festgelegt und direkt damit begonnen jeden Tag etwas für *meine Fitness* und etwas für meine Mappe zu tun.” However, some other possibilities were also found in the corpus: “Ich hatte mich erst Anfang dieser Woche entschieden, heute auf *das Fitness* zu verzichten und mit den Kollegen mit zu gehen” “*Das Fitness* hat zum Glück bis 23.30 offen...;-)!” The use of the neuter gender can be explained by the fact that the compound das Fitnesstraining is reduced. But despite the ellipsis, the gender assignment remains unchanged, namely neuter. Some other possibilities are the reduction of das Fitnesscenter and das Fitness-studio.	Form of the word. Loanwords with a final hard consonant are masculine in Russian. «Читаю анкеты уже какой день – каждая вторая занимается *фитнес-ом*». «Да *сам фитнес* это для меня что-то противно пахнущее снобизмом». «приехала на *фитнесс*, а *он* по техническим причинам закрыт».

Training, n	*Тренинг, m*
Suffix analogy. The anglicism in this case is treated like a substantivized infinitive, which normally ends in -ing and has the neuter gender in German. “...und *das Training* folglich erst für morgen angesetzt ist...” “Heute hatten wir *das erste Training* im neu-	Form of the word. Loanwords with a final hard consonant are assigned to the masculine gender «А о многочисленных прикольных моментах *тренинг-а* писать влом, но было весело. :)». «Итак, сегодня был первый из двух дней, и хочется сразу по горячим следам о нем

Training, n	*Тренинг, m*
en Jahr und was soll ich sagen, es war sagen wir es so, es war nicht so toll." "Es gibt zwar keine Wochenpunkte *für das Training*, aber ein gutes Gefühl."	написать, первое впечатление *о тренинг-е*, Каптереве, группе». «Это прототип номер один, пока не слишком юзер-френдли, но я его буду еще как-то *для тренинг-а* перерабатывать».

Shopping, n	*Шоппинг, m*
Suffix analogy. The anglicism in this case is treated like a substantivized infinitive, which normally ends in -ing and has a neuter gender in German. "Hier ist *echtes Shopping* möglich"	Gender assignment due to word ending. Loanwords with a final hard consonant are masculine. «В этом году *шоппинг оказался удачным* и каждый купил то, что хотел :)))». «Вырвалась на *пятичасовой шоппинг* в МЕГУ. Ух! Красота :))».

Trend, m	*Тренд, m*
Syllabicity. Monosyllabic borrowings in German are usually masculine. "Denn *dieser Trend* sammeln, statt lösen hält an." "*Der klare Trend* von morgen: Das Me&Myself-Forum."	Gender assignment due to word ending. Syllabicity. The consonant stem is the mark of the masculine gender in the case of one-syllable nouns. «*Первый модный тренд* на сегодня: ура, apple iphone». «При всём при том, *тренд этот был* создан сравнительно недавно, порядка десятилетия назад».

Compilation, f	*Компиляция, f*
Suffix analogy. Nouns ending in -tion are normally feminine in German. “Andere Lieder *der Compilation* werden aber korrekt ausschließlich unter Compilations angezeigt.” “*Eine ganze Compilation* mit Mixen der genannten Funky Diven könnt Ihr Euch hier anhören und downloaden – CD-Cover inklusive.”	Gender assignment due to word ending. Loandwords ending in -я are feminine in Russian. «При *обычной компиляции* все так и происходит». «U103 – это *компиляция, ориентированная* на российских диджеев, промоутеров и всех любителей отечественной танцевальной музыки».

Hit, m	*Хит ,m*
Syllabicity. Monosyllabic borrowings in German in most cases are masculine. “Vor ein paar Tagen war “I Bet You Look Good On The Dancefloor“, *der erste Hit* der Arctic Monkeys, mein Lied des Tages.” “Das ist verdammt wenig für solch *einen Hit* mit solch einem Starpower.”	Gender assignment due to word ending. Syllabicity. The consonant stem is the mark of the masculine in the case of monosyllabic nouns. «Вот бы на минике представлена Save me from my Curse, так и осталась она фактически *единственным хитом* со всего альбома». «Про этот трек я уже написал особую статью, так как не мог пропустить *такой неоспоримый хит*».

Drink, m	*Дринк, m*
Sound and rhyme analogy. The lexeme is assigned to the masculine gender in German in analogy to the lexeme der Trunk, which shows a resemblance in	Gender assignment due to word ending. Loanwords with a final hard consonant are assigned to the masculine gender. «Гадюка смотрит удивленно, но быстро

Drink, m	*Дринк, m*
sound image as well as spelling. "Wir wollen nur einen Drink und sind dann auch wieder raus." "Nein, nein, das ist ein Missverständnis, ich wollte Sie nur auf einen Drink einladen."	организовывает мне безалкогольный дринк для меня». «Очень важно было держать в руке дринк, и если по неосторожности я ставила стакан на стол, кто-то обязательно налетал и спрашивал где мой дринк и не принести ли мне что-то выпить».

- Semantic criteria[140]
  - Natural gender

Nouns denoting persons acquire gender assignment due to the sex of the person they denote in German as well as in Russian:

die Lady, die Queen, der Daddy

мадам f, детектив m

In the case of German *das Baby, das Girl and Girlie*, the nearest lexical synonym influences gender assignment: *das Kind, das Mädchen*. Schlick[141] states that in the case of nouns denoting persons, it is not the natural gender but the nearest lexical synonym that denotes the gender. However, this hypothesis is criticised by linguists: Schulte-Beckhausen (2002:39) arrives at the conclusion that the criterion 'natural gender' is solid and can be applied independently. She formulates the following rule:

> Lehnwörter, die Personen bezeichnen, erhalten bei ihrer Übernahme ins Deutsche im allgemeinen das Genus nach ihrem natürlichen Geschlechet (maskulin oder feminin). (Schulte- Beckhausen 2002:41)

This rule can be also applied in Russian.

But even in the case of gender assignment, the criterion of natural gender can sometimes be supported by some other means, namely particular suffixes help to define the gender to which nouns are ascribed.

---

140 See also Carstensen 1965; Nettman-Multanowska 2003; Schulte-Beckhausen 2002; Pyo 1997; Aristova 1978, etc.

141 See also Schulte-Beckhausen 2002.

The following suffixes take the masculine in German:[142]

-ist, -boy, -master, -er (by professions), -nik, -man

Cowboy, Heimtrainer, Cartoonist, Showmaster, Beatnik, Superman.

In Russian:

-ист, -ер/-ор, -мен, -бой, -ник

байкер, бармен, баскетболист, инструктор

Feminine gender:

German: *-ess, -woman, -in*

Designerin, Stewardess, Wonderwoman;

Russian: -ка, -ша, -ица,-есса

клоунесса, сноубордистка, тренерша

One more way of defining the gender of a noun denoting persons exists in Russian: compounds are created where one of the components denotes sex. Here are the examples found in the corpus: *тётка-тренер, баба-тренер, дама-тренер*.

There is also a syntactic way of distinguishing the gender of nouns denoting persons. In context the determiners – in German, articles and pronouns; in Russian, pronouns or adjectives – help make the gender of the noun coincide with the sex of the person denoted. As an example we can take the word 'DJ', introduced in both German and Russian, which can refer to either a woman or a man.

Der/dieser DJ; die/diese DJ

этот/тот/мой/знаменитый DJ; эта/та/моя/знаменитая DJ

Here are some examples:

Trainer, m	*Тренер, m*
Gender assignment due to the word ending. Natural gender. "Aber *der Trainer*. Der ist sympathisch." "Ich werde mein volles Einführungstraining *mit dem Trainer* Markus absolvieren."	Gender assignment due to the word ending. Natural gender. Loanwords with a final hard consonant are masculine. «Завтра второе и последнее бесплатное

142 See Русская грамматика 1980, Duden, Grammatik der deutschen Gegenwartssprache 1998.

Trainer, m	*Тренер, m*
“war ne erkältung bei mir am start (was ich in meiner entschuldigung *für meinen trainer* etwas hochgepusht hatte ^^"")” If the natural gender of *Trainer* is feminine, a native suffix -in as a marker of the feminine gender is attached. Ein Trainer – eine Traine-r*in* “*meine trainerin*, die sandra, hat mich zunächst mal gründlich vernommen - wie groß ich bin, wie viel ich wiege, was meine beweggründe fürs studio sind, ob ich irgendwelche probleme mit gelenken, sehnen usw. Habe.” “*Von meiner Trainerin* habe ich gehört, daß sie ihre Hunde nicht barfen möchte, da sie so viel unterwegs ist und es für sie daher nicht praktikabel ist.”	занятие *с тренер-ом*, где он мне распишет план по дням, впишет этот план в спец-файл и этот файл положит в спецкоробку прямо в зале, чтобы я, придя в зал, не слонялся рандомно из угла в угол, а знал что мне делать и подо что ложиться». «На выходные Ирина куда-то уехала и мы остались *без тренер-а*». If the natural gender of *Trainer* is feminine, several ways of realizing feminine gender are possible in Russian in contrast to German, where normally a suffix -in is attached. In the corpus, some interesting examples were found showing a wide range of possibilities concerning gender markers in Russian. The first possibility is the attachment of the native suffix that stands with the feminine gender in Russian. In this case the suffix -ша is attached: «Прискакала *тренер-ша*[143] – маленькая накачанная женщина».

Model, n	*Модель, f*
The choice of gender may in this case be influenced by the lexeme das Mädchen. Pronominal correlation is relevant for the gender distinction in this case. In context Model can be *es, er* or *sie* in terms of the	During the transition from English into Russian, the word acquired -ь at the end. Nouns with the stem ending in -ь can be either ‚masculine or feminine‚. The choice of gender in this case may be influenced by the

143 The following nouns denoting feminine gender are marked in Russian. They all have negative connotation, which is not true for German.

Model, n	*Модель, f*
natural gender, but the gender assignment of the word is the same in all cases, namely neuter. Alternatively, the choice of gender can be chosen in analogy to das Modell. "Schon wieder ist *ein* junges Model verhungert."	natural gender of the phenomenon it denotes. As a result модель in the genitive singular acquires the ending -и, which is the marker of the feminine gender. In context, pronominal correlation should be taken into consideration: она модель/он модель: «Такой *модел-и* пожизненно платят миллионные гонорары». «Падайте ниц перед *модель-ю* =)». «Так *он модель*! Я его нашла в афише лондонских моделей!». One more way of defining the gender of a noun denoting persons exists in Russian. Compounds are created involving a component word denoting sex. «У *девушек-моделей* существуют параметры 90—60—90».

Designer, m	*Дизайнер, m*
Gender assignment due to the word ending. Natural gender. The suffix -er is typical of nouns denoting professions. They are of masculine gender. "Ich fand den Gedanken recht spannend, sich mal vor Augen zu führen, was *einen Designer* eigentlich ausmacht." "Und zwar wird ein T-Shirt quer durch die Welt geschickt, *von einem Designer* zum nächsten, und *jeder Designer* darf sich auf dem T-Shirt verewigen."	Gender assignment due to the word ending. Natural gender. Loanwords with a final hard consonant are assigned to the masculine gender. «Тамошний *дизайнер* в качестве ключевого элемента... *посадил* зайцев, практически точно таких же!». «Мля, мне главное завтра где-нибудь случайно *этого дизайнера* не встретить...». Although there is actually no corresponding noun of a feminine gender, the word with the

Designer, m	*Дизайнер, m*
The corresponding noun of feminine gender is provided: Designerin “Das Bild ist in Bremen entstanden, es ging da eigentlich primär um superschweren Silberschmuck irgend einer Hamburger *Designerin*.”	feminine suffix -ша is often used in colloquial speech: «просто суперски талантливая дизайнерша... с которой мы поругались по глупости.... в мае этого года....». Pronominal correlation is also relevant for gender distinction in context. Here also, compounds are created with a component-word denoting sex, as in the case of *trainer*: «Какая-то *дама-дизайнер* привезла с собой в студию собаку, породистую настолько, что следы вырождения налицо, и показала собакин золотой зуб, который ей за несколько часов до съемок вставил собачий стоматолог». «Вот и к нам в офис пришла *тётка-дизайнер*, особа, приближённая к супруге босса».

– Nearest semantic equivalent

In some cases the choice of gender is influenced by the next lexical synonym in the recipient languages or by a translation equivalent. This happens mostly in cases when borrowings are not marked for a particular gender with suffix/inflexion or there is no graphical or phonological similarity with the native equivalent. The use of this criterion in gender assignment is questionable. Linguists do not have any common opinion about what cases should be applied; as Carstensen (1980:55 ff) puts it:

> ..mit dem Prinzip der nächsten lexikalischen Entsprechung einige Probleme verbunden sind [...] Es bleibt in der Mehrzahl dieser Fälle sehr schwierig, dieses lexikalisch-semantische Prinzip nachzuweisen [...] das Prinzip der nächsten lexikalischen Entsprechung zwar in einigen, jedoch keineswegs in allen Fällen maßgebend ist -

das Image – das Bild; der Computer – der Rechner; die Story – die Geschichte

view (вью) м.р. – вид ; emergency (эмёрдженси) ж.р. – необходимость.

In the corpus, a number of examples of anglicisms whose gender is defined due to the closest semantic equivalent were found in German, but none in Russian. In fact this criterion is not typical of the Russian language. Here are some examples of gender assignment based on the nearest semantic equivalent in German and other (formal) criteria in Russian:

Playlist, f	*Плейлист, m*
Semantic criteria. The nearest semantic equivalent. The gender of this noun is probably influenced by the lexeme die Liste, whose meaning is close to the meaning of the anglicism. On the other hand sound and rhyme analogy between Liste and list played the decisive role in gender assignment. “Zum Rausschmeißen eines Stückes muß diese Box *die dazugehörende Playlist* zeigen.” “es geht schlichtweg um *eine Playlist* für Traumtänzerinnen”	Gender assignment due to the word ending. Loanwords with a final hard consonant are assigned to the masculine gender. «Загружаешь хоть *сохраненный плейлист,* хоть сами файлы и всех делов». «В каждый момент времени у меня есть только *один плейлист, в котором* содержится 5-6 (при удачных обстоятельствах – 10) песен».

Label, n	*Лейбл, m*
Semantic criteria. The closest lexical synonym das Etikett influences the gender of the borrowing. The first meaning of the word is “1) Etikett das auf ein Produkt oder dessen Verpackung aufgeklebt wird.”[144] On the basis of analogy	Gender assignment due to the word ending. Syllabicity. The consonant stem is the mark of the masculine gender in the case of monosyllabic nouns. «Сидели недавно с товарищами и

144 Duden - Deutsches Universalwörterbuch 2003.

Label, n	*Лейбл, m*
the second meaning appears "Etikett einer Schallplatte" where the native synonym 'Etikett' plays the central role. Due to metonymy the meaning is transferred into 'Schallplattenfirma', but the gender remains the same. "Irgendwann hatte ich einfach genug von den bescheuerten Cover-Vorschlägen mit denen *das Label* ständig ankam." "im Oktober 06 hat die Band die erste CD veröffentlicht, und damit wir möglichst unabhängig sind, haben wir im gleichen zuge auch *unser eigenes plattenlabel* gegründet."	размышляли: «Не открыть ли *свой лейбл*?» «не решает всех проблем, но при наличии согласованной стратегии между артистом и *его лейбл-ом* можно значительно увеличить продажи пластинки». «Для это *лейбл должен* не просто сидеть и ждать, когда к нему придут те, кто завтра принесет ему золотые горы».

Single[145]*, f*	*Сингл, m*
Gender assignment due to the nearest semantic equivalent. In this case the choice of gender can be influenced by the noun die Schallplatte. "*Neue Single* heißt "Rocksong" und ist ein Popsong… zufällig bei YouTube gefunden." "Als kleinen Vorgeschmack haben sie auf ihrer MySpace Seite bereits *die neue Single* reingestellt."	Gender assignment due to the word ending. Syllabicity. The consonant stem is the mark of masculine gender in the case of monosyllabic nouns. «У нашей замечательной тернопольской группы Холодне Сонце наконец-то *вышел новый сингл*, ураааа!!!!» «Оказывается есть *такой сингл, который был* саундтрэком к фильму Vision Quest».

145 Here only one meaning of the word is taken into consideration.

– Semantic categories

All nouns belong to some semantic field. The most common term defining the field in some cases influences gender distinction of borrowings:[146]

der Gin, der Whiskey, der Rum – der Drink/der Alkohol/der Trunk

die Crimson Rambler – die Rose

кольраби f – капуста f, авеню f – улица f, салями f – колбаса f

There are cases when borrowings have two or three different genders, which is in fact typical of the first stage of integration. “Die Unsicherheit bei der Genuszuordnung ist umso größer, je weniger das englische Wort dem Benutzer vertraut ist.”(Gester 2001:81):

Die/das Trademark, der/die Glamour, der/das Quiz, Break, Match

The anglicisms mentioned above are relatively new in the German language, so different criteria for gender assignment may apply in this case. Over time, one criterion – and hence one gender – normally wins out.

However, in some cases different genders can have a distinguishing function:

das Single (Einzelspiel bei Tennis) – die Single (Schallplatte) – der Single (nicht Verheirateter)

Such instances are not typical of Russian.

Several semantic equivalents can also have their impact on the loanword:

der/das Lunch – der Imbiß oder das Essen.

It is also relevant to mention that in Russian, formal criteria for gender assignment are more significant than semantic ones. When a borrowing does not show any formal, graphical or phonological analogy with the native words, it is assigned to a particular gender due to a semantic criterion.

The following table sums up all the possible criteria for gender assignment in Russian and German.

---

146 See also Carstensen 1965; Nettman-Multanowska 2003; Schulte- Beckhausen 2002; Pyo 1997; Aristova 1978, etc.

Table 32: Criteria for gender assignment

	Russian	*German*
Formal criteria	Suffix analogy	Suffix analogy
		Sound and rhyme analogy
		Graphical analogy
	Syllabicity	Syllabicity
	Word form/ending	Word form/ending
Semantic criteria	Natural gender	Natural gender
	Nearest semantic equivalent	Nearest semantic equivalent
	Semantic categories	Semantic categories

The next table presents all the possible ways of gender assignment from the most used to the least used in German and Russian.

Table 33: Frequency of use of different criteria for gender assignment (from the most frequent to the least)

Russian	*German*
Word form/ending	Nearest semantic equivalent/Suffix analogy
Syllabicity/Suffix analogy	Syllabicity
Natural gender	Natural gender
Semantic categories/Nearest semantic equivalent	Word form/ending
	Semantic categories/Sound and rhyme analogy/Graphical analogy

As can be seen from the table, some common tendencies concerning gender assignment in both languages can be singled out. Criteria such as syllabicity, suffix analogy and natural gender play a decisive role in gender assignment in both languages. Even so, in Russian the majority of the anglicisms (about 80 percent) are assigned to one of the three genders according to the formal criterion of word form/ending, while in German the semantic criterion (nearest semantic equivalent) together with the formal criterion (suffix analogy) occupy the leading position.

6.2.2. Genitive Singular[147]

In German the inflexion paradigm of borrowed nouns is not changed in any of the cases except for the genitive singular, while in Russian the nouns adopt different inflexion paradigms in all six cases: *Именительный, Родительный, Дательный, Винительный, Творительный, Предложный.*

The anglicisms accepted into the system of German nouns do not adhere strictly to the rules of German morphology, where it is stated that nouns are to take the inflexions -(e)s or -en in the genitive. In some cases anglicisms do not take any endings at all. Carstensen (1980) found the examples of the use of apostrophe -s applied to borrowings found in German, although no such instances were found in the corpus analysed.

In Russian there are no extra rules governing anglicisms in the genitive case. Normally they are declined according to the general rules of Russian. Indeclinable nouns naturally do not acquire any inflexion in the genitive singular.

6.2.3. Plural Formation

- Plural -s

One more interesting point to discuss in the integration of loanwords into the systems of Russian and German is plural formation. As is known, most English nouns form their plural with the help of the suffix *-s*.

As far as German is concerned, some nouns can also form the plural with the help of *-s*, which is why the suffix does not seem foreign to the system of the German language and is easily accepted and used: *Tickets, Bands, Basics, Charts, etc*. In some cases two forms of the plural are applied, namely a native one and *s*-ending. Some examples are shown below.

In the Russian language there is no plural marker *-s,* which is why although the suffix *-s* can be preserved in loanwords, it is not percevied like a plural-forming suffix. The following ways of forming the plural form of English borrowings with the ending *-s* are possible (Pyo 1997):

---

147 See Русская грамматика 1980; Современный русский язык 2002; Duden, Grammatik der deutschen Gegenwartssprache 1998.

- The plural *-s* is preserved but treated like part of the stem; the Russian plural ending *-ы* is added to form the plural: *виндоус – виндоусы, комикс – комиксы.* These nouns are treated as belonging to the masculine gender.

- In the case of nouns that are treated as feminine, the suffix *-s* is substituted by the Russian *-а, -ка, -я*: *aerobics – аэробика, economics – экономика.*

- Native plural formation

Some nouns with the equivalent suffixes in German form their plural according to the rules of German word formation.[148] For example, borrowings ending in *–ion* take the feminine in German and form their plural like native nouns ending in *-ion*: *die Version-Versionen.*

If a noun is transferred in a singular form and is declinable in Russian, the typical Russian plural endings *-ы/-и* are added: *аккаунт – аккаунты, аська – аськи, бункер – бункеры.*

In the case of pluralia tantum in German, the original form of the word is normally preserved: *Jeans – jeans; Shorts – shorts, Basics – basics, Lyrics – lyrics.* Meanwhile in Russian two ways of adoption are possible (Pyo 1997): supplementation, when the original form with the *-s* ending is supplemented by the Russian plural marker *-ы/-и*: *джинсы, чипсы, бутсы, памперсы;* or alternatively the ending *-s* is substituted by the native one: *shorts – шорты.*

- No plural marking

In German there is a group of borrowings that have no plural marking. Such a tendency is based on a suffix analogy and is shown in masculine nouns ending in *-er*: *der Designer – die Designer, der Trainer – die Trainer, der Toaster – die Toaster.*

Such a tendency is not typical of Russian, where all nouns should be marked for plural with particular endings.

- Deviations

Even so there are still some deviations in form, for example all German nouns ending in *–y*, where several coexisting variants are possible: *Hobbys/Hobbies, Partys/Parties, Babys/Babies, Storys/Stories.*[149] Other examples include *CD/CDs, Cover/Covers, Newcomer/Newcomers,Grills/Grille, Puddings/Puddinge, Tests/Teste, Toasts/Toaste, Remixs/Remixes.*

148 Duden, Grammatik der deutschen Gegenwartssprache 1998.

149 As far as nouns ending in -y is concerned, both variants mentioned above were found in the analysed corpus.

Here are some examples of different plural formation strategies in both German and Russian:

Playlist

In German the form of the plural generally coincides with that in English, although some examples with the plural ending -n (in analogy to die Liste – die Listen) were found. In Russian the native plural ending is attached.

Playlist → Playlist-s

"Ach ja, Tags: wie bei Mystrands oder Last.fm steht Euch die Möglichkeit zur Verfügung, Künstler, *Playlists* und Songs mit zutreffenden Bezeichnungen zu versehen."

Playlist → Playlisten

"Ich hatte auf meinem Mac eine Reihe iTunes *Playlisten* für den iPod."

Плейлист → Плейлист-ы

«Последние *плейлисты* выдохлись, а совсем старые еще не ожили».

Remix

In DUDEN the plural form with e-ending is to be found. In the corpus analysed, though, forms with the original s-suffix and forms ending in -en prevail.

Remix → Remixe

"Hab mich gefragt, ob es davon irgendwelche *Remixe* in der Richtung Electro- oder Filter-/Funky-House was gibt..."

Remix → Remixes

"Also ich hab mir heute mal wieder den Vollassi gegeben und bin dann auchmal über einige *Remixes* gestolpert."

Remix → Remixen

"Der Release kommt im EP-Format mit sieben Songs und *Remixen*, die exklusiv hier erhältlich sind."

Ремикс → Ремикс-ы

«так что убил немного времени от нечего делать прослушал все *ремиксы* на Катю Чехову – по проводам».

Jeans

A pair-word jeans, in German Jeans, the Russian джинсы has no singular form. In both German and Russian the plural ending -s (-с) is preserved. As in

Russian the ending (suffix) -с has no plural meaning, an extra plural ending -ы is added to the word.

Jeans → Jeans

"Dazu trägt man eine hautenge *Jeans*, so daß der Stiefel über der *Jeans* getragen wird."

Джинсы → Джин-с-ы (double plural formation)

«Нэ....они, правда, те *джинс-ы* красивые были и сидели хорошо... еще б не расползались... и было б совсем сщастье))».

6.3 Verb

Borrowed verbs in both Russian and German are integrated into the system of conjugation.[150]

The most frequently used ending in German is *-en* (*shoppen, streiken, testen, surfen*), although some cases with *-ieren* (*trainieren*), *-(e)l(n)* (*googeln, sporteln*) are also to be found .On the whole, all borrowed verbs belong to the weak conjugation: *testen – testete – getestet.*

In Russian, verbs take the suffixes *-ить/-ать/-овать* (*бэкапить, кликать, спонсировать*) and belong to one of the two conjugations (first or second) according to the suffix.

Past participles are formed in German with the help of the prefix *ge-* and suffix *-t* (*ge-styl-t*), although in our corpus one example of a so-called 'hybrid' was found where the double formation of the past participle is to be observed, namely a typical English formation with the suffix *-ed* plus the German prefix *ge-* (ge-flash-ed).

6.4 Adjective

Whether adjectives are inflected or not mainly depends on the function the adjective takes in a sentence and the degree of integration.

Already integrated adjectives in an attributive position are inflected just like native ones in German as well as in Russian:

"Gestern bin ich bei einer cool*en* Party gewesen."

«Со звуковым нормальным долби*ным* окружением».

150 See Duden, Grammatik der deutschen Gegenwartssprache 1998.

Adjectives that fulfil a predicative function or are used attributively as constituents of a lexical unit are not inflected.[151]

“Überleben ist schwierig, kann man bei diesem *online* Spiel feststellen.”

«Дорога через Хаос – ролевая *онлайн игра*».

Adjectives that have vowel endings like sexy, crazy are not normally inflected in German according to the rules of German grammar (Gester 2001:94).

“Doch solch ein *sexy* Paket hat auch seinen Tribut und der ist eindeutig bei der Kamera zu finden, die zwar mit zwei Megapixeln auf den lechzenden Käufer wartet, aber einen Blitz vermissen lässt, wodurch die Fotos “in die Tonne gekloppt”.

Through integration into the system of German and Russian, adjectives sometimes take the native suffixes. For German the following suffixes are typical: -isch, -lich, -ig (chat-technisch, sportlich, rockig), for Russian- -н, -ск, -ов (тестовый, нехайтековский, дефолтный):

“nina hat mich *chat-technisch* leider versetzt, wir wollten heute darüber reden ob wir am wochenende fahren oder nicht..”

“Nichr wirklich *sportlich* aber süß wie ein Honigkuchen…”

“Der Opener „As I please” mag auch nach 10 maligem Hören nicht so richtig zünden – sehr schnell, sehr laut, sehr *rockig*, aber nicht wirklich mitreißend und eine Prise zu unmelodiös.”

«Когда мне предложили *тестовое* задание – статуя Свободы, ограничение – 5000 треугольников – я был в ступоре, не зная, как сделать модель именно с таким бюджетом».

«Надоело получать *нехайтековскую* зарплату и делать однообразную работу».

«Утешает одно, вроде Амик у меня получился не такой несчастный как большинство *дефолтных* Цианов, рекламирующих на Латсе парики и одежки срочно всех спасти из рабства».

Adjectives that do not take native endings (such cases are not normally typical of Russian) are used predicatively.

As far as degrees of comparison are concerned, the way they are formed in German is similar to English and at this point there are no difficulties. The comparative degree is formed with the help of the suffix -er and superlative -est.

---

151 Adjectives as constituents of a lexical unit are looked upon as a part of a compound.

“52 Schulen aus Österreich – Slowenien – Ungarn – Deutschland – Kroatien – Italien – Ukraine zeigen sich von ihrer *creativsten* Seite”.

“Irgendeine unsinnige Umfrage hat herausgefunden, dass sie den *sexiesten* Akzent haben, obwohl ich mir echt nicht vorstellen kann, auf tiefbairisch angebaggert zu werden, ohne zu lachen.”

“Meine erste Belohnung wird eine neue Hose sein, eine die etwas enger sitzt und mich wieder *sexier* macht;-)”

In Russian, as all adjectives fit into an inflexion paradigm, no difficulties concerning the formation of the degrees of comparison are encountered. Borrowings build up the degrees of comparison in the same way that native adjectives do:

«Более/менее креативный/креативнее – самый креативный».

«Мы не задумывали, не дай Бог, замочить Дмитрия Михалыча или что-то вроде этого, нами были запланированы гораздо *более креативные* вещи...»

«Листовки придумывайте пока, а то придётся мне *менее креативным* мозгом придумывать».

«А давай оригинальнее, а? *Креативнее*, друг мой, *креативнее*! А руки мне целовать не надо)))) Помаду размажешь».

«Я освободился и вошёл в один из *самых креативных* периодов своей жизни».

To draw a line it should be stated that not all criteria of gender assignment are applicable in Russian. Even so, some common tendencies concerning gender assignment can be singled out, for criteria such as *syllabicity, suffix analogy* and *natural gender* play a decisive role in gender assignment in both languages. On the other hand, the following main factors regarding gender assignment can be stated: in Russian the majority of anglicisms are assigned to one of the three genders according to the formal criterion of word form/ending, while in German the semantic criterion (nearest semantic equivalent) together with the formal criterion (suffix analogy) are the principal aspects. It is also important to mention that in German some dubious cases of gender assignment can be found in particular with newly borrowed nouns when a noun is assigned to different genders simultaneously according to several criteria, which is why a noun can sometimes take two or three genders[152] – which seems a nonsense for Russian where gender assignment is based mostly on formal criteria allowing no deviations.

152 Still it should be mentioned that such cases are rare.

Due to the similarity of the plural formation process in English and German (in German the plural form of nouns can be also formed with the help of the suffix *–s*), the original plural form of an anglicism can be preserved, remaining unchanged. In Russian it should be either substituted or supplemented by a native suffix. In some cases in German, nouns even take no ending or several variants coexist. On the whole there is a wider range of possibilities for forming the plural of anglicisms in German in comparison with Russian.

As far as the system of declension is concerned, the German language is also rich in deviations from the norm, as in the case of the genitive case, when the *-s* ending can be either preserved or dropped. In Russian, by contrast, all borrowed nouns take native suffixes to fit the declension paradigm.

In the case of adjectives and verbs, common tendencies can be pointed out, namely verbs take native suffixes in both German and Russian to fit into a conjugation paradigm. The same can be said about adjectives.

To sum up, judging by the examples taken from the corpus analysed consisting of *blog* entries, Russian is a more conservative language in relation to borrowed units, requiring them to adapt to its grammatical structure by acquiring native suffixes, endings, etc. By contrast, in German several uncertain cases concerning gender, inflexions, etc. were found. Accordingly, the system of the German language is generally more flexible towards borrowings and new lexical units.

7. Semantics

To begin with, it would be relevant to quote Miroslaw Jablonski, who states that

> Lexikalische Einheiten werden nie von Sprache zu Sprache als vollständige "dictionary entries" entlehnt. Die Entstehung eines Wortes kann nur in konkreten Lebenssituationen geschehen." (Jablonski 1990:120)

It is important to recognize that any word, or any anglicism in our case, undergoes certain changes in its meaning when transferred from English into German or Russian. Both qualitative and quantitative, these changes occur both in the denotative and connotative parts of the meaning.

The main aim of the present chapter is to analyse authentic spontaneous texts by average speakers, namely *blog* entries, and to trace the basic tendencies concerning the adoption of anglicisms into German or Russian on the semantic and stylistic levels. The texts in question constitute a solid and reliable material for studying connotations, as the connotation of a lexical unit depends on such factors as context and speaker. The analysed corpus offers the opportunity to reveal the connotative potential of anglicisms, as each time we deal with individual contexts and different speakers with their own perception of anglicisms. Another point of the analysis is to state whether the labels attached to a lexical unit in dictionaries differ from or coincide with the perception of individual speakers in a real communicative situation. With regard to denotation, it is also essential to state if there are any differences between the individual perception and the definition given in the dictionary.

In this chapter, anglicisms from the German and Russian parts of the corpus are contrasted in order to state the differences between them and point out their similarities.

The well-tested tools of semantic description were employed with the essential terminology outlined at the beginning of the chapter and the analysis of the examples coming afterwards.

7.1. Types of Meaning

To begin with it is necessary to introduce the basic semantic terms, and more specifically, the terminology concerning the types of meaning. This is all the more appropriate at this point, as according to Alan Cruse (2000:46), "several scholars have proposed ways of classifying meaning into types, and the various proposals by no means agree in their details."

It is a linguistic tradition to differentiate between the *denotative* and *connotative* parts of the sense/meaning of a lexical unit.[153]

Denotation is a conceptual constituent of the sense, while connotation lies beyond the conceptual frames.

Therefore, we can state that in contrast to the *denotative meaning*, which is the same for all the members of a community, the *connotative meaning* of a word is individual and depends on the speaker's perception of reality.

A classification of connotations has been given by Hansen et al. (1990:19ff); they differentiate between *stylistic*, *expressive,* and *regional* connotations. Cruse (2000:58ff) in his turn, speaks about *expressive meaning* and *evoked meaning*, implying dialect and register peculiarities. Other linguists suggest *regional*, *temporal,* and *social* connotations.

In the present research, the above classifications were summed up and the following types of the connotative meaning were singled out: *stylistic connotation* and *expressive connotation.*

Stylistic connotation:

- elevation of meaning (formal, literary, poetic, archaic, foreign, terms) / degradation of meaning (colloquial, jargon, slang, vulgar). The labels from dictionary entries will be compared with the speakers' perception and the similarities or differences will be analysed;
- belonging to a certain register[154] (technical terms, computer terms, official language, formal / informal, etc.).

Expressive connotation (attitude / feelings of the speaker):

- estimation (positive – appreciative, jocular, euphemistic; negative – derogatory, taboo; and neutral);
- association[155] (exotic, ironic, aggressive, friendly, etc.).[156] This part of the connotative meaning is of great interest for the present research, as it is observed in numerous examples from the analysed corpus.

---

153 See also Lyons 1995, Welte 1993.

154 We further imply the subdivision of register into field, mode and style. See also Cruse (2000:61).

155 Yang conducted research into the speaker's associations with anglicisms to be followed by a study by Silke Gester (Yang 1990, Gester 2001).

156 Compare Которова (1998:78).

7.2 Stylistic Potential of Anglicisms in *Blogs*

It is a tradition to differentiate between *lexical (linguistic)* and *situational (extralinguistic)* context.[157] With regard to anglicisms, it is the *situational* context that is of paramount importance, as the stylistic features of each anglicism vary depending on the situation it is used in. Here the following factors play the decisive role: *the speaker, the addressee, the situational background, the intention of the speaker, the text type, etc*. Within the framework of the present research based on a study of *blogs*, the text type is obviously definite and invariable, as well as the addressee[158]; the intention, or the text function is in most cases informative, which is in line with the nature of a *blog* and its aims. It is the situational background or both the situational background and the speaker (producer) that differentiate a *blog* entry from another one. In the case of borrowings, the situational context in the recipient language influences the exposure of the hidden stylistic potential, which is not normally revealed in the source language.

7.2.1 Stylistic Devices

Here are some examples of *blog* entries, in which the stylistic potential of anglicisms is revealed in the context:

- Metaphor:

"Jedenfalls war gestern Abend *der Chat wieder fast nur rosa vor lauter Flüsterern*. Einer von den Jungs, den ich scheinbar so beeindruckt habe, lies nicht locker und war am Ende."

"Gut... werde jetzt noch ein wenig *durch die Weiten des WWW surfen* und dann irgendwann zur Schule fahren... "

"Die meisten meiner Einträge für Freunde geschrieben und deswegen einfach bei Interesse fragen und *ich hadde dich.*"

"hab ich schon erwähnt ... dass ich es absolut nicht mag ... wenn man mitten in einer msn-unterhaltung *offline geht*?"

«Дисклеймер», свисающий со столика, гласил: «Настоящие подковы на счастье». Поодаль стоял такой же столик, но без дисклеймера. Поддельные подковы на несчастье?»

157 See also Cruse 2000, Lipka 2002.
158 See Chapter 1 for details.

- Metonymy:

«Правда с этим трудно, ходила по магазинам – ну ничего не нравится, из того *«сэкэндхэнда», которым завалены магазины*, ничего не нравится, а то, что более или менее нравится стоит просто сумасшедших денег».

Irony:

“Und zweitens, weil *"fans"* von mir meine Aufmerksamkeit wollten”

“Dann erzählte sie ausgiebig von ihrem Mann (DER ARME!), der seine Hemden selber bügelt und ja sowieso Hausmann ist, weil sie immer berufstätig war und das Geld verdient (die haben bestimmt ne riesige Villa, bei SO einer intelligenten *Business-Frau* als Brötchenverdienerin)”

“Einzig mein *Outfit* hat mich etwas gestört, denn normalerweise empfange ich nicht so gerne Gäste mit fettigen Haaren und schmutzigen Klamotten, die Hände noch nass vom Toiletteputzen...”

- Personification:

«Писала вчера сочинение, как ежик, старалась, мало того что *Лингву затерроризировала, так еще и гугль спрашивала»*.

«В результате *боулинг нам ставил пиво-соки-чай* за счет заведения».

7.2.2 Expressive Connotation

Given below are a number of examples where the expressive connotation of anglicisms comes to light only in the context and does not appear in dictionaries:

- Negative connotation:

“Handy kein Kredit mehr (in der Türkei läuft alles via PrePaykarte). Ein trauriges SMS von einem anderen Handy aus. Bis der Lohn kommt keine Möglichkeit mehr mir zu schreiben.”

“Zweifel kamen hoch! Stimmt die Story? Ist es nur ein Trick um an Geld zu kommen (aber nicht mit mir), oder ist er mich schon leid? Neue Woche neue Touristin?”

“Auf Grund dessen, dass ich während der Klausurenphase wieder 3kg zugenommen habe, habe ich mich entschlossen bis Ostern auf Süßkram und Fastfood zu verzichten”.

«Напечатанные *офсетным* способом тиражом от 20000 экземпляров - от депутатов, заказчиков, подрядчиков, супермаркетов... В общем от всех, кто хочет получить деньги. Фактически те же счета».

«И вообще, я и училась, и работала, Масяныш сначала была слишком маленькой для садика, потом год болела *нон-стоп*, няни дорогущие и тоже болели. Короче говоря, было весело».

- Positive connotation:

Here are some interesting examples:

«Своих наличных средств мало, есть *джип*. И нет, пропить его нельзя, на чем я буду тогда работать и девок катать?»

The use of the anglicism '*Jeep*' emphasizes the author's material well-being in spite of the lack of cash.

«и тут... мы начали потихонечку понимать, что комод несколько тяжелее, чем нам бы хотелось, но мы не сдавались. Все-таки мы же *байкеры*, а не балерины – должны осилить!» (....but we are bikers, not ballet-dancers....)

Here the anglicism 'байкер' ('bikers') as a symbol of strength, fearlessness, etc. is used in contrast to the word 'балерина' ('ballet-dancer') which evokes opposite associations.

7.2.3 Stylistic Interference

Anglicisms in *blogs* can be the subject of stylistic interference. Hans Galinsky (Carstensen, Galinsky 1975:71) distinguishes the following functions of the stylistic interference of anglicisms:

- Providing national American colour settings, actions, and characters:

«Что там московский гей-парад! В Новой зеландии пройдет санкционированный порно-парад, 30 порно звезд проедут *топлесс* на *байках* по центру города. И никаких вам идейных бабушек и омона - даже скучно».

"Ich schmeiße jegliche Filmprojekte, die ich momentan habe hin (zu schade, dabei haben sich die großen Hollywood-Studios ja praktisch um die Finanzierung gerissen), um zusammen mit Frau S. "Passenger Rattlesnake" zu drehen. Dieser spannende *Action-Liebes-Suspense-Doku-Road-Movie* spielt im australischen *Outback*. Eine Gruppe fährt im *Jeep* über eine staubige Straße und hört die ganze Zeit seltsame Geräusche".

- Establishing or enhancing precision:

There are a number of examples, in which loanwords are inserted in texts for the sake of the precision of expression – when there is no equivalent in the native language or the translation is not possible or does not meet the author's expectations. In such cases lexical units are generally borrowed to fill in the lexical gap.

“Er steckte mir irgendwann, dass er nur einen *One-Night-Stand* wollte – daraufhin warf ich ihn aus meiner Wohnung.”

“... gefunden, aber ich hoffe hier auf die ultimativen Expertenstimmen: freches grinsen: Nun ist es also wieder so weit, es ist bald Freitagabend und das berühmte erste *Date* steht an... ...und ich habe keine Ahnung, was ich anziehen soll. ... ”

«Если КОНЬЯК разбавить водой, то он сразу теряет запах и сильно меняется во вкусе. А водкой – одни плюсы. А если в *шейкер* положить 5 кубиков льда и налить туда не 50 г ВИСКИ, а 35, то будет казаться, что там все семьдесят. Так же и с разными КОКТЕЙЛЯМИ: просто недоливали, клали лед, и – все!»

«*Тест-драйв:* вторая, и я надеюсь, последняя серия. По мотивам предыдущей серии. Ездил сегодня на три *тест-драйва* и опосредованно тестировал четвертую машину».

- Providing or facilitating intentional disguise (euphemisms):

«А чё, будет *дефлор-тренажёр*, вполне себе продукт, будет пользоваться спросом :)».

«пришли мы к полуночи, и может группа устала толи не знаю, но пела заунывно... нам не понравилось, отправились в караоке-бар *дринькать*».

“Ich bin jetzt auch *Single*. Kannst du mir nicht ein paar Tipps geben? ” Die Kassiererin mustert mich fragend, während mir Fluchtgedanken durch den Kopf schießen.”

“Shit happens...”

- Effecting brevity to the point of terseness:

«В субботу *тестдрайвила* новый сивик хэтч. Жестковат, шумноват, ноофигенный. Ждем-с....»

“Und dann eines von mir, auf der Hochzeit wo wir *gebabysittet* haben. Hach. Süüüüüss :-) Oberniedlich.”

- Producing vividness, often by way of metaphor (see the examples below);
- Conveying the tone:

“Aber die nächsten Wochen wird es nicht anders werden, ich springe ja ständig für irgendjemanden ein. Andererseits...*Money, Money, Money*...Urlaub spare ich mir auf die Art auch an und dann werd ich im Herbst mit Daniel weg-fahren".

- Creating or adding to the variety of expression;

"Dieses schöne rote *Top* ist von der deutschen Designerin Katrin Schnabl. Irgendwie erinner mich dieses *Oberteil* mit dem intesiven Rot an einen roten Lippenstift".

"ich gehe gern *einkaufen*. sehr gern sogar. ich bekomme auch meistens ganz gut hin, zumindest wenn es sich um nahrungsmittel und der gleichen handelt. Klamotten *shoppen* verabscheue ich abgrundtief".

"Nach diesem ersten Text beginnt die eigentliche *Geschichte* als Rückblick, zum Schluß schließt die *Story* wieder an diese Szene an".

«Магазин хороший, большой выбор, приятные *скидки* и дискотная карточка (стандартный маркетинговый ход, ведь имея *дисконт*, в следующий раз я пойду именно в этот магазин)».

«Шансы встретить эту вещь на финальной *распродаже* стремятся к нулю. Потому что сотни таких же желающих уже побывали в этом магазине, и у кого-то из них нашлась достаточная сила воли, чтобы не экономить и не ждать *сейла* ...»

«У нас в городе есть 2 *татуировщика*, делающих *наколки* половине молодежи. Большинство татуировок, которые можно увидеть в наших клубах – их работы. Оба – классные парни».

7.2.4 Neologisms

An extensive use of neologisms is a characteristic feature of the style of *blogs*. The absence or general ignorance of the spelling and punctuation norms by the authors encourages them to be creative in coining new words. That is why *blogs* are marked with a great number of neologisms, a large part of them being loans. Consider the following examples:

«Я тут подумала - я не хочу *бодибилдить*, ну нафиг, это скучно».

«все комментарии *скринятся* по умолчанию»

"Die Tätigkeit Band-Gründen ist momentan unglaublich verbreitet. Ich glaube, ich bin Mitglied in fünf oder sechs abenteuerlichen Combos, hach, dass wird ein Durcheinander-*Gefeature* und Kollaborieren, wie es selbst in den ver-hurtesten Hip-Hop-Crews noch nicht vorgekommen ist!"

7.3 Denotative and Connotative Meaning of Anglicisms in *Blogs*

At this point a concluding line under the theoretical part of this chapter is being drawn and the next part turns to the actual analysis of the examples taken from the analysed corpus[159]. The above-mentioned theoretical points will be applied to them in order to distinguish the differences and similarities concerning the semantic and stylistic processes that anglicisms undergo in German and Russian in contrast to the language of their origin.

- *Fitness*

The lexeme Fitness is the first lexeme under consideration. Given below are some examples from the corpus, which will help to define the term:

1. "Genau das habe ich mir schon eine ganze Weile gedacht und daher habe ich am 03.03.2008 beschlossen ich muss mal wieder was für meine *Fitness* tun.

Hab mich also bei der Website 1-2-sports.com angemeldet um meine sportlichen Aktivitäten zu protokollieren und mir durch die dort angebotenen Wettbewerbe eine weitere Motivation zu verschaffen."

2."Nach langer Suche nach einem Sportgerät, das gleichzeitig auch jung und alt Spaß macht, ist es mir eingefallen: das Trampolin müsste dafür die optimale Lösung sein. Es lässt sich einfach im Garten aufstellen und muss auch nicht vor Regen oder sonstiger Witterung geschützt werden. Aus eigener Erfahrung weiß ich, dass das Springen nicht nur unheimlich viel Spaß macht, sondern dass es auch schnell anstrengend wird, was einen aber nicht daran hindert weiterzumachen. Man tut also was für seine Kondition und seine *Fitness*!"

3."Dieser Effekt zeigte sich um so deutlicher, je älter die Teilnehmerinnen an diesem Test waren. So hatten 65jährige, die besonders viel Kaffee tranken, ein um 30% geringeres Risiko für abnehmende Gedächtnisleistung und unter den 80jähringen sank die Gefahr sogar um 70%."

Dass diese Wirkung des Koffeins auf Gehirne von Männern nicht nachweisbar sei, liege möglicherweise daran, dass weibliche Körper sensibler reagieren und der Stoffwechsel das Koffein anders verarbeite als bei Männern.

Demenzerkrankungen können der Studie zufolge durch Koffein zwar nicht verhindert werden, aber es kann den kognitiven geistigen Abbau verlangsamen. Im Vergleich zu Medikamenten gegen den geistigen Abbau habe Koffein auch

159 Some Russian examples have been translated into English. Other examples, however, have been left as they are to preserve their authentic colouring.

weniger Nebenwirkungen. Na denn Mädels, auf zum nächsten Kaffeetratscherl - tut was für euere geistige *Fitness* :-)"

4."*Fitnessbeginn* 7.2.08. Nun war ich schon ca. 26 x im *Fitness*. Das heisst ich war im Durchschnitt bissl. mehr als 2.5 x pro Woche also fast 3 x pro Woche im *Fitness*. Mein Stoffwechsel kommt langsam in Schwung was dann auch das Abnehmen und die Fettverbrennung beschleunigen wird die nächsten Wochen und Monate."

5."Ich habe 2 Überweisungen zu 2 Ärzten und einen Termin schon, sowie eine Empfehlung zu einem anderen. Hier habe ich Fortschritte gemacht. Ich gehe mittlerweile 2mal zum *Fitness* und bin kurz davor, 3mal zu schaffen. Hier habe ich große Fortschritte gemacht, daher sehe ich diesen Punkt als erledigt. Mit gesunder Ernährung und Fitnessgrundsätzen habe ich mich zu wenig beschäftigt."

6."Vielleicht etwas zu meiner *Fitness*... ich betreibe schon seit meiner frühen Jugend Sport und war vom 13-17 Lebensjahr Leistungssportler an der DHFK Leipzig im Bereich Leichtathletik/ 7-Kampf. Momentan habe ich mich mehr auf den Ausdauersport konzentriert und laufe regelmässig 3x wöchentllich zwischen 10 und 15km. *Fitness* und Ausdauer sollten also ausreichen vorhanden sein."

On analysing the lexeme *Fitness* in the above examples from the point of view of its denotative meaning, we can conclude that German bloggers use this lexeme in three meanings. It can be defined as "*health*" or "*the state of being fit*" (examples 1-3); it can also mean *"the place where one can train to reach the state of being fit and healthy, like gym or something of the kind"* (examples 4-5), or, as is clear from example 6, it can denote *"a particular sport activity*".

Such are the meanings of the lexeme *Fitness* in German *blogs*. Now it is relevant to pass on to the Russian examples in order to contrast them with the German ones.

1. «И еще. Спустя года три после родов она опять стала заниматься *фитнессом*. НО! Она пошла на занятия, чтобы отвлечься от будничной жизни, сменить обстановку, разрядиться, отдохнуть от семьи, побыть одной... Тысячи поводов и на самом последнем месте – приобретение хорошей формы и похудение. Допускаю, что в её подсознании есть еще какие-то причины набора лишнего веса. Мною описаны только те, которые наиболее заметны были для меня».

2. «В августе прошлого года перестал ходить на хастл. Так сложились обстоятельства. С января хожу на *фитнесс*, нагрузки побольше, но того

позитива нет совершенно. Вижу одна девочка из начинавших уже преподает. Правда от другого клуба».

3. «Мне тут сказали, что обязательно нужно заниматься *фитнессом*. Качать мышцы спины. А я НЕ ХОЧУ. В смысле на *фитнесс* не хочу. Я знаю, что я до него тупо не буду доходить. А если и буду доходить, то это будут походы типа «да здравствует сауна!»…»

4. «А вот мои знакомые инструкторы из команды Золото Белого Моря "Коллекции Приключений" http://www.active-life.ru/ (компания, с которой мой старший активно проводит летние и зимние каникулы уже 6 лет) сегодня вернулись с Белого Моря из лыжно-байдарочного похода Ледовый Гамбит. Вот где был *фитнесс* и преодоление и среды и себя. Жду их отчетов и горжусь ими! Это уникальные люди. Очень уважаю то, что они делают и для детей и с ними, и просто по жизни! Вот они».

5. «В это время я мыла полы. Романтично так, по сельски. две косицы-жопа вверх, юбка заткнута-да и нет ее вовсе. ползаю по полу, *фитнесс* такой у меня, подползаю к двери в детскую-возюкаю тряпкой по полу в коридоре-чу! тишина, странное, сопение. носок вижу-у нас косяк кривой, зазор между дверью и полом отменный-протираю тряпкой-глаз!»

6. «И всё! Снова вид сзади. Теперь уже я был вынужден лёгким (пишу без стёба) движением пододвинуть даму в сторону прохода. Всё-таки в херовый *фитнесс* она ходит – даже напряжением косой мышцы живота не ответила. Скорее всего, потому что их заводят скучающие жёны бизнесменов, а им это создание абсолютно безынтересна. Но упёртая бабёшка попалась – продолжала тыкаться в мою тележку и задницу парня».

As is clear from the *blog* entries, the Russian language has developed the following meanings of the lexeme *Fitness*: 1. *"a particular set of physical exercises"* (examples 1-3); 2. *"physical effort"* (examples 4-5); 3. *"a place where one can have physical training"*.

The German and Russian meanings of the lexeme *Fitness* are compared in the following table:

German	*Russian*
the place where one can take exercise to reach the state of being fit and healthy, like a gym or other facilities	a place where one can get physical training
a particular sport activity	a particular set of physical exercises

German	*Russian*
"health" or " the state of being fit"	____________________
____________________	physical effort

On the whole, we can state that German and Russian bloggers distinguish two meanings, which nearly coincide. At the same time, each language has independently developed one additional meaning, which is unique to it.

Compare the meanings distinguished by the bloggers with definitions from English, German and Russian dictionaries[160]:

Fitness	*Fitness*	*Фитнес*
1)the state of being healthy and strong so that you are able to do hard work or sport 2)the degree to which someone or something is suitable or good enough for a particular situation or purpose	Gute körperliche Verfassung, Leistungsfähigkeit (aufgrund eines planmässigen sportlichen Trainings)	Система физической подготовки с целью достижения хорошей спортивной формы, коррекция фигуры, укрепление организма, включающая комплексы специальных упражнений, занятие йогой, рациональное питание, соблюдение режима дня и т.д. (the system of physical training, which helps to reach a good physical form, keep in shape and strengthen the

160 The definitions have been taken from Oxford Advanced Learners Dictionary of Current English 2005, The Concise Oxford Dictionary of Current English 1995,Longman Dictionary of Contemporary English 1995,Duden- das große Fremdwörterbuch 2003, Duden - Deutsches Universalwörterbuch 2003, Anglizismen-Wörterbuch Bd. 1-3 1993-1996,Толковый словарь русского языка конца XX века. Языковые изменения 1998, Словарь иностранных слов 2004.

Fitness	*Fitness*	*Фитнес*
		organism; it includes special physical exercises, yoga, balanced nutrition, observance of daily routine etc.

Only one meaning – the first meaning of the polysemantic word *fitness* – has found its way into German and Russian. The way the borrowed lexeme is interpreted differs in the two languages, which can be represented with the help of the following chart:

English: state .... so that

German: state ...... achieved through

Russian: system ...... for the purpose of ...

The main difference between the English and German variants of '*Fitness*' is the reverse order of *cause* and *effect*:

E. the state of being healthy and strong → ability to do hard work or sport

G. gute körperliche Verfassung ← planmäßiges sportliches Trai ning

As far as Russian is concerned, the process of adoption is more complicated. The stress is made on the seme '*physical training*' rather than on the seme '*state/körperliche Verfassung*':

R.комплексы специальных упражнений хорошая спортивная форма,
занятие йогой, → Система физической → коррекция фигуры
рациональное питание, подготовки укрепление организма,
соблюдение режима дня и т.д.

It is obvious that while in English and German the stress is laid on the effect or the result, the process and its means play the decisive role in Russian.

Another important point is that the German lexeme *Fitness* has one more variant, the shortening of the form *Fitnesstraining*.

Fitnesstraining – sportliches Training zur Erhaltung oder Verbesserung der körperlichen Leistungsfähigkeit.

In the majority of the examples from the corpus, the lexeme *Fitness* is used in the sense of *Fitnesstraining* and not in its original sense.

“Ich habe heute festgelegt und direkt damit begonnen jeden Tag etwas für meine *Fitness* und etwas für meine Mappe zu tun.”(original sense)

“ah schön ich bin gerade zurück vom *fitness* und bin einfach nur noch happy :) es stimmt was mein arzt sagt: sport mach wirklich glücklich.”(used in the sense of Fitnesstraining)”

“Ich weis nicht, woher ich heute die viele Energie habe, aber nachdem ich zweieinhalb Stunden im *Fitnes* war und meinen Frust immer noch nicht abgebaut hatte, musste ich mich noch an einem Sandsack auslassen.” (used in the sense of Fitnesstraining)

This fact also explains the use of the neuter gender instead of the feminine one.

If we compare the Russian Фитнес with the German Fitnesstraining, both lexemes have much more in common from the semantic point of view than Фитнес and Fitness:

Система физической подготовки,

включающая комплексы специальных упражнений, = sportliches Training

занятие йогой, рациональное питание,

соблюдение режима дня и т.д.

с целью достижения хорошей, zur Erhaltung oder Verbesserung

спортивной формы = der körperlichen Leistungsfähigkeit.

коррекция фигуры,

укрепление организма

Generally speaking, the Russian *Фитнес* and the German *Fitnesstraining* are almost identical in their denotative meaning. Still, the definitions given in German and Russian dictionaries do not cover all the range of meanings found in real communication, namely in *blogs*, as shown in the table below:

Meanings found in German and Russian blogs	*Meanings in the German dictionary*	*Meanings in the Russian dictionary*
A place	-	-
Particular activity/set of	+	+

exercises		
The state of being fit	+	-
Physical load	-	-

With regard to the connotation of the word Fitness / Fitnesstraining, it belongs to the neutral vocabulary in German as an older borrowing, whereas in Russian it was only adopted in the late nineties and still appertains to the modish vocabulary. Therefore, Russian speakers often attach a certain degree of elevation to it, or sometimes even degradation. The example below reveals the essence of the lexeme Фитнес in Russian:

«Странно как-то. Читаю анкеты уже какой день – каждая вторая занимается *фитнесом*. Может и правда люди на сайтах знакомств все определенной категории и там нет такого разнообразия характеров как в оффлайне? Но не бывает так в жизни. Да сам *фитнес* это для меня что-то противно пахнущее снобизмом».

(It seems strange. I have been looking through profiles for several days already. A half of the women there do fitness training regularly... Fitness to me means something that "stinks" of snobbery.)

With respect to the native counterparts of the lexeme Fitness, it does not have complete synonyms in either of the languages. The term is of such a complicated and collective nature that it can only be explained with the help of several native units as in definitions given above.

- *Glamour*

1."Ihr Auftreten ist immer sehr prunkvoll! Nicht immer im Sinne von viel Schmuck und eleganter Kleidung, mehr durch ihr gesamte Erscheinung, denn *Glamour* kann man ja auch nicht an einzelnen Dingen festmachen."

2."vom winter mal ganz zu schweigen. muss weihnachten und silvester veranstalten, damit er wenigstens ein bisschen *glamour* hat."

3."Die nächsten sechs Stunden verbringe ich damit Journalisten zu erklären, warum sie kein Aftershowbändchen bekommen. „Ich will aber eins". „Du bekommst keins und damit Schluss. Keine weitere Diskussion." Falls mich also irgendjemand mit der BAMBI-Tasche sieht. Ich habe sie mit wenig *Glamour*, aber viel Schweiß erworben."

4.“Mit dem *Glamour* ist das so eine Sache. Im Alltag findet er selten Platz und bleibt besonderen Anlässen und Momenten vorbehalten. Denken wir nicht alle direkt an *Bling Bling*, lange Roben und perfekt sitzende Frisuren?!”

5.“Ich bin ein Luxusweibchen geworden in Dubai. Ich brauche ein wenig *Glamour*, ein klitzekleines bisschen Luxus. Sonst werde ich gaaanz schnell unzufrieden. Mein Mann weiß das, deshalb wird er mir auch die neuen *Handschuhe* schenken :-) Ich bin die glücklichste Frau auf der Welt!!”

As is clear from the examples, the following synonyms can define the lexeme Glamour in German from the average speakers’ point of view: luxury, style, manner, gorgeousness, magnificence, gloss. From here we can state that the word is an evaluative concept; it has become popular due to the fact that it alone comprises many ideas associated with the luxurious way of life or style as such.

In contrast to a similar tendency sometimes observed in Russian, the negative side of the term is very prominent in a number of examples from the Russian blogs. As a matter of fact, the term is being intensively discussed in blogs, and there are actually two points of view on its connotation. Some bloggers believe its meaning and connotation to be positive, others share the opposite opinion. Perhaps it is not so much the term that is being discussed but rather the concept behind it. Anyway, Russian bloggers offer the following definitions:

1. *«Гламур* – манерность, блеск, красивая картинка, зачастую в противовес содержанию, нередко даже деньги, секс, продажность и глупость. В общем, веяние времени…»[161] (Glamour is but airs and graces, flashy lustre, a pretty picture, often in contrast to the content; sometimes also money, sex, bribability and silliness)

or another one:

2. «Человек *гламурного* мышления, есть существо, которое считает акты потребления — достижениями» — К. Крылов».[162] (a person of the glamorous way of thinking is the one who considers an act of consumption an achievement)

3. «Все, кто ругает *гламур* – дураки. Потому что *гламур* – это просто современный стиль. Быть *гламурной* значит быть современной, т.е. не анахроничной клушей из двадцатого века и тем более не кисейной барышней века девятнадцатого». (Everyone who criticizes glamour is stupid, because glamour it is just the modern way of life….)

---

161 Taken from URL:http:// www.diana-cafard.blogspot.com. (17 October, 2006).

162 Quoted from URL:http://www.voffka.com. (18 October, 2006).

The first definition already represents two opposite sides of the term *Glamour*; on the one hand, it is related to *gloss, appearance, preciosity,* but on the other hand, the author of the definition notes that the features listed are in most cases superficial, and behind them there are money, sex, venality, corruption, silliness, etc. *Glamour*, as it were, is only a cover to hide not too attractive things. The next definition also sustains this idea, though the stress here is also laid on the word *consumption* and the world of *consumers*.

However, the third definition is quite opposite, as it refers *glamour* to the modern life style. It assigns a definitely positive connotation to the term. It is clear that nowadays '*modern style'* actually comprises the concepts that are mentioned in the other two definitions.

To sum it up, the following table of associations with the term *glamour* in German and Russian can be drawn up:

German	*Russian*
Luxury Style Manner Gorgeousness Magnificence Gloss	Preciosity Appearance Consumption Money Sex Modern Style Gloss

Generally speaking, the associations that the term brings up for German and Russian bloggers are apparently similar. Still the term tends to be negatively tinged in Russian.

Consider the definitions from dictionaries:

Glamour	*Glamour*	*Гламур*
1)the attractive and exciting quality that something has because it is connected with wealth and success 2)strong personal attractiveness	Blendender Glanz, auffällige betörende Aufmachung	О ком-либо/ чём-либо чарующем, обворожительном, пленительном, иногда илюзорном, обманчивом; что-либо нарочито красивое в противоположность бытовому, ординарному

With regard to the quantitative changes, the number of meanings has been reduced from two to one in both German and Russian.

The German definition of *Glamour* is mainly based on the second meaning of the lexeme in English – "strong personal attractiveness". *Glamour* in German is associated with appearance, positive impression or general outward appeal, like its synonyms *Glanz* and *Aufmachung*.

Here is another definition of *Glamour* from Wikipedia:

Glamour - Heute als Attraktivität bzw. Faszinosum verstanden, bezeichnet Glamour ein besonders prunkvolles oder elegantes Auftreten oder Selbstdarstellen in der Öffentlichkeit, das sich von Alltag und Durchschnitt abhebt. Eine Person, Veranstaltung oder ein Kleidungsstück kann glamourös sein.

The Russian definition of *Glamour* given in the table above[163] is based on the first English meaning. It has nevertheless undergone certain changes. In the original definition, the stress is laid on the seme *quality,* while in Russian – on the seme *something or someone.*

The above definition, however, does not appear really up to date and does not reveal the true meaning of the word in Russian. That is why another Russian definition of *Glamour* from the Internet encyclopedia "Wikipedia" should be quoted here:

Гламур – оценочное понятие (оценка при этом может быть как положительной, так и отрицательной, в зависимости от взглядов говорящего), означающее близость к общепринятым стандартам "роскоши", "шикарного", внешне "блестящего". (Glamour is an evaluative concept (the evaluation can either be positive or negative depending on the speaker's point of view), which denotes a certain degree of association with the generally accepted standards of "luxury", "stylishness", or outward "lustre").

If we compare the original definition of *Glamour* with the Russian definition from Wikipedia, we shall be able to conclude that both in Russian and English, *Glamour* stands for something (a quality or a concept) that is closely associated with luxury, wealth, style, and attractiveness.

People's associations with the term and its definitions from German and Russian dictionaries are summarized in the following table:

163 The definition was taken from «Словарь иностранных слов» 2004.

German bloggers	*German dictionary*	*Russian bloggers*	*Russian dictionary*
Luxury Style Manner Gorgeousness Magnificence Gloss	Appearance Positive Impression Outward general qualities Gloss	Preciosity Appearance Consumption Money Sex Modern Style Gloss	Luxury Wealth Style Attractiveness

On the whole, there are only slight differences in the denotation of this term in both the languages. This is probably due to the fact that this anglicism is relatively new in them. The connotation of the word *Glamour* will be analysed below.

Native counterparts

The German language has a nearly complete synonym to Glamour – Glanz. Still, Glamour is often regarded as a modish word, so its use is the matter of prestige.

Russian offers no native correspondence to this word. The term is completely new not only for the Russian language, but also for the Russian reality. The borrowing was prompted by the changing lifestyle in society. More and more people are willing to demonstrate their wealth and prosperity. More are more people are concerning themselves about fashion, style, etc. The term Glamour has been borrowed to define the new lifestyle.

Connotative meaning

With regard to the connotative meaning, we are dealing here with opposite tendencies in German and Russian. In German the lexeme has acquired a positive connotation and in Russian a negative one.

The negative connotation of the word Glamour in Russian is obvious in the two above-mentioned definitions from the blogs. To sum it up, the following concepts are associated with Glamour in Russian: superficial luxurious appearance (in a negative sense), money, consumption as the aim of life, label-hunting, attaching great importance to clothes, accessories, cars, houses, etc.

Given below are a number of quotations from Russian blogs, which plainly reveal the negative attitude of their authors to the phenomenon of Glamour and to the word itself. Glamour is widely discussed on the Internet and in blogs, which testifies to its controversial nature and negative impact on society.

«Итак, *гламур*. Зажмурься и произнеси это слово вслух – какие зрительные образы проносятся в урбанизированном подсознании? Девочки в розовом, стразы от Swarovski, журналы Vogue и Glamour…»[164]

«Лет пять назад такое понятие если и существовало, то только в зачаточном состоянии и не все это замечали. Сейчас *гламур* это образ жизни для многих, да какой нах образ – сама жизнь. Настоящие чувства уходят в небытие. Пословица «встречают по одежке» стала не пословицей, а законом, который теперь называется дресс код. Аппетиты девиц растут. Негхиты не помогают. Помогает лишь серебристый бентли или для большинства неискушенных масс подержанный хундай. Что это? Глобальное повышение уровня жизни или тлетворное влияние запада? Как с этим бороться? В каких глубинках найти поселения староверов, которые ещё верят в сбербанк, социальные льготы и бесплатную любовь?»[165]

«В отношении этих веяний, действительно, никакой иронии быть не должно, а должно быть изничтожение явления и его запрет. *Гламур* в его нынешнем виде тоже безобидным назвать нельзя. Общество потребителей, наверное, хорошо для экономики, но. Нужно думать всё же о чём-то высшем, о национальных идеях и ценностях».[166]

«Далее мама почти за руку повела меня в магазины, в которые бы в здравом уме и памяти зайти бы не решилась. Магазины мягко говоря *гламурного* (вас не передергивает от этого слова?) содержания».[167]

«Насмотревшись рекламы. ... Господа, а вы хоть раз слышали в нормальном человеческом общении слово «*гламур*», кроме как в глумливо-издевательком контексте? Я – точно нет».

«Не на вижу *гламур* во всех его проявлениях! Эти удодные мальчики пестрящие своими переливающимися серьгами, с не единой волосинкой на груди и в жопе наверно тоже бреют))) хаааааа я валяюсь))))) Не люблю *гламур*, люблю простоту!»

«Другое дело если *гламурчик* для души и для себя. Кому-то нравится антиквариат, кому - путешествие, а кому - симпатичная кофточка. Но в последнее время что-то все стали на одно лицо: силиконовые губки, оранже-

---

164 Quoted from URL:http://www.voffka.com (18 October, 2006).

165 URL:http://beon.ru/dating/126-822-glamur-read.shtml (15 December, 2006).

166 URL:http://i-foster.com/2007/02/18/glamur-nadumannaya-problema/ (29 October, 2005).

167 URL:http://sestrra.livejournal.com/14617.html (13 February, 2006).

вый загар, стразы везде, и неоновые расцветки. Немного напрягает мой бедный мозг. Короче, я против *гламура*. Но слегка».

German blogs, on the contrary, reveal no negative attitude to the phenomenon of Glamour. It is always associated with Faszination, with something that one would be happy to possess. Such attitude can be observed in the following examples:

"am samstag vormittag war ich mit meinem schwulen freund und bruder in nem designer möbelgeschäft. da er ja in 14 tagen sein neues haus bezieht und sich noch inspirieren lassen wollte. ja da gehen wir dann durch die wundervollen riesigen räume einer alten fabrik, umgeben vom edelsten vom edlen. ach es war wirklich *glamour*. momentan lebe ich aus beruflichen gründen auf sparflamme, und meine anschaffungen kommen somit von ikea, was ja auch recht lustig ist. aber dies ist halt schon was anderes."

"Tja, wir alle werden älter und es zieht uns am Samstagabend dann doch mal eher an den heimischen Herd als in die Großraumdisko im Industriegebiet. Wer den aufregenden Glitzer der Disko-Kugeln trotzdem nicht vermissen möchte, kann sich diese Abzugshaube aus Glas und Edelstahl von DR Cooker zulegen, die nicht nur Kochgerüche entfernt, sondern auch diesen gewissen Hauch von *Glamour* in die Küche bringt."

Hence the conclusion: the borrowing Glamour has undergone certain changes in its denotative meaning in German and Russian; still, the borrowed variants lie close to the original and to each other. With regard to the connotative meaning, the German and Russian variants of Glamour are pure opposites[168].

- Sale

1.1"Zur Zeit hat Threadless, einer meiner Favoriten-T-Shirt-Shops, einen Holiday *Sale* am laufen."

1.2"Nach der Anprobe entschied ich mich für eine Hose, die mit dem Schild -*Sale*- versehen war."

2."Gestern brachte der Postbote neben dem H&M Blumentop noch etwas: ein schönes schwarzes Kleidchen. Ich habe es in *Wenke's Blog* gesehen und mich verliebt. Außerdem war es im *Sale*. Nach dem Anziehen schnappte ich meinen Einkaufskorb und ging in den Supermarkt."

3."Endlich mal wieder ein Tagesoutfit für euch. Ich habe mir im *sale* im H&M diesen Pullover mit der etwas zwiespältigen Farbe gekauft. Damit er nicht

168 The conclusion is limited to the examples from the corpus analysed.

so plastikmäßig aussieht habe ich den neuen Ledergürtel (den auch die Diana *hier* trägt) darübergelegt."

4."habe mir jedoch stadtverbot erteilt, denn es ist wie immer *sale* und ich kann dem shoppingangebot nur schwer widerstehen....und ich muss doch fuer meine ausfleuge sparen, echt gemein....und hier kann man shoppen.....und alles ist so guenstig...naja, ab und an muss man sich ja auch mal was goennen......"

5."Einen ganz entscheidenden Vorteil hat es aber für mich: Im clearance und im *sale* sind die Größen XS und S im Überfluss zu finden! Bleibt nur zu hoffen, dass bei mir die drei Wochen nicht ansetzen!"

1. «Совершенно неожиданно – фееричный повсеместный *сейл* и выпадающие с многочисленных витрин цифры и знаки, вроде – 70%!, -50%!, и более скромные – 30%!, которые на этом пире номинальной халявы смотрелись просто как скаредные предложения негибких продавцов».

2. «Потому что каждый день в половине магазинов половина товаров на *сейле*. А назавтра - другая половина. А на послезавтра - в другой половине магазинов. Только и успевай выяснять «где какая рыба и почем»...»

3. «Сдал рубашку, произведённую компанией point zero взад в магазин les ailes. сделанная из тонкого хлопка, она явно была не рассчитана на кнопки, более подходящие к джинсе. тётки помычали-побурчали типа «никадатакованебыло», но взяли её назад. денег назад давать не стали. вариантов замены не нашлось, ибо ацтой ацкий (hugo boss от 150 бакарей в расчёт я не брал, так как не *сейл* я нынче), и пришлось брать от них кредит ноут, по которой, как я понял, я могу отжать какую-нибудь тряпочку в ихих в магазинах на 67 рублей. чего я решил вдруг покупать себе рубашку этого сраного нулевого понта? не знаю, бес попутал. теперь вот и рубашки нет, и денег нет».

4. «Никто не заводит меня случайно в ряд с мороженным и не говорит – ой, давай купим эту пачку, она на *сейле* (мороженное съедается за один вечер несмотря на размер пачки)».

5. «Моя сестра hguna дай йий Боже здоров'ячка приодевшись на европейских *сейлах* была так великодушна, что передала с барского плеча мне обносочков своих – класные джинсы disel».

6. «Мобильник на шнурке – для пятиклассников, в кобуре на ремне – для сантехников (можешь туда ещё гаечный ключ прицепить). Если есть деньги, то можно пройтись по бутикам в период *сейлов* и одеться от брендов, это придаст доволнительные баллы».

A study of the above examples reveals certain similarities with the analysis of the denotative meaning of the word *sale*. Two main meanings can be pointed out: (1) *sale* means "*a definite period of time when prices are reduced" (*examples 1.1, 3 German, 3, 5, 6 Russian); and (2) "a *special offer (special price) much cheaper than usual"* (examples 1.2, 2, 4, 5 German, 1, 2, 4 Russian).

Consider the definitions from dictionaries:

Sale(9)	*Sale*	*Сейл*
3) a period of time when shops sell their goods at lower prices than usual	Einen in der Schaufenster-werbung zunehmend verbreiteten Anglizismus, der für Sonderangebote steht, insbesondere für den Abverkauf von Saisonware (früher:Winterschlussverkauf, Sommerschlussverkauf).	Распродажа товаров по сниженным ценам (Selling of goods at discount prices)

The number of meanings that found their way into German and Russian has been drastically reduced. The two languages have borrowed only one meaning out of nine.

Some qualitative changes in the meaning of the borrowed word have also taken place.

In English, the word *"sale"* in the above meaning stands first of all for a particular period of time when goods are sold at lower prices. In German and Russian the accent is made both on the period of time and prices. By *Sale* one understands *a period of time* in the first place: *WSV* or *SSV* in German, and *сезонная распродажа* in Russian; and secondly, *selling goods at lower prices*: *Reduziert* or *со скидкой*.

The meanings derived from the *blog* entries and dictionaries completely coincide, which is a truly rare case.

Both German and Russian have native correspondents of the word *sale*:

Der Sale = WSV, SSV, reduzierte Ware

сейл = распродажа, скидки

As the native synonyms completely cover the needs of the language, no borrowings seem to be necessary. *Sale* is nonetheless popular for a possible reason of the economy of language means, as a one-syllable word is more practical in use than the native constructions. Also, we should not underestimate the influence of the American culture and way of life in this case.

Both German and Russian *bloggers* sometimes express their negative attitude to the word *Sale*:

"Tja, wo er (oder sie oder es) Recht hat, hat er (oder sie oder es) Recht. Mir ist am Mittwoch folgendes in Karlsruhe aufgefallen. So ein Zettel wurde anscheind an jeden zweiten Laden geklebt, welche sich mit dem Wort *Sale* penetrant hervorheben wollen, eigentlich idiotisch, weil's alle ~~Idioten DrecksLä~~den leider machen und es eigentlich nur nervt. Ich schlage "*SALE*" als das Unwort der letzten Jahre vor."

«Или вот это – крутят сейчас постоянно – ненавижу больше остальных – в гуме (цуме и прочей херне) кончаются сезонные *сейлы*? Что, извините, кончается? Сезонные продажи? Нет такого слова в русском языке».

- *Shopping*

1."...nicht, was Sie jetzt schon wieder denken. Einfach vom *Shoppen*. Ja, ich gehe gerne einkaufen. Dieses Einkaufen, das man so gemeinhin als *Shopping* bezeichnet. Denn einkaufen selbst meint doch eher das Einkaufen von Lebensmitteln oder ähnlichen Mitteln zum Leben. Jetzt könnte man natürlich sagen, dass auch Kleidung zu den Mitteln zum Leben gehört. Aber das ist ja wohl für alle ausser Mode- Pardon Fashionjunkies übertrieben. Also reden wir vom *Shoppen*. Vom lustvollen. Meistens. Manchmal. Nie."

2."Ich – als Männchen – habe früher nie so recht verstanden, was eigentlich "*Shopping*" ist. Ich bin mir nicht sicher, ob ich es heute richtig verstehe. Vielleicht bin ich hormonell einfach falsch ausgestattet. Aber zumindest hat mir das Zitat "Wenn es beim *Shopping* nur darum ginge, einzukaufen, hieße es 'Buying'!" dem femininen Verständnis dieser Beschäftigung näher gebracht. *Shopping* ist nicht möglichst effizientes Eínkaufen sondern eine erlebnisbetonte, oft stark sozial geprägte Beschäftigung, die man am besten zusammen mit einer oder mehreren guten Freund/innen genießt."

3."Ich liebe *Shopping* wirklich über alles. Für mich gibt es fast nichts schöneres, als durch Läden zu streifen und sich von oben bis unten einzukleiden."

4."*SHOPPING*...Frauen lieben es und Männer hassen es eher, aber es gibt ja auch Ausnahmen unter den Männern Doch was tun, wenn es schon bald zur Kaufsucht wird? Sie haben immer den Drang, etwas bestimmtes kaufen zu müssen? Kaufen Sie sich Dinge, die Sie auch wirklich brauchen? Und liegt es überhaupt in Ihrem Budget? Wenn Sie sich alles gut einteilen, dann ist zwischendurch etwas Luxus auch ok… ansonsten mal auf die Bremse treten und weniger shoppen, am besten die Kreditkarte zu Hause lassen!"

5."Wir haben uns dann auch recht schnell wieder vertragen...aber nötig gewesen wäre es echt nicht. Heute dagenen war ein total-sonnig-schöner-*Shopping*-Tag. Waren sieben(!!)Stunden in der Stadt und haben eingekauft wie die Irren. Hab mir eine neue Cordhose (very stylisch!!), neue Flip-Flops von Bufallo (ja, ich hab zuviel Geld!), eine Tasche von Esprit(Schnäppchen), einen Zehenring(ist sofort kaputt-gegangen dank Megazehen) und ein neues, schmalziges Buch gekauft. Mein Freund hat sich ne Hose, ein Buch, ein Hörspiel und eine Sonnenbrille geleistet. Sind insgesamt ca. 150€ losgeworden. War aber trotzdem total schön. Und oft macht man so Shopping-Sessions ja auch nicht, oder?"

6."Heute nach der Schule Freundin geschnappt und ab in die Stadt. Wollt mir nur für meine Jeans ein neues Lederband holen – daraus wurden 4 Stunden Shopping und jede Menge Spaß :-)"

1. «Я люблю *шоппинг*. Люблю прийти в магазин просто так, когда ничего сообо и не нужно и потратить чуть ли не последние деньги на то, что мне, по сути, не нужно. А потом прийти домой и любоваться на то, что приобрёл».

2. «как известно, люблю *шопинг*, просто гулять по магазинам, даже если нихрена не куплю. выходные так провожу)»

3. «чем меньшим обладаешь, владеешь, тем больше стремишься к владению.неважно, чего именно не хватает: собственности, машины, семьи, стабильности.. но если есть ощущение незаполненной пустоты, то ее просто необходимо чем-то заполнить. *шоппинг* – это наше замещение заполнения этой пустоты. это сублимация участия в празднике, владения собственностью. Чем больше пустота, тем больше сублимации. Насколько же глубоки пустоты в консьюмер-обществах...»

4. «я веду к тому, что у нас случился неожиданный долгожданный *шоппинг*. ага, вот так. мы сорвались и поехали в мегу. у Алинки было три тыщи от зарплаты, у меня – четыре. непонятно откуда взявшиеся. что такое *настоящий шоппинг*. это когда 1)с любимой подружкой, с которой вкусы хоть чуть-чуть совпадают и уровень любви к брождению по магазинам примерно одинаковый; 2) с перерывом на обед в мак-даке, или подобном заведении, когда забываешь о диете, заказываешь любимый молочный коктейль и двойной чиз, а Алинка даже два; 3) когда есть деньги, и ты знаешь, что можешь купите вот это, это и еще вооон то, НО; 4) не покупаешь

всю эту милую, но ненужную чушь, а рыщешь в поисках сокровищ. настоящих. очень нужных и будуще-любимых; 5) выходишь из торгового центра счастливой, ты улыбаешься, ты довольна собой, ты отлично провела время, ты не купила ничего ненужного, а самое главное 6) не ожидала! очень ждала, мечтала о *шоппинге*, но не думала, что он случится сегодня».

5. «А если просто посмотреть по событиям, то, годики были насыщенными, прожила одни сложные отношения, побывала в замечательных местах, познакомилась с велликолепными людьми, которые стали мне настоящими друзьями, и нашла новые, яркие отношения, которые хочу и буду хранить, как самое важное в жизни!!!! Сейчас. радость моя работает, и я его не вижу и не слышу, и такое ощущение что половину меня оторвали, что нет меня, нет настороения и т.д. Вот думаю сходить поднять настроение *шоппингом*=))))))))))))))0».

It cannot be denied that both in German and Russian Shopping means the process of going from one shop to another in order to buy things. Still, from the above quotations we can add the following features to the denotational component of this word:

German	*Russian*
- excitement - together with friends - for pleasure - going from one shop to another without intention to buy anything -obsession about buying things	- for a good mood - together with friends - for pleasure - going from one shop to another with no intention of buying anything - a feeling of possession

As is clear from the table, almost all associations related to the word Shopping in both the languages are positive, except for one. In German it is an obsession with buying things ("Doch was tun, wenn es schon bald zur Kaufsucht wird? Sie haben immer den Drang, etwas bestimmtes kaufen zu müssen?") and in Russian it is a feeling of possession («чем меньшим обладаешь, владеешь, тем больше стремишься к владению, неважно, чего именно не хватает: собственности, машины, семьи, стабильности, но если есть ощущение незаполненной пустоты, то ее просто необходимо чем-то заполнить. *шоппинг* – это наше замещение заполнения этой пустоты, это сублимация участия в празднике, владения собственностью»).

Upon the whole, speakers of both the languages understand this lexeme practically in the same way. They regard shopping as a leisure activity, which is done together with friends for fun and pleasure.

The following table provides dictionary definitions:

Shopping	*Shopping*	*Шоппинг*
1) the activity of going to shops to buy things	Häufig mit einem Stadtbummel verbundener Einkauf in verschiedenen Läden und Geschäften, bes. Von Waren, die nicht dem täglichen Lebensunterhalt dienen	Посещение магазина или магазинов с целью совершения покупок/ процесс покупки, закупка товаров (a visit to a shop or several shops with the aim of buying something / the process of buying / making a purchase)

It is relevant to begin with listing the reasons for borrowing the word *Shopping* and describing its native correspondents in German and Russian. There is no doubt that both the languages have preserved the synonyms of this word. In German it is *Einkaufsbummel* in the first place, and in Russian – the following noun phrases: *поход за покупками, поход по магазинам*.

In both the languages *Shopping* is a relevantly new borrowing appertaining to modish words. It is becoming increasingly popular from day to day. The lexeme is particularly widely used in German. So at this point it would be relevant to compare the borrowing *Shopping* with its native correspondents in German and Russian, to distinguish their shades of meaning, and to state the reasons why the borrowing is so popular.

Einkaufsbummel	*Shopping*
Spaziergang [durch eine Stadt], den jmd. Macht um dabei Einkäufe zu erledigen.	Häufig mit einem Stadtbummel verbundener Einkauf in verschiedenen Läden und Geschäften, bes. Von Waren, die nicht dem täglichen Lebensunterhalt dienen

Einkaufsbummel and Shopping appear to be complete and interchangeable synonyms. Yet the use of the native lexical unit is becoming somewhat restricted under the influence of the borrowing, as the native word is perceived as less prestigious.

Unlike German, Russian has no complete synonyms to the borrowing. The following noun phrases are used instead: поход за покупками, поход по магазинам. Therefore we can speak here of the economy of language means. The use of one word is preferable in this case to the use of a whole phrase, and furthermore, as in the case of German, the use of the native counterpart is restricted because the borrowing is believed to be more prestigious and modish.

On comparing dictionary definitions with the bloggers' perception of the word *Shopping*, we can state that dictionaries register only a part of its implied meaning, namely the process of buying things. Additional meanings and associations are left out, but the above examples clearly reveal them.

Here are some more quotations from blog entries, which present the whole idea of shopping as a hobby, pastime, or a passion, rather than just a process of buying things:

«Мне вот лично кажется, что *шоппинг* – удел бездельничающих зевак: иду в магазин, не знаю, зачем, что увижу, то прикуплю». (I personally think that shopping is something for idle gapers. I aimlessly enter a shop and then buy everything that comes into view.)

«*Шоппинг* – не цель жизни. Это всего лишь еще один способ отдыха». (Shopping is not the goal of our life; it's just another way to take a rest.)

"*Shoppen* bzw. *Shopping* ist heutzutage nicht nur Zeitvertreib und notwendiges Übel, sondern Spaß für viele. Es ist nicht nur etwas, dass Frauen genießen, auch Männer und Kinder haben viel Spaß daran und verbringen Stunden mit ihrem neuen Hobby."

Due to the fact that the loanword is treated like a modish word in both German and Russian, we can observe a certain degree of elevation of its meaning in the above examples.

- *Fast food*

1."Als ich noch jung war... haha viele von euch würden jetzt sagen ich bin noch jung... konnte ich absolut kein *Fast Food* essen. Ich war eins von den Kindern die vielleicht einmal im Jahr zu McDoof gegangen sind und das einzige was ich da runter kriegen konnte, waren Pommes und eventuell auch Chicken McNuggets, daher vermisse ich es auch nicht. Aber heute hatte ich seltsamerweise Hunger auf Burger (obwohl ich früher gar keine mochte), also hab ich die

Gemüsebratlingsmischung genommen, die diese Woche im Aldi im Angebot war und hab erstmal schöne fettige Bratlinge gemacht. Während dessen habe ich Brötchen aufgebacken und Gurke und Tomate in Scheiben geschnitten. Als die Brötchen fertig waren hab ich sie mit Ketchup und Senf bestrichen und mit Salatblättern, Gurken - und Tomatenscheiben und Bratlingen belegt. Ich muss sagen, tausendmal besser als die wenigen Burger die ich probiert hab."

2."Heute ließ ich mich mal wieder hinreißen und besuchte ein *FastFood Rastaurant* auf der Lindauer Insel. Den Namen dürfen wir hier aus Werbetechnischen Gründen nicht erwähnen."

"Woher kommt eigentlich der Name *Fast Food*? Für mich ganz klar, man bekommt dort schnell etwas zu Essen. Tja eigentlich! Doch nicht so in diesem auf der Insel in der nähe des Bahnhofs gelegenen Restaurants oder sagen wir eher "Fresstempels". Mein vorhaben: Kurz rein - schnell einen CheeseBurger und ein paar Hühnerteile bestellt und dann nach Hause und den kulinarischen Schmaus genießen."

3."Wenns ums Essen geht, zählt für mich in 95% der Fälle dass es schnell geht. Gott sei Dank muss *fast food* nicht unbedingt junk food sein, aber auch das ist eine Definitionsfrage. Spaghetteria, Tiefkühlpizza und Co. laufen für mich zum Beispiel unter *fast food* aber nicht junk food. Wer will kann gerne eine gewisse Genussfeindlichkeit aus meinem Kochverhalten ableiten. (Und wenn es nur wegen der Überleitung ist.)"

4."tja und zum Abendessen hatten wir mal richtigen *fast food* ;) .. Hamburger, Hot Dogs und Pommes und natürlich eine Cola dazu ;)…"

5."Tja, gestern haben wir uns jedenfalls einen gemütlichen *Fast-Food-Abend* gemacht und zwar mit zwei richtig schönen Burgern - sehen sie nicht lecker aus? Sie hatten es auf jeden Fall in sich ..."

6."Vorher hatte ich von einem leckeren *Fast-Food* gehört, welches alle möglichen *Fast-Foods* in sich vereinen sollte: Yufka. Mein Hunger trieb mich nun dazu, den Laden zu suchen, wo es diese Köstlichkeit der neuen Welt zu kaufen gab. Da Marburg ja bekanntlich winzig ist, fand ich die Bude schnell und bestellte mir ein Yufka Chicken Nuggets. Man kann sich ein Yufka so vorstellen: Man nehme ein Lamacun, kippt da Chicken Nuggets, Salat und Kraut, sowie Pommes und viel Soße rein und fertig ist das Yufka. Lecker, ungesund aber lecker, wobei man hier das zweite „lecker" mit einem langen ersten e aussprechen sollte, welches sich über fünf Sekunden ziehen sollte."

1. «Что-то меня сегодня потянуло что-нибудь занимательное написать. Причём касаться это должно всех, ну или почти всех. Да, некоторые этого

стыдятся и стесняются, но делал это каждый. Да-да, это именно *фаст фуд* (а вы что подумали?) :) Эта кошмарная, но всё-таки такая вкусная америкосовская еда. И это действительно касается всех, ведь *фаст фуд* – это быстрый и дешёвый способ относительно вкусно перекусить. Согласитесь, ведь удобно на переменке или на перерыве выбежать к ближайшим палаткам и купить там что-нибудь горячее. Для меня, например, важно, что бы еда была горячая, поэтому я и не ем в нашей студенческой столовой, где по идее горячая еда всегда холодная».

2. «Всё-таки я не понимаю. Вот прайм-стар. *Фастфуд фастфудом* – салаты, сэндвичи, все как полагается. При этом они позиционируют свою продукцию как natural food. Внимание, вопрос: в чем, собственно говоря, фишка? По мне так *фастфуд* он и есть *фастфуд*. Бутерброд по определению не может быть полезным, будь то макдональдс, прайм стар или шаурма. Причем стоит это все недешево (ну, по крайней мере, я считаю, что 150 руб за бутерброд - это недешево). Платить за иллюзию того, что сэндвичи которые ты ешь, дико полезные?? Посему из чувства протеста против *фаст-фуда* съела вчера в прайм-тайме суши и салат (тот, который завернут в лепешку)».

3. «В *фасту-фудах* я ем редко, очень редко, только в критических ситуациях, когда белки и углеводы в организме практически на нуле, а времени на восполнение оных в нормальном месте нет. Сегодня в обед как раз была такая ситуация: все свое обеденное время я провел в бессмысленных переговорах с мудаками, и поэтому времени на еду не осталось, а в офисе надо быть в 13-00 как штык. На бегу принял решение забежать в ближайший к работе *фаст-фуд* и купить что нить на вынос, да бы съесть в офисе».

4. «Сидим, смотрим телевизор, идет реклама McDonald's. Хочу заметить, что не являюсь поклонницей всех этих хот догов, чисбургеров и прочих *фаст фудов* (не буду лукавить, могу раз-два в месяц зайти перекусить такой едой), но то ли проголодалась я тогда, то ли уж больно реклама хороша была... короче))) – Хочу гамбургер! – говорю я мужу. – Гамбургер – это нездоровая пища! – отвечает любимый. – А, я хочу гамбургер, я его хочу! – уже с ноткой каприза в голосе, и с надеждой, что мой любимый сбегает в рядом находящийся McDonald's и принесет мне его. – Хотеть гамбургер – это ненормально! Тебе любой психиатр скажет, что хотеть гамбургер – это не-нор-маль-но!!! – отвечает моя радость».

5. «ЛАДОННАЯ ДИЕТА. Ее суть состоит в том, что за день вы можете съесть только то, что помещается у вас на ладони. Слава небесам, я нена-

вижу *фаст-фуд*, а то бы каждый раз оправдывала бы себя тем, что бигмаки, и иже с ним, как раз аккуратно ложатся в ладонь».

6. «Посещать *фаст-фуды* сейчас стало также модно, как медитировать под расслабляющие напевы Будда-бара. И это несмотря на все увещевания диетологов отказаться от вредной «быстрой еды»! Впрочем, при желании компромисс между назидательным гласом медиков и собственными предпочтениями достижим. Ведь даже в дебрях *фаст-фудов* можно найти правильные блюда».

On the basis of the above examples it is possible to distinguish the following meanings of the word-combination *fast food*:

1) *Particular kind of food:*

The Germans include here *Pommes, Chicken, McNuggets, Burger, Spaghetteria, Tiefkühlpizza, Hamburger, Hot Dogs*; and the Russians – *салат, сэндвич, бутерброд, хот дог, чисбургер, биг мак.*

2) *Fast food restaurant:*

In German no shortening of the form has been found, while in Russian the word *restaurant* is contracted (examples 3, 6).

3) *Quick service*

This meaning has been only found in the German part of the corpus (example 2).

Speakers of both the languages generally associate American dishes with *fast food*. In German, some Italian, Turkish, and Chinese dishes can also belong here. As Russians have not widely adopted these cuisines, the word-combination *fast food* is mostly associated with *McDonald's* and similar fast food restaurants. Hence in German *fast food* implies a much greater variety of dishes than in Russian.

As the table below demonstrates, the word-combination *fast food* has more meanings in *blog* entries than in dictionaries.

Fast Food	*Fast Food*	*Фаст Фуд*
Food such as hamburgers which is quickly prepared in a special restaurant	a) <o. Pl.> (in bestimmten Schnellgaststätten angebotene) Schnellgerichte; b) Schnellgaststätte:	Блюда быстрого приготовления, обычно предлагаемые специализированными заведениями

Fast Food	*Fast Food*	*Фаст Фуд*
		(Dishes, which can be quickly prepared and which are served in special catering establishments)

Both in *blog* entries and dictionaries the term *fast food* refers to the food that is served in special catering establishments. So we can assume that in German and Russian the meaning of the term proceeds from the particular kind of place where one can have a snack; whereas in English it is the other way round – the seme 'food' comes first and only then it entails an association with the catering establishment.

German / Russian:

particular catering establishment ⟶ *fast food*
⟵

English

An explanation lies in the fact that in Germany and Russia such restaurants as McDonald's or Burger King appeared first and only then the food that was served there was termed fast food. In the US, however, traditional American hamburgers had appeared long before the above-mentioned restaurants.

With regard to the connotation of the term fast food, it has a definitely negative colouring both in German and Russian. It means first of all unhealthy food, which can lead to putting on weight:

«Бутерброд по определению не может быть полезным, будь то макдональдс, прайм стар или шаурма». (A sandwich cannot be healthy by definition…)

«Иногда бывают дни/недели, когда нет времени (да уж что говорить и желания) пойти в продуктовый магазин. В такие моменты я питаюсь ресторанной едой, которую безмерно люблю (да-да и этот ужасный *фаст-фуд* тоже жалую, хотя знаю, насколько это *вредно*), ну, а если есть силы, то освобождаю холодильник, морозилку и полки от разных запасов». (I like this awful fast food, although I know how harmful it may be…)

«Плохой хавчег. Вот это самое страшное – ведь в «Макдональдсе» можно нажраться от пуза, а через час ходить голодным. Просто *еда там хреновая* – всякие трансжиры и пр». (….food there is worthless….)

“Ich lebe einfach total *ungesund*, so gut wie *fast* jeden Abend ess ich *Fast-food* oder der Gleichen.”

“ich esse gerne dann bist du einer gut und viel und eigentlich fast alles außer *fastfood* und mcdonalds und so ein kram das *macht dick* und *fett* lach und *es schmeckt nicht*”

- *Cool*

1.“Von mir ließ er dann bald ab und setzte sich gegenüber neben ein junges Mädchen. Gaffte sie genau so an wie alle anderen und setzte sich dann *cool* hin. Seine Beine waren übrigens doppelt so lang wie seine Arme, ihr könnt euch also vorstellen wie *cool* das aussah, als er das eine Bein auf der gegenüberliegenden Seite seines Platzes parkte und eine Hand an der Haltestange festmachte. Dabei natürlich immer *cool* zu dem Mädl neben sich blickend. Ich beneidete sie nicht. Und ich war froh zwei Stationen weiter aus dem Bus wanken zu dürfen.”

2.“...diesen Spruch fand ich so *cool* (und er passt gerade so gut!), da muss ich ihn einfach von *Suse*vkopieren**:**
Wir Frauen sind wie ein Engel!Doch bricht man uns einen Flügel, fliegen wir auf unserem Besen weiter!!!!”

3.“Die ersten kleinen Schneefälle waren nicht ganz so berauschend für mich und mein Burnsmobil, da wir eine kleine Begegnung mit nem Stop Schild nicht vermeiden konnten. Zum Glück hinetrließ das Schild nur leichte Kratzspuren an der Stoßstange und meinem Ego, das ich doch eigentlich ein guter Autofahrer gerade im Winter bin! So holt uns Gott immer wieder auf den Boden zurück und lässt uns wissen… keep cool ohne mich geht garnichts! Ja, *cool* bleiben fiel mir nicht ganz so leicht, als ich mich bei dem zuständigen Polizeibeamten nachts um halb 2 wegen so einem blöden angefahrenen Straßenschild bei minus Graden rechtfertigen musste warum ich diese Straße um diese Uhrzeit befahre…… wat? Aber Gott sei Dank, es ist nichts schlimmeres passiert – mir und auch dem Polizisten nicht!”

1. «Всем приветС)сень оч клевый день был правда щас и инглиш фест ехать но у миня оч хорошее настроение так что все *кул*....»

2. «Вай смотрите снег идет!!!*КУЛ КУЛ КУЛ*!!Какое все белое ммм... так красиво=))) Эть иду я из школы домой как ПиНгВиНчЕгГг хех иду , иду , снег идет, идет, РОМАНТИКА*=)))* Никогда не думала что снег может принести столько радости=)Мдя...Это были снежинки ПоЗиТиФфФа=)))»

3. «Да нет, они в этом плане люди серьёзные, я лично знаю 6 контор, которые им платят и пока работают без ДОСА. Дешевое фуфло. С вероят-

ностью 99% могу сказать, что это какой-то школьный *кул* хацкер хочет стать смотрящим Интернета».

4. «ПРив=) я снова с вами. Я не оч. Чет ся так хреного чуствую. Мне Рита подарила значоГ с Джеком повелителем тыкв. ОоОО я мего=))) Я так норм в школе принцып. ВАгиф сцуко не хочет как я поняла телефонами менятся. И у меня сломались большие найшники *Фак мой мозг* шас собиру деньги и куплю се их. А потом диск st1m (аахаха вспомнила=)))А еще сень бабушка кудато свалла и я стояла морозилась на улице потом пошла на площадку и поиграла с какимето пацанами в 33. Я их выйграла я *кул*=)))»

First of all it is necessary to mention that both in Russian and German the lexeme cool belongs to the informal style and is mainly used by the younger generation.

According to the above examples, the following meanings of the word cool are distinguished in German and Russian:

German	*Russian*
-calm, relaxed (example 1(1) ,3) -very good, super (example 2)	-very good, super (example 1, 2, 4) -well-qualified with the tinge of self-importance (example 3)

In the English language the word *cool* is polysemantic. Depending on the dictionary, three to five or even more meanings are distinguished. Here are two meanings that have found their way into German and Russian:

cool (CALM) adjective: *calm and not anxious or frightened; not influenced by any strong feeling*;

cool (GOOD) adjective, exclamation INFORMAL: *excellent; very good.*

Both meanings in German and the first one in Russian were borrowed directly from English without any significant changes.

Here are the definitions found in German and Russian dictionaries:

German	*Russian*
1.[stets] die Ruhe bewahrend, keine Angst habend, nicht nervös [werdend], sich nicht aus der Fassung bringen lassend; kühl u. lässig, gelassen 2.keine Gefahren bergend, risikolos, sicher 3.keinen, kaum Anlass zur Klage gebend, durchaus annehmbar, in Ordnung 4.in hohem Maße gefallend, der Idealvorstellung entsprechend	1.отличный, хороший (excellent, good)

As is clear from the table, four meanings of the lexeme *cool* are registered in the German dictionary. Two of them are new meanings, not to be found in English (meanings 2 and 3), though in *blog* entries only meanings 1 and 4 have been found.

In contrast to German, a new meaning of this word appears in Russian *blogs*, which is not registered in dictionaries. It refers to naming persons, who think that they are so well-qualified in some particular field that they feel extremely self-important and purport to have advantages or power over others. The Russian synonym that suits here would be "крутой" or "классный". The adjective *cool* is normally used in compounds denoting professions or other activities related to computers. Therefore we can conclude that the word *cool* in this meaning pertains to the computer jargon.

Moreover, when used in this meaning, the word can sometimes acquire a negative or derogatory connotation (see the examples above).

Some other examples:

«вчера гендир где-то услышал, что сегодня какой-то день, празднуемый *кул-хакерами*, поэтому сегодня у всей фабрики нет инета... кроме программеров :)»

«решил тут глянуть рейтинг своего жж на яндекс.блогах. собственно вот: рейтинг блогов рейтинг блогов бугага, я просто супер-мега-*кул-блоггер* :)»

«Ну что же здарова *кул-хакЁр!!!*Ты ещё не *кул-хакер*???Ты ещё не натянул сервак http://www.whitehouse.gov/??? Ты ещё даже не научился выкидывать ЛОМОВ из чата??? Ну так что же, не беда, этому ты научишься позже...»

The following table summarizes the meanings of the word *cool* found in dictionaries and *blog* entries:

	Dictionary	*Blogs*
Russian	1 borrowed meaning	1 borrowed meaning + 1 newly developed meaning
German	2 borrowed meanings + 2 developed meanings	2 borrowed meanings

In this chapter the most illustrative examples of anglicisms that have found their way into the German and Russian languages have been analysed . The analysis has served the purpose of revealing the semantic and stylistic potential of borrowings with the same English cognate in two different languages. It has also demonstrated that any foreign lexeme adopted by a language undergoes both qualitative and quantitative semantic changes in both the denotative and connotative parts of its meaning.

The same anglicisms occurring in new surroundings, namely in the systems of the German or Russian language, cannot be expected to 'behave' in the same way as they do in English. For instance, if the meaning of a lexeme is degraded in Russian, it can be at the same time elevated in German. The same can be said about the expressive connotation. The way a lexeme is interpreted in different languages varies drastically. These differences do not only depend on linguistic factors but also and more importantly on extralinguistic ones, as the vocabulary of any language is the reflection of reality, people's way of life, their mentality, etc. Hence the conclusion: though we can trace certain common trends in the adoption of anglicisms by the two languages on the semantic level, i.e. the reduction of the meaning of polysemantic words, the influence on native counterparts in syntagmatic relations etc., still the way a borrowing behaves in the recipient language is individual and mostly depends on the extralinguistic reality, which is by no means the same in any two languages. The most important fact to mention here is that as the above examples confirm, dictionaries propose only a limited number of meanings and associations in contrast to live speech, or *blogs* in the present research.

Furthermore, there is always a great difference between the stylistic labels that dictionaries propose and the stylistic peculiarities that are revealed directly in the context. A lexeme that is stylistically neutral or unmarked for any particular connotation in the source language can be interpreted as degraded or elevated from the stylistic point of view in the recipient language, or else it can acquire a new connotation. Here, in stylistics, the context plays the crucial role – in contrast to semantics, where extralinguistic factors such as people's way of life, their mentality and the speaker's perception matter more. In the case of anglicisms, it is the situational context that is of paramount importance. Therefore the stylistic features of a borrowing depend on its linguistic surroundings or on the context rather than on the peculiarities of a particular recipient language. So one and the same borrowing can have either similar or different stylistic features in German and Russian depending on whether it occurs in similar or distinct situational contexts. On the whole, *blogs* as a new text type have definitely contributed to the disclosure of the stylistic potential of the anglicisms under study.

Conclusion

Given in the present paper are the details of my research into two linguistic problems, which were dwelt upon in equal proportions. The first problem lies in the necessity to describe a new form of communication and a new text type in the Internet, namely *a blog* (a blend of the term *web log*), and to distinguish its characteristic features. A comparative analysis of anglicisms in German and Russian blogs is the second major issue of my paper.

There is little doubt that the Internet as a way of communication between individuals is steadily growing in popularity. It seems that it is becoming so widespread that it is superseding the traditional ways of communication, like letters or even telephone. Therefore it appears to be of utmost importance to get a deeper look into it from the linguistic point of view, to focus on the possibilities of communication that the Internet offers the users nowadays, and to state why people are so attracted by it.

The most important feature of any type of communication is feedback, which can only be achieved through an opportunity to realize oneself in communication and to get the message across. The traditional and well-known forms of communication in Internet such as e-mails, chats or forums undoubtedly offer such opportunity. But as the progress goes on, new types of communication emerge to meet the needs of the users. People want to publish whatever they like in whatever form and whenever they fancy, and at the same time to get feedback and recognition. This is how the idea of blogs appeared. Blogs revived the genre of the diary, adjusting it to modern reality and to the needs of Internet users. Due to blogs a private genre was turned into a public one. A number of features set blogs against handwritten diaries – the style, the lexis, the form, the communication formulas and the vital importance of feedback (one writes for many!). On the other hand, however, the two types of diaries still have much in common, i.e. the chronological order of entries, truthfulness, subject matter and unchangeability of entries. These features bring them closer to each other.

If we compare blogs with other forms of communication in the Internet, like forums or chats, they basically serve the same purposes – to inform, to publish and to create a network. But the main feature that helps differentiate between these genres, let alone their form, is that blogs are still more personal. Not only does it concern the information published, but also the personal data about the author, which is generally available. In the case of chats and forums, nicknames are normally used. If we have a look at a blog, it virtually offers us a CV of the author. This makes blogs closer to traditional diaries, on the one hand, and to personal home pages, on the other.

The reasons for keeping a blog also differ. Here we can mention the need for self-expression, the sense of freedom in writing whatever one wishes, the general accessibility of the Internet and easiness in creating blogs. There are also some peculiarities of their layout and form. Generally speaking, Internet has developed its unique code, which is determined by hybrid spelling, a greater tolerance to spelling mistakes, the negligence of punctuation marks and the simplicity of syntactic constructions. All these features find their realization in blogs, alongside a wide use of anglicisms. They make blogs an integral part of the Internet culture, both written and oral. (As it was stated, written and oral features overlap in blogs). The following features make blogs closer to verbal discourse: grapho-stylistic means (various grapho-stylistic means are able to reflect the emotional side of the conversation nearly as well as paralinguistic means); an extensive use of interjections, onomatopoeic means, capital letters, etc. to reflect the author's emotions. Sometimes these means appear as emotional as mimicry or gesticulation in face-to-face communication. Then the author can create a feeling of personal presence, as in face-to-face conversation, using direct addresses or describing each detail of the setting (though a rather rare case, it is still possible). Also, given the reader's possibility to comment on the entries, which means the author's getting feedback and a chance to react, a kind of dialogue appears on the Internet, stemming from a pure monologue genre – the diary.

A very natural question to ask at this point is 'Who is the blogger?' For the purpose of this research, I have analysed a substantial number of blogs, which allows me to state that neither age nor any other criteria can prevent a person from creating a diary on the Internet. However, the statistical data I have gathered plainly reveal that an average blogger is a teenager who keeps an online-journal describing events happening in their private life.

Upon the whole, blogs are like a bridge between the Internet and the printed culture, a result of cooperation between the writer and the readers, a reflection of the state of things in modern society and culture. The analysis of the blogs has revealed that they actually constitute a new text type with its own unique features, and that they can be called a new form of communication.

All the above-mentioned features of *blogs* make them invaluable material in a study of anglicisms. Made up of spontaneous texts created by common users, blogs amply reflect the peculiarities of the Internet language. Hence, we can rightly assume that the anglicisms that occur in them belong to the everyday vocabulary of the user and were not inserted on purpose. Furthermore, as proven by several linguists, the number of anglicisms used in a text directly depends on its subject matter. The blogs studied have given me an opportunity to distinguish between topic-oriented and non-topic-oriented entries, which is in perfect conformity with the purpose of the present research.

As far as *anglicisms* are concerned, the German and the Russian linguists have exhaustively studied the problem. My research, however, focuses on two points, which apparently require further elaboration. First, to make a comparative analysis of the German and Russian languages, tracing the common tendencies and stating the differences; and, second, to collect statistical information on the use of anglicisms in a new text type, which is a part of the Internet culture, and to use this information in a sociolinguistic research.

The use of single lexical units of one language in a speech act carried out in another language is called *a borrowing*. In my research, I have analysed *long-term borrowings*, which found their way to dictionary entries, as well as *on-the-spot borrowings*, which were inserted in texts spontaneously and can be regarded as neologisms. I have also studied borrowings on the syntactical level or *code-mixers*, which are relatively rare and demand an advanced knowledge of the foreign language from the speaker. In the framework of my research, the definition of an anglicism goes as follows: an anglicism is a phenomenon found in German and/or Russian on the lexical or syntactical level, the form and/or meaning of which can be traced back to the English origin.

The reasons for borrowing are traditionally subdivided into linguistic and extralinguistic ones. As a rule, one single reason cannot be pointed out; there is essentially an interaction of several linguistic and extralinguistic factors going on at the same time. Taken in their entirety, these reasons sustain and motivate the growing number of anglicisms in other languages.

Upon the whole, there are a great many ways to classify loans in general and anglicisms in particular. The criteria of classification can be based on the form as well as the meaning, on the relevance for communication and on the relationship between loans and native lexical units; also, some particular stages of incorporation are introduced. Still, as the number of loans is growing from day to day, the adoption sometimes does not go the way it theoretically should – not all the stages are accomplished or, as the general knowledge of the English language is growing with non-native speakers, sometimes it becomes difficult to say whether the form or the content or none of them appear unusual to the speaker. In addition, this tendency concerns the relationship between loans and native vocabulary units. The modern trend is to supplement the vocabulary, as due to the technical progress and other factors more and more notions appear that are named with the help of the English language.

Here, it is necessary to sum up once again the results obtained from the comparative analysis of the anglicisms from the point of view of their integration on the graphical, morphological, semantic, and stylistic levels. All the examples cited in my paper and all the conclusions I have drawn are based on the material of the analysed corpus of blog entries, which were chosen for the analysis. At this point two parts of my paper – the description of blogs as a new text type and the comparative analysis of anglicisms – come together.

Generally speaking, comparative analysis as such was not made in all fields of graphics owing to the differences in graphical systems. Some peculiarities concerning the adoption of anglicisms in German and Russian were discussed separately. As German and English use the same Latin alphabet, the integration of anglicisms into the graphical system of German is not as complicated as it is in Russian, since most anglicisms preserve their original spelling. A basic rule applied to anglicisms is that nouns are capitalized. In Russian, however, the process of integration is really complicated, as stated above. Four ways of transition are possible: *transplantation,* which means that anglicisms are transferred into Russian in their original form, preserving the Latin spelling; *hybrid spelling* – an anglicism preserves its original spelling, namely its stem, but in order to function normally in the grammatical system, inflexions are added to it, which are written in Cyrillic; *transliteration* – each letter of the source word is reproduced with the corresponding letter in Cyrillic; and *transcription* – the sound image of an anglicism is reproduced with the letters which can express these sounds in writing more precisely. The pronunciation of the word is realised in writing, yet most anglicisms introduced into the graphical system of the Russian language are transferred according to both *transliteration* and *transcription.*

With regard to the spelling of compounds, I have drawn the following conclusions: in German, a better understanding of compounds plays the decisive role in the choice between different spelling possibilities; what matters more in Russian is how meaningful the constituents of a compound are. Compound nouns (N+N, N+Adj.) tend to be written in one word in German, while in Russian separate spelling prevails. In the case of compound nouns (N+Acronym) in both the languages, the majority of the examples are written through a hyphen. The same is true of compounds consisting of more than two components. Only 23.8% of German compounds and 49.1% of Russian compounds, which only consist of English material, are hyphenated.

In some cases (13.13%) German uses linking elements for the creation of compounds with the help of borrowed material. This phenomenon is not typical of the Russian language at all.

With regard to the spelling of particular letter combinations, the tendency of adjusting the original spelling to the native one takes place both in Russian and German. In Russian it occurs through transferring the original Latin spelling in Cyrillic, and in German – through the adjustment of the original letter combinations to the most near-native ones.

German and Russian are both synthetic languages, hence some common tendencies in the word-formation process. First, the mechanism of *shortening* works in the same way in both the languages. As far as composition is concerned, compounds are formed in a different way in English and Russian. Unlike Russian, the first component modifies the second one in English. This pattern has nonetheless found its way into the system of the Russian language and is becoming increasingly popular nowadays. The structure of German and English compounds is identical and poses no questions. Another point to mention here is that while in German many-member compounds are fairly widespread, the Russian language prefers less bulky noun-phrases. With respect to derivation, its means are not as productive in German as they are in Russian. Prefixation, on the other hand, is widely used by verbs in both the languages, and also by adjectives in Russian.

The next point is gender assignment. Not all the criteria of gender assignment are applicable in Russian. Still, we can trace some common tendencies and state that *syllabicity, suffix analogy,* and *natural gender* play a decisive role in gender assignment in both the languages. The differences are as follows: in Russian the majority of anglicisms are assigned to one of the three genders according to the formal criterion of the word form/ending, while in German the semantic criterion (the nearest semantic equivalent) alongside the formal criterion (the suffix analogy) hold the leading position. Also, there are certain cases in German when nouns (especially newly borrowed ones) are assigned to several genders at the same time according to different criteria. This is impossible in Russian, where gender assignment is mostly based on formal criteria, which allow of virtually no deviations.

Plural formation in English and German is based on the same principles, namely that in German plural noun-forms can also be formed with the help of the suffix *-s*. That is why the original plural form of an anglicism is normally preserved. In Russian however, it should either be substituted or supplemented by a native suffix.

As far as the declension system is concerned, a number of deviations from the norm can be found in German, as with the Genitive case, when the *-s* ending can either remain or fall out. In Russian, on the contrary, all borrowed nouns take native suffixes to fit the declension paradigm.

German and Russian verbs and adjectives display common tendencies, such as taking native suffixes to fit the conjugation / declension paradigm.

To sum it up, all borrowed units in Russian should fit the grammatical structure of the language in any case – through acquiring native suffixes, endings, etc. No deviations or dubious cases are allowed. This tendency is clearly observed in the Russian blog entries. In German blogs, on the contrary, several dubious cases concerning gender, inflexions, etc. appear, which allows us to state that the system of the German language is generally more flexible with borrowings and new lexical units than the system of the Russian language.

The next point of the analysis was the semantics of the borrowed units. The results clearly show that during integration into the systems of German and Russian a lexeme undergoes both qualitative and quantitative semantic changes, both in the denotative and connotative components of its meaning. Besides, the same anglicisms occurring in new surroundings, i.e. in the system of German or Russian, undergo different changes in most cases, and different processes take place. For instance, while the meaning of a lexeme in Russian is degraded, it can be at the same time elevated in German. The same can be said about expressive connotations. The ways a lexeme is interpreted in the two languages vary drastically. These differences depend not only on linguistic factors, but also, and more importantly, on extralinguistic ones, as the vocabulary of any language is the reflection of reality, people's way of life, their mentality, etc. Hence the conclusion: though we can trace certain common trends in the adoption of anglicisms on the semantic level, such as the reduction of the meaning of polysemantic words or influence on native correlates in syntagmatic relations, the way a borrowing functions in a recipient language is individual and mostly depends on extralinguistic factors, which cannot be claimed to be the same in any two languages.

The previous conclusion is further sustained by the stylistic aspect of my research. I have proved that there always is a wide discrepancy between the stylistic markers that dictionaries propose and the stylistic peculiarities that are directly revealed in the context. A lexeme that is stylistically neutral or not marked for any particular connotation in the source language can appear stylistically degraded or elevated in the recipient language, or acquire new connotations. Every instance of borrowing is individual, and the context as it is plays the decisive role. In the case of anglicisms, it is the situational context that is of paramount importance. So we can state that the stylistic features of a borrowing depend on the context or on the linguistic surroundings it occurs in, rather than on the peculiarities of a particular recipient language. Hence the similarity (or dissimilarity) of stylistic features of one and the same borrowing in German in Russian directly depends on how similar its situational contexts are in these two languages.

Upon the whole, the results, which were obtained from the comparative analysis of the two languages, allow us to draw certain parallels between the adoption of anglicisms in the German and Russian languages despite the noticeable differences of these languages on all levels (graphical, morphological, semantic and stylistic). At the same time, the peculiarities of each particular language undoubtedly play an important role in the integration of anglicisms, and extralinguistic factors should not be underestimated either. These conclusions have become possible in the course of an in-depth study into a particular text type – *the blog*, with its entries written notably in a language that can be called spontaneous and living.

With regard to the hypotheses advanced in my paper, the results of the research have not confirmed all of them. The first hypothesis, *the number of loans in one language definitely exceeds the number of loans in the other one*, has not been confirmed, as in the course of the analysis it became clear that the number of loans depends first of all on the topic of the text, and even if the general number of all loans is larger in one language, the number of unique loans can at the same time be larger in the other language.

The next hypothesis was that *the number of anglicisms in topic-oriented blogs exceeds the number of anglicisms in non topic-oriented blogs.* The results of the research have confirmed this hypothesis.

With regard to the interrelation between the age and sex of bloggers and the number of anglicisms they use, it is possible to draw the following conclusions. The number of inserted anglicisms does not depend on the writer's age, and it cannot be asserted that the younger the blogger is the more anglicisms he/she uses. The hypothesis about the dependence of the number of anglicisms on the writer's sex has not been confirmed by the results of the research. Therefore, neither the blogger's sex nor age definitely influences the number of anglicisms in the blog entries. Some other factors play a decisive role here and, most importantly, the topic of the text.

Speaking of what anglicisms bloggers actually choose depending on their age and sex, I have proved that there are, as a matter of fact, no "female" or "male" topics; it is possible, however, to single out certain topics, which particular age groups prefer to others.

The Internet as a new medium influences not only the bloggers' lexis but also their interests. That is why age and sex distinctions do not really work in blogs as far as the number of anglicisms is concerned. As I have already mentioned, the subject matter of the text is the most important factor that influences the use of anglicisms. For instance, anglicisms that are directly related to the Internet culture, computers, progress, etc., find their place in the blog entries of all users, regardless of their age, sex or nationality.

Upon the whole, the results of the comparative analysis of anglicisms in German and Russian on the example of a new text type, *the blog*, can be considered sufficient and reliable, as they have served to establish the general tendencies concerning the adoption of borrowings on all levels in the spontaneous speech of the average speakers of two European languages, that seemed to have more differences than common features. The results of the present research, however, demonstrate that the Internet language, or the language of blogs in our case, brings German and Russian closer to each other in general, and in the way they treat borrowings in particular. Here we can speak with a high degree of certainty of *globalization* on the linguistic level in the Internet.

Appendix 1: Complete List of Anglicisms (Russian)

Nouns

1. аватары
2. аврал (over all)
3. адаптер
4. админ
5. айпишник
6. аквааэробика
7. аккаунт
8. альтернативщик
9. аниме
10. антиперспирант
11. антиспам
12. антиспам-движок
13. апгрейд
14. арт-рок
15. ассемблер
16. аська
17. аудиотрек
18. аэробика
19. байкер
20. бан
21. банда
22. банер
23. банкомат
24. бар
25. баскет
26. баскетболист
27. бейсбол
28. бейсболка
29. бенчмарк
30. бизнес
31. бизнес-семинар
32. бильярд
33. бит
34. блог
35. блоггер
36. блогосфера
37. блокбастер
38. боди-бар
39. бодибилдинг
40. бодикомбат
41. бодипамп
42. бокс
43. бонус-трек
44. борд-кросс
45. боулинг
46. браузер
47. бренд
48. бренд-менеджер

49. бум-бокс
50. бункер
51. бутсектор
52. бутсы
53. бэкап
54. вай-фай
55. веб-камера
56. велоспорт
57. велотренажёр
58. видеокарта
59. видеокассета
60. видеоклип
61. видюшка
62. винамп
63. винд
64. винда
65. виндоус
66. винт
67. винчестер
68. вирус
69. гипермаркет
70. гламур
71. гол
72. голкипер
73. гольф
74. гольфы
75. гранж
76. даэри
77. девайс
78. демка
79. детектив
80. дефолт
81. джаз
82. джакузи
83. джинса
84. джинсики
85. джинсы
86. джип
87. джоинт
88. диджей
89. дизайн
90. дизайнер
91. диксиленд
92. диск
93. дисклеймер
94. дискомфорт
95. дисконт
96. дисконтная карта
97. диско-клуб
98. дискотека
99. дисторшин
100. дистрибьютер
101. длинк
102. допинг
103. допинг-препарат
104. дос

105. драйв
106. драйвер
107. драфт
108. зомби
109. зум
110. имидж
111. инди-лейбл
112. инет
113. инетик
114. инсайд
115. инсталлер
116. инсталяшка
117. инструктор
118. интернет
119. интернет-газета
120. интернет-карта
121. интернет-клип
122. интернет соединение
123. интернет торговля
124. йогурт
125. кантри
126. карвинг
127. кард-ридер
128. квест
129. кейс
130. кёрлинг
131. клик
132. клинап
133. клип
134. клипмейкер
135. клоун
136. клоунесса
137. клуб
138. клубешник
139. клумба
140. кодек
141. коктейль
142. колледж
143. коммент
144. комментарий
145. коммунити
146. комп
147. компакт-диск
148. компания
149. компашка
150. компик
151. компорт
152. компьютер
153. контроллер
154. конфигурация
155. корт
156. креатив
157. кроссовер-кабель
158. кроссовки
159. кроссы (кроссовки)
160. кулер

161. лаптоп
162. лейбл
163. лидер
164. лизинг
165. лог
166. локалка
167. лузер
168. луз фит
169. лэптоп
170. маркетинг
171. матч
172. мегамолл
173. медиа-бизнес
174. мейби
175. меморис
176. метросексуал
177. микро-шорты
178. микс
179. микшер-софт
180. мини-бикини-купальный-сезон
181. митинг
182. мобильник
183. модель
184. модельер
185. модем
186. моник (монитор)
187. монитор
188. мотивация
189. мувик
190. мультитрек
191. мэн
192. навигатор
193. Нет
194. ник
195. нокаут
196. ноут
197. ночной клуб
198. нью-метал
199. нью-эйдж
200. ок
201. онлайн-дневник
202. онлайн-магазин
203. органайзер
204. офис
205. паб
206. памперсы
207. панк
208. панк-группа
209. панк-рок
210. панк-формация
211. парковка
212. партишн
213. пас
214. патерн/ паттерн
215. пауэрлифтинг

216. пеар
217. пейджер
218. перформанс
219. пиар-компания
220. пиарщик
221. пиджак pea-jacket
222. пиджачок
223. пикчерофф
224. пирсинг
225. ПК
226. плейер/плэер
227. плейлист/плей-лист
228. плей-офф
229. поп-группа
230. поп-звезда
231. попкорн
232. поп-музыка
233. попса
234. порно-экшн
235. порт
236. пост
237. постинг
238. постпанк
239. пресс-релиз
240. принтер
241. провайдер
242. прогрессив
243. продакт плейсмент
244. продюсер
245. промо версия
246. промокассета
247. промоушен
248. профайл
249. реал
250. реалити шоу
251. регги
252. регги-звук
253. регги-тематика
254. регулар
255. рейтинг
256. релаксед фит
257. релиз
258. ремикс
259. ресет
260. респект
261. ретейк
262. ритейл
263. рок
264. рок-барабанщик
265. рок-гимн
266. рок-группа
267. рок-драйв
268. рок-дэмка
269. рок-музыка
270. рок-обработка
271. рок-опера

272. рок-студия
273. рок-театр
274. рок-хитмейкер
275. ролики
276. роуминг
277. роутер
278. рэп
279. рэп-культура
280. сайт
281. саунд
282. саунд-драма
283. саунд-продюсер
284. саундсистема
285. саундтрек
286. свитер
287. сейл
288. сейф-ячейка
289. секонды
290. секондхенд
291. секс
292. сендвич/ сэндвич
293. сервак
294. сервер
295. сервис
296. сервис центр/ сервис-центр
297. сериал
298. серфинг
299. сет
300. сингл
301. системный хард
302. скан
303. сканер
304. ска-саунд
305. скверик
306. скейт
307. скейтборд
308. скиборд
309. скриншот
310. скутер
311. сингл
312. слоган
313. смайлы
314. смит
315. смс
316. смс-викторина
317. смска
318. смс-ка
319. сноуборд
320. сноубординг
321. сноубордист
322. сноуборд парк
323. сноуборд-слалом
324. снэплинг
325. сокет
326. софтвер
327. софт-джойс

328. спам
329. спамоборона
330. спарринг
331. спонсор
332. спорт
333. спортзал
334. спортклуб
335. спортсмен
336. старт
337. стартап
338. степ
339. степ (снаряд)
340. степ-аэробика
341. степ-платформа
342. стоп
343. страйкбол
344. стресс
345. стрип-бар
346. студия
347. супермаркет
348. супер (маркет)
349. сэмпл
350. сэмплер
351. танга
352. татуировка
353. ТВ-канал
354. тенденция
355. терминал
356. тест
357. тест-драйв
358. техно-корни
359. течхаус
360. топ (предмет одежды)
361. топик
362. топ (топ 100)
363. топ-менеджер
364. трабл
365. трансвестит
366. трафик/ траффик
367. трек
368. трек-лист/ трек лист
369. трекер
370. трейлер
371. тренажёрный зал
372. тренажёры
373. тренажёрка
374. тренд
375. тренер
376. тренерша
377. тётка-тренер
378. баба-тренер
379. дама-тренер
380. тренинг
381. тул
382. туннель
383. тюнер

384. уикенд
385. установочный диск
386. утилита
387. утилитка
388. фаворит
389. фак
390. файл
391. файловая система
392. фанки-диско-коммершиал хаус
393. фанарт
394. фанат
395. фаст фуд
396. фен
397. фильм
398. фитнес
399. фитнес клуб
400. фитнес-фанатка
401. фитнес-центр
402. фитнесс-центр
403. флаер
404. флеш
405. флэш-бек
406. флэш-диск
407. флеш-карта.
408. флэшка
409. флешмоб
410. флеш-память
411. фолк
412. фолк-метал
413. фолк-рок
414. фольк
415. фольклор
416. фотомодель
417. френд
418. френд-лента
419. френдолента
420. фривей
421. фронтмен
422. футбол
423. футболка
424. фьюжн
425. хай-кат
426. хард
427. харддрайв
428. хардрок
429. хакер
430. хеппи энд
431. хеппи бёздей
432. хиппи
433. хит
434. хит парад
435. хоккей
436. хот-спот
437. центр
438. чарт

439. чат
440. чекдиск
441. чемпионат
442. чоппер-круизер
443. чип
444. шампунь
445. шейкер
446. шейпинг
447. шопоголия
448. шоппинг
449. гранд шоппинг
450. шопофоб
451. шорты
452. дресс шорты
453. шортики
454. шоу
455. шоу-бизнес
456. экстрим
457. электро-прогрессив
458. этно-шоу
459. юзер
460. юзеринфо
461. юзернейм
462. юзерпик
463. яху
464. bluetooth
465. CD
466. cd-болванка
467. CD компиляция
468. CDROM
469. CD-Rom´ы
470. chat
471. CD-привод
472. dvd/ DVD
473. DVD-Audio
474. dvd диск
475. DVD плеер
476. e-mail
477. firewall-ы
478. flashback
479. fm-радиостанция
480. house´a (Genitiv)
481. IP
482. IP адрес/ IP-адрес
483. ipod-video
484. job offer
485. luxary
486. minimal techno
487. mixed CD
488. mp3
489. nickname
490. partition
491. opensource-can
492. post-production
493. progressive´a
494. r´n´b

495. rock´n´roll
496. sale
497. techno
498. UPS'ы
499. USB-дивайс
500. USB-драйв
501. USB-кабель
502. USB-модем
503. USB-порт
504. USB-устройство
505. user´ов
506. VIP-карта
507. Wi-Fi
508. wintalk
509. WOW
510. XP-шка

Verbs

1. бэкапить
2. детектился
3. дефрагментировать
4. законнектиться
5. инсталировать
6. инсталяться
7. кликать
8. креативничать
9. парковаться
10. пикниковать
11. попиарить
12. проапгрейдить
13. расфрендить
14. серферя
15. скопировать
16. смс-ить
17. смситься
18. спаринговаться
19. спонсировать
20. тест-драйвить
21. тестить
22. фанатеть
23. форматировать
24. форматить
25. чекаться
26. хакать
27. шопить/шоппить

Adjectives

1. андеграундный
2. антивирусный
3. аэробный
4. баннерный

5. бескулерный
6. блюзовый
7. бутовый
8. вельветовый
9. виндовая
10. виндоуский
11. виртуальный
12. гигабитная
13. гламурный
14. глэм-фэшн
15. гуд
16. дефолтный
17. дизайнерский
18. джинсовый
19. со звуковым нормальным долбиным окружением
20. драйвовый
21. запаркованный
22. енд-юзерский
23. инспирирована
24. интернетное
25. клубный
26. компьютерный
28. корпоративный
29. креативный
30. кул
31. лайв
32. локальный
33. модельный
34. мотивационный
35. небрежно-пиксельный
36. нехайтековский
37. онлайн
38. полупопсовый
39. попсовый
40. продюсерский
27. роковый
28. сексуальный
29. спортивный
30. супер
31. теннисный
32. тестовый
33. трансовый
34. тренажёрный
35. трендовый
36. фолковый
37. хай_течный
38. down-to-earth

Appendix 2: Complete List of Anglicisms (German)

Nouns

1. Admin
2. Afterwork-Chillout-Abend
3. All-inclusive-tickets
4. Alltagsbusiness
5. American Football
6. Ausdauer-Training
7. Baby
8. Babybild
9. Babymassage
10. Babyratte
11. Baby-Shop
12. Babyszene
13. Backstage
14. Backup
15. Badminton
16. Badmintonturnier
17. Band/ (Tanz)kapelle
18. Vorband
19. Bandkollege
20. Bandmädchen
21. Bandmitglieder
22. Bar
23. Barfrau
24. Basics
25. Basketball/Korbball
26. Beat
27. Bergtour
28. Bikini
29. Blog Editor
30. Blog-Eintrag
31. Blog/ blog
32. Bluescreen
33. Bluetooth-Modul
34. Bluetooth-Tastatur
35. Board (snowboard)
36. Bodentraining
37. Bodybutter
38. Bodylotion
39. Bodyshop
40. Bonus Track
41. Booking (Buchung)
42. Bootmenü
43. Bootloader
44. Bootvorgang
45. Boyband
46. Bloggen
47. Bonus DVD
48. Bowling
49. Boygroup
50. Boxen

51. Brenner
52. Browser
53. Browser game
54. Buchtipps
55. Bug
56. Buttons
57. Cartoon/Karikatur
58. cable guy
59. Cash
60. Cashmere
61. Cashmerepulli
62. CD
63. Doppel-CD
64. CD-Image
65. CD-Inlet
66. CD-Qualität
67. CD-Regal
68. Challanger
69. Chat
70. Chatroom
71. Chatverhalten
72. Chart
73. Charterfolg
74. Check
75. Cheerleader-Team
76. Chillen
77. citybus
78. clean install
79. Clip
80. Club
81. Club-Mate
82. Coach
83. Cocktailbar
84. Cocktailsoße
85. Cola
86. Comedy
87. Comicladen
88. Community
89. Compilation
90. Computer/ Rechner
91. Computeranschluss
92. Computer Band
93. Computerchaos
94. Computer-Expert
95. Computer-Gehäuse
96. Computerkenntnisse
97. Computerladen
98. Comuterschaden
99. Computershop
100. Computerspiel
101. Computertüftler
102. Connection
103. Cover
104. Coverversion
105. Cowboy
106. Crash

107. Creolenohrclips
108. Crosstrainer
109. Cut Copy
110. Dad
111. Dancefloor
112. Date
113. Datenrate
114. Deejay
115. DJ
116. Top-DJ
117. Demoaufnahme
118. demo-mp3-Dateien
119. Demoversion
120. Design
121. Designer
122. Designerfälschung
123. Designer Outlet
124. Desktop genus
125. Disaster/ Desaster
126. Disco
127. Display
128. Doc
129. Download
130. Downloadlink
131. Downloadserver
132. Down Phase
133. Driver
134. Duty-free shop
135. DVD
136. DVD-Regal
137. DVD-Spieler
138. Einkaufstour
139. Email/ e-mail
140. Entertainment-Product
141. Event
142. Groß-Event
143. Fairplay
144. Fan
145. Fanhysterie
146. Fashiongirl
147. Fashiontipp
148. Fashion-Victims
149. Fastfood/ Fast Food
150. Features
151. Feedback
152. Fernsehshow
153. Film
154. Filmverweiß
155. Firewall
156. Firewire
157. Firmware-Update
158. Fitness
159. Fitnesscenter/ Fitness-Center
160. Fitness-Check
161. Fitness club

162. Fitnesshalle
163. Fitness-Studio/ Fitnesstudio
164. Flatrate
165. Flock
166. Framework
167. Flair
168. Folkpopstück
169. Freelancejob
170. Frickelfrackel-Sample-Elektro
171. Friesbee
172. Fuck interj.
173. Fuck off
174. Funk
175. Game das -Spiel
176. Gedankensplitter
177. Gerätetraining
178. Gildenhomepage
179. Gimmick
180. Glamour
181. Grill
182. Grillen
183. Grunge
184. Hacker
185. Hammersong
186. Handball
187. Hardliner
188. Hardware
189. Hause-Track
190. HDD
191. Headset (Kopfhörer)
192. Heimtrainer
193. High Heels
194. Highlight Höhepunkt
195. HipHop
196. Hit
197. Hobby
198. Hobbyfotograf
199. Homepage
200. Homepage Shop
201. Hometrainer
202. Horrortag
203. Horror
204. Hotline
205. Hot Pants
206. Hp
207. Icons
208. Image
209. ICQ
210. In-Fashion
211. Inline-Skater
212. Intervalltraining
213. Insider
214. Internet
215. Internetadresse
216. Internetaktivität

217. Internet Community
218. Internet-Installations-CD
219. Internetleitung
220. Internetgebühren
221. Internetseite
222. Interview
223. Jammerstories
224. Jeans (pl. used as sg.)
225. Job
226. Jobsuche
227. Jobwechsel
228. Joghurt
229. Joggen
230. Jogger
231. Jogging
232. Joggingschuhe
233. Jogging-Sessions
234. Joggingweg
235. Kassetenrekorder
236. Keyboard
237. Keyboarderin
238. Kids pl.
239. Kraftsport
240. Krafttraining
241. Label
242. Lady
243. Laptop
244. Lappi
245. Layers Look
246. Layout
247. Lautsprecherboxen
248. Lichtshow
249. Lieblingsband
250. Lieferservice
251. Light Version
252. Link
253. Liveperformance
254. Live Video
255. Location
256. Longdrink
257. Login
258. Logo
259. Seematrosen Look
260. Look-a-likes
261. Lyrics
262. Mail
263. Mail-Account
264. Mailadresse
265. Mailbox
266. Mailkontakt
267. Mail-Software
268. Mainboard
269. Mainstream-Pop
270. Management
271. Manifestation
272. Männerfindetip

273. Marken-Shops
274. Masterkeyboard
275. Message
276. Messenger
277. Midlife-Crisis
278. Mighty Mouse
279. Milchshake
280. Miss-America-Look
281. Mix
282. Modedesigner/ Mode-Designer
283. Mode-Einkaufs-Freaks
284. Model
285. Modulupdates
286. Monitor
287. Mountainbike
288. Mp3-Player
289. Musical
290. Musicplayer
291. Musikvideo
292. Nachtportierjob
293. Newcomer
294. New look
295. Nick
296. Notebook
297. Okay/ OK/ O.K./ ok
298. One-Night-Stand
299. Onlinebanking
300. Onlinebestellung
301. Open air
302. Outfit
303. Outlet
304. Overall
305. Park
306. Party
307. Partyanimateure
308. Partygemeinde
309. Party-Übermonster
310. Patch
311. PC
312. PC-Pool
313. PC-Spiel
314. PC-Tastatur-Layout
315. PDF-Creator
316. Pepsi
317. Peeling
318. Pferdesport
319. Pflegeset
320. Picking
321. Piercing
322. Pingpong
323. Plattendeal
324. Playlist
325. Player
326. Playmobil
327. Pole-Position

328. Polo (Polohemd)
329. Pop
330. Pophymn
331. Poplieder
332. Popup
333. Posting
334. Powerbook
335. Prepaykarte
336. Private Party
337. Probetraining
338. Producer
339. Production
340. Product-Key
341. Programmcode
342. Projekt
343. Pudding
344. Pulli
345. Punk-Mode
346. Punkrockversion
347. RAM
348. Remix
349. Punk
350. Reallife
351. Rebound
352. Registry
353. Return-Taste
354. Rezepttips
355. Rock
356. Rock-Legende
357. Rockfestival
358. Sachsen-Ticket
359. Sale der
360. Salzpeeling
361. Sampler
362. Scans (from scanieren)
363. Scheck
364. Schmuddelreporter
365. Schock
366. Schockzustand
367. Screenshot
368. Self-made-Genie
369. Server
370. Server-Update
371. Service Bereich
372. Session
373. Set
374. Sex
375. Shirt
376. Shit
377. Shopping
378. Shöpchen
379. 50-Cent Shop
380. Samstagvormittagshopping
381. Extrem-SSV-Shopping
382. Shopping-Fieber
383. Shopping-Rausch

384. Shopping tour
385. Shoppingqueen
386. Shoppen
387. Show
388. Bühnenshow
389. Showdown
390. Shortcut
391. Sicherheitstraining
392. Sicherheits-Update
393. Signing
394. Single
395. Single-Dasein
396. Maxi-Single
397. Single-Veröffentlichung
398. Site
399. Skitour
400. Sms
401. Snooze-Taste
402. Snowboard
403. Snowboarden
404. Snowbombing
405. Softwarekonzern
406. Sommertops
407. Song
408. Cover Song
409. Songschreiber
410. Songtexte
411. Sound
412. Soundblaster
413. Sound Qualität
414. Spamm
415. Special Edition
416. Special Guest
417. Spezialsoftware
418. Sport
419. Sportart
420. Sporthosen
421. Sportkurs
422. Sportler
423. Sport-Monster
424. Sportsachen
425. Sportsblick
426. Sportsgeist
427. Sportunfähigkeit
428. Spot
429. Sprintstrecke
430. Squash
431. Squash Courts
432. Star
433. Start
434. Startnummer
435. Startseite
436. Steak
437. Steal
438. Sterberate
439. Store

440. Story
441. Stream
442. Streikzeit
443. Ärztestreik
444. Strechmaterial
445. Strongmen-Sport
446. Stress
447. Studentenjob
448. Studio (from Fitnessstudio)
449. Styling
450. Stylistin
451. Support
452. Support-Team
453. Surfer
454. Surfen
455. Surround-Sound
456. Swapping
457. Swim-Suit
458. Synthie(s)
459. Tankini
460. Tanzsport
461. Tatoo
462. Techno
463. Team
464. Teamkameradin
465. Teamspeak
466. Teenager
467. Teenagerzeiten
468. Teeniemode
469. Teeny
470. Tennishalle
471. Test
472. Testballons
473. Tester
474. Testphase
475. Testag
476. Thrashmob
477. Tip/ Tipp
478. Tipp-Runde
479. Toast
480. Toaster
481. Top
482. Top Ten
483. Touch
484. Tour
485. Track
486. Trailer
487. Training
488. Trainer
489. Trainerassistent
490. Trainingseinheiten
491. Trainingsimpuls
492. Trainingsplan
493. Trainingsprogramm
494. Tray-Icon
495. Treiber CD

496. Trance
497. Trekkingtour
498. Trend
499. Trick
500. Trip
501. T-Shirt
502. TV
503. TV-Computer-Kompatibilität
504. TV-Team
505. Uggs
506. Unterhosendesigner
507. Clamupgrade
508. Update
509. Kernelupdates
510. Upload
511. USB-Stick
512. User
513. Videoclip
514. VIP-Tour
515. Voice-Funktion
516. Volleyball
517. Wakeboarden
518. Waldtour
519. Walken
520. Walker
521. Walking Programm
522. WWW
523. Wassersport-Saison
524. Webadresse
525. Webbrowser
526. Weblog
527. Webseite
528. Websitecreator
529. Weight Watchers
530. Weltcuprennen
531. Weltklasse-Entertainer
532. Whirlpool
533. Windows
534. Windowsanwender
535. Windows-Desktop
536. Windowsfreunde
537. Windows-Setup
538. Windowsuser
539. Windows Update Patch
540. Wintersport
541. WLan
542. Wochenendtrip
543. Word Format

Adjectives

1. chat-technisch
2. clean (unschuldig)
3. clubtauglich
4. designed
5. cool
6. to be down
7. digital
8. erquickend
9. fair
10. fit
11. geflashed
12. happy
13. high
14. hi-tech
15. jobtechnisch
16. kreative
17. live
18. monstermäsig
19. offline
20. online
21. real
22. rockig
23. gestylt
24. sexy
25. shopping
26. sportlich
27. top
28. tough
29. trance-ähnliches
30. trendy
31. trendig
32. unfair
33. wild
34. wildfremd
35. wow

Verb

1. abblocken
2. antesten
3. babysitten
4. bannen
5. bloggen
6. booten
7. bowlen
8. chatten
9. checken
10. coachen
11. cool down
12. cutten

13. downloaden
14. einloggen
15. eintippen
16. filmen
17. flirten
18. fuzzen
19. gegoogelt/googeln
20. herumklicken
21. jetten
22. joggen
23. interviewen
24. killen
25. klicken
26. mailen
27. mitstreiken
28. mixen
29. outen
30. rauspicken
31. relax
32. rocken
33. scannen
34. shoppen
35. shoppen gehen
36. megashoppen
37. sit back
38. sporteln
39. squashen
40. stoppen
41. streiken
42. stylen
43. surfen
44. testen
45. tippen
46. trainieren
47. training machen
48. walken gehen
49. wegklicken

Appendix 3: Complete list of anglicisms (subdivided according to age group, topic and nationality)

	-25 ru	*-25 de*	*25-35 ru*	*25-35 de*	*35-ru*	*35-de*
general	даэри зомби лузер мейби ок реал респект сейф секс слоган старт стресс татуиров ка тест топ трабл фак флаер хеппи бёздей шампунь шоу гуд	Baby Babybild Buchtipps Citybus Bate Fan Fuck fuck off Highlight Hobby Horror Interview Light version Ok Okay Park Sex Shit Sicherheits- training Service bereich sorry Stress Test Tester Trick Tip cool cool down fair fit happy high live real to be down[169]	аврал детектив креатив памперсы парковка пикчерофф рейтинг респект секс сервис стоп стресс супермаркет топ тест уикенд флеш флешмоб френд хеппи энд креативни- чать парковаться расфрендить WOW	Baby Babymassa ge Babyrate Babyszene Booking Check Comicladen CU Date Down Phase Event Fan Flair Fuck Highlight Lieferser- vice ok Okay o.k Reallife Rezepttips Sachsen Ticket Salzpeeling Schock Schockzust and Self-made genie Sex Snowbom- bing Sorry Spot Star Story	детектив джип джойнт инсайд клумба лидер меморис митинг ок памперсы парковка пеар перформанс секондхенд секс сервис сервис центр скверик супермаркет центр шейкер шоу запаркован- ный попиарить down-to- earth	Crash Fantasy- Blödheiten Gedanken- Splitter Hobby Horrortag Jammer- stories Kids Männer- findertip Message Midlife- Crisis ok O.K. okay One-night- stand Pole-Position scheck Session Sex Single-Dasein Start Sterberate Streikzeit Ärztestreik Stress Supermarket Teenager- zeiten Testphase Tipp Tipp-Runde Top Ten Touch VIP-Tour

169 Can also be considered code-switching.

170 Ibid.

	-25 ru	*-25 de*	*25-35 ru*	*25-35 de*	*35-ru*	*35-de*
		unfair wow checken cutten mitstreiken stoppen streiken bye shit happens[170]		Stress Testballons Thrashmob Tip Trick Trip Wochenend -trip cool fair happy kreativ monster- mäsig antesten babysitten flirten jetten streiken wow anyway		wow clean cool sexy tough outen unfair streiken tippen
busi- ness/ finan- ces/ profes- sion	банкомат бенчмарк бизнес лизинг марке- тинг органай- зер спонсиро -вать	Job Studenten- job swapping	бизнес бизнес- семинар дефолт дистрибью- тер кейс офис топ- менеджер job offer post production корпоратив- ный	Freelance- job Job Jobsuche Nactportier- job Jobtech- nisch Teamspeak	бизнес бренд медиа- бизнес офис продакт- плейсмент спонсор корпоратив- ный	Alltagsbusi- ness Job Jobwechsel Online- banking
Internet	аватары аська блог инет инетик интернет интернет -карта онлайн- дневник	Admin Bloggen Browser game Community Email Frewall ICQ Internet Internet-	аккаунт антиспам антиспам- движок аська бан блог блоггер интернет ник	Chat Chatverhalt en E-mail Feedback Gilden- hompage Internet Internetcom munity	аська бан баннер блогосфера бэкап инет интернет интернет газета интернет	Download E-mail Homepage- shop Internet link Nick Posting Spamm User

	-25 ru	*-25 de*	*25-35 ru*	*25-35 de*	*35-ru*	*35-de*
	пост сайт ссылка чат яху	adresse Internetseite Lnk Mail Mailkontakt Message das WWW online bloggen chatten surfen	пост профайл сайт сервер спам спамоборона трафик чат виртуальный онлайн	Internetseite Link Message Shortcut Startseite Webseite chat- technisch online offline googeln mailen	торговля онлайн- магазин пост постинг сайт сервер френд френдолен- та юзер юзеринфо юзернейм юзерпик интернетное законнек- титься	
compu- ter	винчес- тер комп компью- тер монитор файл IP адрес UPS'ы виндовая гигабайт ная проап- грейдить	Klicken PC tippen	винчестер комп компьютер патерн форматирова ние CD-привод форматирова ть компьютер- ный небрежно- пиксельный opensource- soft	Computer Layout PC	апгрейд винт комп компик компьютер монитор тул утилита файл	Computer PC PC-Spiel wegklicken
techni- cal gadgets/ progress	джакузи диск мобиль- ник плеер смс смситься	Bonus DVD CD DVD DVD-Regal DVD- Spieler MP3-Player Notebook Playmobil Sms Toaster	вай-фай диск пейджер принтер роуминг смс-ка тюнер фен DVD смс-ить	CD CD´-Regal DVD Headset Keyboard Lautspre- cher-boxen Masterkey- board Prepaykarte Sms Whirlpool	диск зум принтер скан сканер смс- викторина смс-ка DVD DVD-плеер долбиный хайтечный нехайтековс кий	Brenner CD DVD Sms Snooze-Taste hi-tech

	-25 ru	*-25 de*	*25-35 ru*	*25-35 de*	*35-ru*	*35-de*
music/ show-business	Дикси-ленд попса поп-звезда хит	Band Boyband Poplieder Punk Rock Single Song Techno Trance trance-ähnliches	сингл фольклор	Mix Single Song	клип шоу-бизнес rock n roll	Musical Sound Track
fashion/ beauty/ clothes	бикини дизайн модель топ	Pulli Trend designed shoppen shoppen gehen	джинсы дизайн дизайнер имидж модель сейл топ футболка шопоголия шоппинг шопить	Design Shirt shoppen	модель модельный	gestylt
hobbies/ free time occupations	бар диско-клуб дискотека клуб клубешник	Cocktailbar Party private party	ночной клуб пикниковать	Bar Club Party	бар паб стрип-бар	Club Disco Party
TV	реалити шоу	TV		TV-Team		Fernseh-show
sports	аэробика баскет бильярд боулинг скейт спорт тренер	Single Ausdauer-Training Pferdesport Snowboard Snowboarden squash Sport Sportler Sportsachen Sportunfähi	бутсы тренажёрный зал тренер сноуборд сноубординг спорт спарринговаться	Basketball Single Snowboard Tanzsport	снэплинг тренер дама-тренер тренинг фитнес футбол	skitour Sportlich-keit Walken Walking Programme joggen walken gehen

	-25 ru	*-25 de*	*25-35 ru*	*25-35 de*	*35-ru*	*35-de*
		gkeit Tennishalle Training Trainer Wintersport				
food	йогурт коктейль сендвич	Cocktail- soße Fastfood Milchshake Pepsi Pudding Toast	попкорн		коктейль сендвич	Fast Food Grill Grillen Steak
film	сериал	Cartoon Film filmen	блокбастер порно-экшн сериал трейлер фильм	Film	сериал фильм	Film
educa- tion	колледж ретейк					
names for professi ons/ people	диджей мэн трансвес- тит	Barfrau Cable guy Doc Insider Single	байкер метросексу- ал	Cowboy Dad Lady Schmuddel- reporter Single Teeny	клоун клоунесса	Hobby- fotograf Teenager
building	бункер		туннель фривей		терминал	

References

A. Linguistics

Adamzik, Kirsten (1995). Textsorten-Texttypologie: eine kommentierte Bibliographie. Münster: Nodus-Publ.

Adamzik, Kirsten (ed.) (2000). Textsorten: Reflexionen und Analysen. Tübingen:Stauffenburg-Verl.

Adamzik, Kirsten; Christen, Helen (eds.) (2001). Sprachkontakt, Sprachvergleich, Sprachvariation: Festschrift für Gottfried Kolde zum 65. Geburtstag. Tübingen: Niemeyer.

Adamzik, Kirsten (2004). Textlinguistik. Eine Einführende Darstellung. Tübingen: Niemeyer.

Adler, Manuela (2004). Form und Häufigkeit der Verwendung von Anglizismen in deutschen und schwedischen Massenmedien. Jena: Univ., Diss.

Altenberg, Bengt; Granger, Sylviane (2002). Lexis in Contrast.Corpus-based Approaches. John Benjamins Publishing Company Amsterdam/Philadelphia.

Auer, Peter (ed.) (1999). Code-switching in Conversation. Language, Interaction and Identity. London, NY: Routledge.

Bauer, Laurie (2004). A Glossary of Morphology. Edinburgh: University Press.

Bechet- Tsarnos, Valerie (2005). Wirtschaftsanglizismen. Tübingen: Narr.

De Beugrande, Robert-Alain; Dressler, Wolfgang Ulrich (1981). Einführung in die Textlinguistik. Tübingen: Niemeyer.

Bloomfield, Leonard (2001). Die Sprache. übers., kommentiert und hrs. von Peter Ernst und Hans Christian Luschützky unter Mitwirkung von Thomas Herok. mit einem Geleitw. von Andre Martine. - Dt. Erstausg. - Wien: Ed. Praesens.

Bohmann, Stefanie (1996). Englische Elemente im Gegenwartsdeutsch der Werbebranche, Marburg: Tectum Verlag.

Bräuer, Gerd (2003). Schreiben als reflexive Praxis: Tagebuch, Arbeitsjournal, Portfolio. Freiburg im Breisgau: Fillibach-Verlag.

Brinker, Klaus (1997). Linguistische Textanalyse. Eine Einführung in Grundbegriffe und Methoden. Berlin: Erich Schmidt.

Brinker, Klaus (2001). Linguistische Textanalyse. Eine Einführung in Grundbegriffe und Methoden.Berlin: Erich Schmidt.

Busse, Ulrich (1993). Anglizismen im Duden: eine Untersuchung zur Darstellung englischen Wortguts in den Angaben des Rechtschreibdudens von 1880-1986. Tübingen: Niemeyer.

Carstensen, Broder (1965). Englische Einflüsse auf die deutsche Sprache nach 1945. Heidelberg: Carl Winter Universitätsverlag.

Carstensen, Broder; Galinsky, Hans (1975). Amerikanismen der deutschen Gegenwartssprache: Entlehnungsvorgänge und ihre stilistischen Aspekte. Heidelberg: Carl Winter Universitätsverlag.

Chang, Youngick (2003). Anglizismen in der deutschen Fachsprache der Computertechnik. Peter Lang.

Chesterman, Andrew (1998). Contrastive Functional Analysis. Amsterdam/Philadelphia: John Benjamins Publishing Company.

Cruse, Alan (2000) Meaning in Language. An Introduction to Semantics and Pragmatics. Oxford: OUP.

Don Alphonso, Kai Pahl (eds.) (2004). Blogs! Text und Form im Internet. Berlin: Schwarzkopf & Schwarzkopf Verlag GmbH.

Dimter, Matthias (1981). Textklassenkonzepte heutiger Alltagssprache: Kommunikationssituation, Textfunktion u. Textinhalt als Kategorien alltagssprachlicher Textklassifikation. Tübingen: Niemeyer.

Duckworth, David (1979). Der Einfluss des Englischen auf den deutschen Wortschatz seit 1945. in: Braun, ed.

Eichler, Wolfgang (1989). Deutsche Grammatik : Form, Leistung und Gebrauch der Gegenwartssprache. Frankfurt am Main: Athenäum.

Field, Fredric W. (2002). Linguistic Borrowing in Bilingual Contexts. John Benjamin B.V.

Fink, Hermann (1995). Semantische Explorationen: Eine empirische Untersuchung zur "Gebrauchsbedeutung" einiger ausgewählter Anglizismen im Deutschen. Freiberg.

Fink,Hermann (1997). Von Kuh-Look bis Fit for Fun: Anglizismen in der heutigen deutschen Allgemein- und Werbesprache. Frankfurt am Main [u.a.]: Peter Lang.

Fink, Hermann; Fijas, Liane; Schons, Daniel (1997). Anglizismen in der Sprache der Neuen Bundesländer. Frankfurt am Main [u.a.]:Peter Lang.

Fink, Hermann; Fijas, Liane (eds.) (1998). America and her Influence upon the Language and Culture of Post-socialist Countries. Frankfurt am Main [u.a.]: Peter Lang.

Fink, Hermann; Fijas, Liane; Shakhovsky, Viktor (2000). Angloamerikanisches in der russischen Gesellschaft sowie Wirtschafts- und Allgemeinsprache. Frankfurt am Main [u.a.]: Peter Lang.

Fischer, Rudolf-Josef (2005). Genuszuordnung. Frankfurt am Main [u.a.]: Peter Lang.

Fix, Ulla; Habscheid, Stephan; Josef Klein (eds.) (2001). Zur Kulturspezifik von Textsorten Tübingen: Stauffenburg-Verl.

Gester, Silke (2001). Anglizismen im Tschechischen und im Deutschen: Bestandaufnahme und empirische Analyse im Jahr 2000. Frankfurt am Main [u.a.]: Peter Lang.

Gladrow, Wolfgang; Heyl, Sonja (eds.) (1996). Slawische und Deutsche Sprachwelt: typologische Spezifika der slawischen Sprachen im Vergleich mit dem Deutschen. Frankfurt am Main [u.a.]: Peter Lang.

Gladrow, Wolfgang; Hammel, Robert (eds.) (2001). Beiträge zu einer russisch-deutschen kontrastiven Grammatik. Frankfurt am Main [u.a.]:Peter Lang.

Glahn, Richard (2002). Der Einfluß der Englischen auf gesprochene deutsche Gegenwartssprache: eine Analyse öffentlich gesprochener Sprache am Beispiel von "Fernsehdeutsch". Frankfurt am Main [u.a.]:Peter Lang.

Görlach, Manfred (ed.) (2002). An annotated Bibliography of European Anglicisms. Oxford: OUP.

Görlach, Manfred (ed.) (2002). English in Europe. Oxford University Press.

Granger, Sylvianne; Lerot, Jacques; Petch-Tyson, Stephanie (eds.) (2003) Corpus-based Approaches to Contrastive Linguistics and Translation Studies. NY:Amsterdam - New York.

Gregor, Esma (2003). Russian-English Code-Switching in New York City, Wolfgang Gladrow, Barbara Kunzmann-Müller, Heinrich Olschowsky, Georg Witte (eds.), B.21 Berliner Slawische Arbeiten. Peter Lang Verlag.

Gülich, Elisabeth (1986). Textsorten in der Kommunikationspraxis. Werner Kallmeyer (ed.), Kommunikationstypologie: Handlungsmuster, Textsorten, Situationstypen. Düsseldorf: Schwann, 15-47

Hansen, Barbara et al (1990). Englische Lexikologie: Einführung in Wortbildung und lexikalische Semantik. Leipzig: Verlag Enzyklopädie.

Haugen, Einar. (1956). Bilingualism in the Americas: A bibliography and research guide. Montgomery: University of Alabama Press.

Heath, Jeffrey (1989). From Code-Switching to Borrowing: Foreign and Diglossic mixing in Moroccan Arabic. Kegan Paul International London and New York.

Heinemann, Margot; Heinemann, Wolfgang (2002). Grundlagen der Textlinguistik: Interaktion-Text-Diskurs. Tübingen: Niemeyer.

Heinemann, Wolfgang; Viehweger, Dieter (1991). Textlinguistik: eine Einführung. Tübingen: Niemeyer.

Hentschel, Elke (1990). Handbuch der deutschen Grammatik. Berlin; New York: de Gruyter.

Hess-Lüttich, Ernest W.B.; Holly, Werner; Püschel, Ulrich (eds.) (1996). Textstrukturen im Medienwandel. Frankfurt am Main [u.a.]: Peter Lang.

Huber, Oliver (2003). Hyper-Text-Linguistik: TAH: ein textlinguistisches Analysemodell für Hypertexte; theoretisch und praktisch exemplifiziert am Problemfeld der typisierten Links von Hypertexten im World Wide Web. München: Utz.

Hunston, Susan (2002). Corpora in Applied Linguistics. CUP.

Jablonski, Miroslaw (1990). Regularität und Variabilität in der Rezeption englischer Internationalismen im modernen Deutsch, Französisch und Polnisch: aufgezeigt in den Bereichen Sport, Musik und Mode. Tübingen: Niemeyer.

Jackson, Howard (2002). Lexicography: an Introduction. Routledge.

Junker, H. Gerhard (2006). Der Anglizismen-Index : Anglizismen, Gewinn oder Zumutung ?. Ifb Verlag.

Kallmeyer, Werner (ed.) (1986). Kommunikationstypologie: Handlungsmuster, Textsorten, Situationstypen. Düsseldorf: Schwann.

Katamba, Francis (1994). English Words. NY.

Koch, Peter; Oesterreicher, Wulf (1990). Gesprochene Sprache in der Romania: Französisch, Italienisch, Spanisch. Tübingen: Niemeyer.

Krause, W.-D. (ed.) (2000). Textsorten: kommunikationslinguistische und konfrontative Aspekte. Frankfurt am Main [u.a.]: Peter Lang.

Kron, Olaf (2002). Probleme der Texttypologie: Integration und Differenzierung handlungstheoretischer Konzepte in einem Neuansatz. Frankfurt am Main [u.a.]: Peter Lang.

Kupper, Sabine (2003). Anglizismen in deutschen und französischen Werbeanzeigen (zum Umgang von Deutschen und Französen mit Anglizismen. Marburg: Tectum Verlag.

Langner, Heidemarie C. (1995). Die Schreibung englischer Entlehnungen im Deutschen. Frankfurt am Main [u.a.]: Peter Lang.

Lehnert, Martin (1990). Anglo-amerikanisches im Sprachgebrauch der DDR. Berlin: Akademie-Verlag.

Lee,Wan-Ho (1997). Anglizismen in Ostdeutschland : eine Untersuchung am Beispiel der Tageszeitung “Das Volk“ bzw. “Thüringer Allgemeine“ der Jahre 1988, 1990 und 1992. Marburg: Univ., Diss.

Lipka, Leonard (2002). English Lexicology: Lexical Structure, Word Semantics and Word Formation. Tübingen: Narr.

Lyons, John (1995). Linguistic Semantics: An Introduction. Cambrige Univ. Press.

McEnery, Tony; Xiao Richard; Yukio, Tono (2006). Corpus-Based Language Studies. An Advanced Resourse Book. Routledge.

Meyer, Charles F. (2002). English Corpus Linguistics. An Introduction. Cambrige Univ. Press.

Muhr, Rudolf; Ketteman, Bernhard (eds.) (2004). Eurospeak. Der Einfluss des Englischen auf eüropäische Sprachen zur Jahrtausendwende. Frankfurt am Main: Peter Lang.

Müller, Peter O. (ed.) (2005). Fremdwortbildung: Theorie und Praxis in Geschichte und Gegenwart. Frankfurt am Main: Peter Lang.

Myers-Scotton, Carol (1993). Social Motivations for Code-Switching: Evidence from Africa. New York: Oxford Univ. Press Inc.

Nettman-Multanowska, Kinga (2003). English Loanwords in Polish and German after 1945: Orthography and Morphology. Frankfurt am Main: Europäischer Verlag der Wissenschaften.

O' Halloran, Edel (2002). Ist Mode Englisch? : Französische und englische Einflüsse auf die deutsche Mode- und Gemeinsprache im 20. Jahrhundert. Frankfurt am Main [u.a.]: Peter Lang.

Plümer, Nicole (2000). Anglizismus-Purismus-sprachliche Identität: Eine Untersuchung zu den Anglizismen in der deutschen und französischen Mediensprache. Frankfurt am Main [u.a.]: Peter Lang.

Pyo, Sang-Yong (1997). Die Einflüsse des Angloamerikanischen auf das heutige Russische:unter besonderer Berücksichtigung der semantischen und morphologischen Untersuchung der neuen Anglizismen in der russischen Sprache (nach Materialien russischer Zeitungen und Zeitschriften aus den Jahren 1945-1985). Marburg/Lahn: Biblion.

Rehm, Georg (2002). Schriftliche Mündlichkeit in der Sprache des World Wide Web. Arne Ziegler, Christa Dürscheid (eds.), Kommunikationsform E-Mail. Tübingen: Stauffenburg Verlag, 263-309.

Rogers, Henry (2000). The Sounds of Language. An Introduction to Phonetics. Pearson Education Limited.

Rot, Sándor (1991). Language Contact. Frankfurt am Main [u.a.]: Peter Lang.

Sankoff, Gillian (2002). Linguistic Outcomes of Language Contact. J.K. Chambers, Peter Trudgill and Natalie Schilling (eds.), The handbook of language variation and change. Estes, Blackwell Publishers Ltd., 638-669.

Schreiber, Herbert (ed.); Sommerfeldt, Karl-Ernst (2001). Textsorten des Alltags. Frankfurt am Main [u.a.]: Peter Lang.

Schulte-Beckhausen, Marion (2002). Genusschwankung bei englischen, französischen, italienischen und spanischen Lehnwörtern im Deutschen: eine Untersuchung auf der Grundlage deutscher Wörterbücher seit 1945. Frankfurt am Main [u.a.]: Lang.

Schütte, Dagmar (1996). Das schöne Fremde:anglo-amerikanische Einflüsse auf die Sprache der deutschen Zeitschriftenwerbung. Opladen: Westdt. Verl.

Simmler, Franz (ed.) (1997). Textsorten und Textsortentraditionen. Bern [u.a.]: Lang.

Sommerfeldt, Karl-Ernst (ed.) (2003). Textsorten und Textsortenvarianten. Frankfurt am Main [u.a.]: Peter Lang.

Sörensen, Ilse (1994). Englisch im deutschen Wortschatz. Lehn- und Fremdwörter in der Umgangssprache. Cornelsen / Volk und Wissen.

Spitzmüller, Jürgen (2005). Metasprachdiskurse: Einstellungen zu Anglizismen und ihre wissenschaftliche Rezeption. Berlin, New York: de Gruyter.

Stickel, Gerhard (ed.); Eisenberg, Peter (2001). Die grammatische Integration von Fremdwörtern. Was fängt das Deutsche mit seinen Latinismen und Anglizismen an Neues und Fremdes im deutsche Wortschatz: aktueller lexikalischer Wandel. Berlin; New York: de Gruyter, 183-210.

Suter, Hans-Jürg (1993). The Wedding Report: A Prototypical Approach to the Study of Traditional Text Types. Amsterdam/Philadelphia: John Benjamins Publishing Company.

Thaler, Verena (2003). Chat -Kommunikation im Spannungsfeld zwischen Oralität und Literalität. VWF Berlin.

Thomason, Sarah G. (2001). Language Contact. An Introduction. Edinburgh Univ. Press.

Trier, Jost (1973). Aufsätze und Vorträge zur Wortfeldtheorie. Van der Lee and O. Reichmann (eds.), The Hague, Paris: Mouton.

Van Sterkenburg, Piet (ed.) (2003). A Practical Guide to Lexicography Amsterdam/Philadelphia: John Benjamins B.V.

Viereck, Karin (1980). Englisches Wortgut, seine Häufigkeit und Integration in der österreichschen und bundesdeutschen Pressesprache. Frankfurt am Main: Peter Lang.

Viereck, Wolfgang (1980). Das Genus englischer Fremd- und Lehnwörter im Deutschen. Studien zum Einfluss der englischen Sprache auf das Deutsche. Tübingen: Narr, 37-77.

Viereck, Wolfgang (1980). Semantische Scheinentlehnungen des Deutschen aus dem Englischen. Studien zum Einfluss der englischen Sprache auf das Deutsche. Tübingen: Narr, 77-101.

Viereck, Wolfgang (ed.) (1980). Studien zum Einfluss der englischen Sprache auf das Deutsche. Tübingen: Narr.

Viereck, Wolfgang; Bald, Wolf-Dietrich (eds.); Ward, Dennis (1986). The English Contribution to Russian. English in Contact with other Languages. Budapest: Akad. Kiadó, 307-331

Warmbrunn, Jürgen (1994). Englische lexikalische Entlehnungen im Wortschatz der tschechischen Gegenwartssprache. Münster; Hamburg: Lit.

Weingarten, Rüdiger (ed.) (1997). Sprachwandel durch Computer. Opladen: Westdt. Verl.

Weinreich, Uriel (1953). Languages in Contact: findings and problems. NY

Weinreich, Uriel (1976). Sprachen in Kontakt: Ergebnisse und Probleme der Zweisprachigkeitsforschung. München:Beck.

Welte, Werner (1993). Englische Semantik: Ein Lehr- und Arbeitsbuch mit umfassender Bibliographie. Frankfurt am Main [u.a.]: Peter Lang.

Yang, Wenliang (1990). Anglizismen im Deutschen: am Beispiel des Nachrichtenmagazins Der Spiegel. Tübingen: Niemeyer.

Zabel, Hermann (ed.) (2001). Denglisch, nein danke!: zu inflationären Verwendung von Anglizismen und Amerikanismen in der deutschen Gegenwartssprache. Paderborn: IFB-Verl.

Ziegler, Arne; Dürscheid, Christa (eds.) (2002). E-Mail – Textsorte oder Kommunikationsform? Eine textlinguistische Annäherung, Kommunikationsform E-Mail. Tübingen:Stauffenburg Verlag, 9-33.

Zürn, Alexandra (2001). Anglizismen in Deutschen: eine Untersuchung zur Häufigkeit von Anglizismen und deren Inkorporiertheit im Deutschen am Beispiel dreier deutschprachiger Nachrichtenmagazine. Karlsruhe: Univ., Diss.

Аристова В.М. (1978). Англо-русские языковые контакты (англицизмы в русском языке). Ленинград.

Володарская Э.Ф. (2002). Заимствования как отражение русско-английских контактов. Вопросы языкознания - №4: 96-119.

Володарская Э.Ф. (2001). Заимствования как универсальное лингвистическое явление. Вопросы филологии - №1: 11-28.

Дьяков А.И. (2003). Причины интенсивного заимствования англицизмов в современном русском языке. Язык и Культура. Новосибирск: 35-43.

Зеленин А.В. (2003). Англоамериканизмы в русском и некоторых других европейских языках. Русский язык в школе - №5: 94-99.

Земская Е.А. (отв. ред.) (2001). Язык русского зарубежья: Общие процессы и языковые портреты: Коллективная монография. М.; Вена: Языки славянской культуры: Венский славистический альманах.

Комлева И.Л. (2006). Принципы формирования русской компьютерной терминологии. Автореферат диссертации на соискание учёной степени кандидата филологических наук. Москва.

Которова, Елизавета (1998). Межъязыковая эквивалентность в лексической семантике: Сопоставительное исследование русского и немецких языков. Frankfurt am Main [u.a.]: Peter Lang.

Крысин Л.П. (1965). К определению терминов «заимствование» и «заимствованное слово». Развитие лексики русского литературного языка. М., Наука: 104–116.

Крысин Л.П. (1968). Иноязычные слова в современном русском языке. М: Наука.

Крысин Л.П. (1998). Иноязычное слово в роли эвфемизма. Русский язык в школе. № 2.

Крысин Л.П. (2004). Русское слово, своё и чужое. М: Языки славянской культуры.

Кузнецов П.С. (1960). Морфологическая классификация языков. Halle (Saale): Veb Max Niemeyer Verlag.

Мечковская Н.Б. (2001). Общее языкознание: Структурная и социальная типология языков: Учебное пособие для студентов филологических и лингвистических специальностей. М.: Флинта: Наука.

Панов М.В. (2004). Труды по общему языкознанию и русскому языку, под ред. Е.А.Земской, С.М. Кузьминой. М: Языки славянской культуры.

Проценко Е.А. (2004). Проблема переключения кодов в зарубежной лингвистике (краткий обзор литературы за последние десятилетия). Вестник ВГУ, Серия «Лингвистика и межкультурная коммуникация», № 1: 123-127.

Тимофеева Г.Г. (1995). Новые английские заимствования в русском языке. Написание. Произношение. Спб.: Юна.

Филипов К.А. (2003). Лингвистика текста: Курс лекций. С.-Петерб. гос. ун-т. -СПб: СпбГУ.

B. Grammars, Dictionaries

Bartzsch, Rudolf; Pogarell, Reiner; Schröder, Markus (eds.) (2004). Wörterbuch überflüssiger Anglizismen, 6. erheblich überarbeitete und erweiterte Auflage. IFB Verlag.

Carstensen, Broder; Busse, Ulrich (1993). Anglizismen-Wörterbuch: der Einfluß des Englischen auf den deutschen Wortschatz nach 1945. Bd. 1: A – E, Berlin [u.a.] : de Gruyter.

Carstensen, Broder; Busse, Ulrich (1994). Anglizismen-Wörterbuch :der Einfluß des Englischen auf den deutschen Wortschatz nach 1945. Bd. 2: F – O, Berlin [u.a.] : de Gruyter.

Carstensen, Broder; Busse, Ulrich (1996). Anglizismen-Wörterbuch :der Einfluß des Englischen auf den deutschen Wortschatz nach 1945. Bd. 3: P – Z, Berlin [u.a.] : de Gruyter.

Collins Concise English Dictionary. 5th ed, 2006.

DUDEN. Die Deutsche Rechtschreibung. 24., völlig neu bearbeitete und erweiterte Auflage, DUDEN Redaktion. Auf der Grundlage der neuen amtlichen Rechtschreibregeln, ed.,. Duden Band 1; Mannheim: Duden Verlag, 2006.

Duden- das große Fremdwörterbuch. Mannheim:Duden Verlag, 2005.

Duden - Deutsches Universalwörterbuch, 5. Aufl. Mannheim, 2003 [CD-ROM].

Eisenberg, Peter (ed.) (1998). Duden, Grammatik der deutschen Gegenwartssprache , 6., neu bearb. Aufl. Bd.4.Mannheim [u.a.]: Duden Verlag.

Görlach, Manfred (ed.) (2001). A Dictionary of European Anglicisms: A Usage Dictionary of Anglicisms in 16 European Languages. Oxford: OUP.

Hornby A.S. (ed.) (2005). Oxford Advanced Learners Dictionary of Current English. Oxford: OUP.

Kluge Etymologisches Wörterbuch der deutschen Sprache. Tübingen, 2002.

Longman Dictionary of Contemporary English. 3rd Edition, Longman Dictionaries, 1995.

The Concise Oxford Dictionary of Current English. Oxford: OUP, 1995.

Багайцева В.В., Николина Н.А., Чеснокова Л.Д. (2002). Современный русский язык: Теория. Анализ языковых единиц: Учеб. Для студ. Высш. Учеб. Заведений: в 2ч.- Ч.2: Морфология. Синтаксис, под ред. Е.И. Дибровой. М.: Академия.

Баш Л.М., Боброва А.В. (2005). Современный словарь иностранных слов: толкование, словоупотребление, словообразование, этимология. М.: Цитадель-Трейд, ИКТЦ Лада, Рипол Классик.

Вальтер Х., Вовк О., Зумп А., Конупкова Х., Кумпа А., Порос В. (2004). Словарь: Заимствования в русском субстандарте. Англицизмы. М.: ООО Ити Технологии.

Васюкова И.А. (1999). Словарь иностранных слов. М.: АСТ-ПРЕСС.

Диброва Е.И., Касаткин Л.Л., Николина Н.А., Щеболева И.И (2002). Современный русский язык: Теория. Анализ языковых единиц: Учеб. Для студ. Высш. Учеб. Заведений: в 2ч.- Ч.1: Фонетика и Орфоэпия. Графика и орфография. Лексикология. Фразеология. Лексикография. Морфемика. Словообразование. М.: Академия.

Ефремова Т.Ф. (2000). Новый словарь русского языка. Толково-словообразовательный. М.: Рус. яз.

Захаренко Е.Н., Комарова Л.Н., Нечаева И.В. (2003). Новый словарь иностранных слов: 25 000 слов и словосочетаний. М.: Азбуковник.

Лукаш Ю. А (2004). Энциклопедический словарь-справочник руководителя предприятия. (Серия «Библиотека профессиональных словарей»). М.: Книжный мир.

Семенова Н.М. (отв. ред.), Бурцева В.В. (2004). Словарь иностранных слов: свыше 21 000 слов, - 2-е изд., стереотип. М.: Рус.яз.-Медиа.

Скляревская Г.Н. (ред.) (1998). Толковый словарь русского языка конца XX века. Языковые изменения. Российская академия наук, Институт лингвистических исследований Спб: Фолио-Пресс.

Ушаков Д. Н. (ред.) (1935-1940). Толковый словарь русского языка: В 4 т. М.: Гос. Ин-т «Сов. энцикл.»; ОГИЗ; Гос. изд-во иностр. и нац. слов.

Фасмер, Макс (2004). Этимологический словарь русского языка. Мультимедиа-издательство «Адепт».

Черных П.Я. (1994). Историко-этимологический словарь русского языка: 13560 слов: Т.1-2.-2 изд., стереот. М: Рус.яз.

Шведова Н.Ю. (ред.) (1980). Русская грамматика, т.1. М.: Наука.

C. Internet Resources

"Ask Yahoo!" (15 November, 2002). URL:http://ask.yahoo.com/-ask/20021115.html

Barger, John (September, 1999). "Weblog resources FAQ." URL: http://www.open.ge/el/?base=www.robotwisdom.com/&view=0&url='weblogs/index.html'

Blood, Rebecca (7 September, 2000). "Weblogs: a history and perspective" Rebecca's Pocket. URL: http://www.rebeccablood.net/essays/weblog_history.html

Bucher, Stefan (23 September, 2005). "Weblog FAQ." URL: http://www.stefan-bucher.net/weblogfaq/

Corcoran, Neil P (1995). "Orality, literacy and the net". URL: http://www.msu.edu/user/corcora5/essays/ol&n.html

Herring, Susan C; Scheidt, Lois Ann; Bonus, Sabrina; Wright, Elijah (28 December, 2005). "Bridging the Gap: A Genre Analysis of Weblogs". URL: http://www.ics.uci.edu/~jpd/classes/ics234cw04/herring.pdf/

"Just about anyone can use a blog!" (13 June, 2006). URL: http://weblogs.about.com/cs/weblogs101/f/whoblogs.htm

Kresic, Marijana (11 July, 2006). "Kommunikationstheorie und Internet". URL: http://www.websprache.uni-hannover.de/networx/docs/networx-15.pdf/

Lane, Derek R. (17 August, 2006). "Function and Impact of Nonverbal Communication in a Computer Mediated Communication Context: An Investigation of Defining Issues". URL: http://www.uky.edu/~dr-lane/techno/nvcmc.htm

Langham, Don (01 July, 1994). "The Common Place MOO: Orality and Literacy in Virtual Reality". URL: http://www.decem-ber.com/cmc/mag/1994/jul/moo.html

Miller, Carolyn R. (04 November, 2004). "Blogging as Social Action: A Genre Analysis of the Weblog"

URL:http://blog.lib.umn.edu/blogosphere/blogging_as_social_action_a_genre_analysis_of the_web-log.html
Mcneill, Laurie (2005). "Gender under Construction: The Diary on the Internet". URL: http://www.languageatinternet.de/articles/2005/120/
Sanjay, Das (17 May, 2005). "About Blog." URL: http://blogchronicle.blog-spot.com/2005/05/about-blog.html
Schlobinski, Peter (2000). "Anglizismen im Internet". URL: http://www.mediensprache.net/networx/networx-14.pdf
Schlobinski, Peter; Siever, Torsten (2005)."Sprachliche und Textuelle Merkmale in Weblogs". URL: http://www.mediensprache.net/networx/
Schlobinski, Peter (25 May, 2006). URL: http://www.blogger.com/tour-start.g/
Schmidt, Jan (12 June, 2006). "Bloging as Social Action". URL: http://schmidtmitdete.de/pdf/gor05_oneslide.pdf/
Schmidt, Jan; Wilbers, Martin (January, 2006). "Wie ich blogge?!Erste Ergebnisse der Weblogbefragung 2005." Forschungsstelle "Neue Kommunikationsmedien". URL: http://www.fonk-bamberg.de/pdf/fonkbericht06-01.pdf
Skiba, Richard (1997). "Code Switching as a Countenance of Language Interference", The Internet TESL Journal, Vol. III, No. 10, October 1997. URL: http://iteslj.org/Articles/Skiba-CodeSwitching.html/
Wikipedia, the free encyclopedia (15 July, 2006). URL: http://en.wiki-pedia.org/wiki/Types_of_blogs /

Бекетов, Михаил (12 July, 2007). «Интересное интервью про блоггинг». URL: http:// www.dkvartal.ru/beketov/6847/comments/
Бескаравайная, Валерия (15 June, 2005). «Повседневность: век спустя...» URL: http://sociologist.nm.ru/articles/beskaravainaja_01.htm/
«Количество блогов в интернете достигло 35 млн.» (18 April, 2006). Полит.Ру. URL: http://bilingua.ogi.ru/culture/2006/04/18/blogs.html/
«Количество блогов в интернете удваивалось каждые полгода». (05 April, 2007). E-news: Новости Украины и Мира. URL:http://e-news.com.ua/print/147600.html/
Миллер К.; Шеферд Д. (21 June, 2005) «Ведение онлайн-дневника как социальное действие: жанровый анализ блогов». URL: http://www.sociologist.nm.ru/articles/miller-shepherd.htm/
Птица, Александр (01 June, 2002). «Дневники, «Живой Журнал», блоги и все, все, все» ITC.UA URL: http://www.itc.ua/articles.phtml?ID=10097
Сахно О.С. (20 July, 2004). «Дневник как речевой жанр художественной литературы».

URL:http://pn.pglu.ru/index.php?module=subjects&func=viewpage&pageid=790
«Что такое блог». (17 September, 2003).
URL: http://spectator.ru/inter-net/content/blog_is/
«Эволюция блоггеров - экскурс в историю блогов». (12 July, 2007).
URL: http://www.klubok.net/article2199.html/

Hallesche Sprach- und Textforschung

Herausgegeben von Alexander Brock und Annette Schiller

Band 1 Annette Schiller: Die présentatifs im heutigen Französisch. Eine funktionale Studie ihrer Vielfalt. 1992.

Band 2 Gertrud Bense (Hrsg.): Diachronie – Kontinuität – Impulse. Sprachwissenschaftliches Kolloquium Halle 1992. 1994.

Band 3 Wolfgang Boeck (Hrsg.): Sprache, Literatur und Landeskunde slavischer Völker. Funktionale Aspekte in der Beschreibung und Didaktik. 1994.

Band 4 Gertrud Bense (Hrsg.): Kommunikation und Grammatik. 1996.

Band 5 Gisela Hermann-Brennecke / Dietmar Schneider (Hrsg.): Dona Anglica. 120 Jahre Anglistik in Halle. 1997.

Band 6 Max Hans-Jürgen Mattusch: Vielsprachigkeit: Fluch oder Segen für die Menschheit? Zu Fragen einer europäischen und globalen Fremdsprachenpolitik. 1999.

Band 7 Christiane Schiller: Bilinguismus. Zur Darstellung eines soziolinguistischen Phänomens in der Literatur. Dargestellt an Beispielen der regionalen Literatur Preußisch-Litauens: Hermann Sudermann *Litauische Geschichten*, Ieva Simonaityte *Vilius Karalius*. 2000.

Band 8 Gertrud Bense: "Giedojam taw – Wir singen dir". Zur Textgeschichte der preußisch-litauischen Gesangbücher im 18. Jahrhundert. Mit besonderer Berücksichtigung der Liedersammlung von Fabian Ulrich Glaser (1688-1747) und ihrem Umfeld. 2001.

Band 9 Gertrud Bense / Gerhard Meiser / Edeltraud Werner (Hrsg.): August Friedrich Pott. Beiträge der Halleschen Tagung anlässlich des zweihundertsten Geburtstages von August Friedrich Pott (1802–1887). 2005.

Band 10 Julia Balakina: Anglicisms in Russian and German Blogs. A Comparative Analysis. 2011.

www.peterlang.de

Peter Lang · Internationaler Verlag der Wissenschaften

Falco Pfalzgraf (Hrsg./ed.)

Englischer Sprachkontakt in den Varietäten des Deutschen

English in Contact with Varieties of German

Frankfurt am Main, Berlin, Bern, Bruxelles, New York, Oxford, Wien, 2009.
244 S., 26 Tab.
Österreichisches Deutsch – Sprache der Gegenwart.
Herausgegeben von Rudolf Muhr und Richard Schrodt. Bd. 12
ISBN 978-3-631-58132-2 · br. € 42.50*

Dieser Band enthält eine Auswahl von zehn Aufsätzen, welche auf Vorträgen basieren, die in der Sektion *Language & Linguistics* des *Centre for Anglo-German Cultural Relations* (CAGCR) am Queen Mary College der University of London seit Herbst 2006 gehalten wurden. Behandelt wird zunächst die Frage nach der Stellung der Sprachwissenschaft in den britischen *German Studies*. Sodann wird nicht nur der englischsprachige Einfluss auf das deutsche, österreichische und schweizer Deutsch abgedeckt, sondern auch jener des Deutschen auf das Englische. Weitere Beiträge beschäftigen sich hinsichtlich Anglizismen mit deren Integration, mit Problemen ihrer Genusbildung, mit ihrem Vorkommen im Luxemburgischen, mit ihrer Rolle in einer multiethnischen Jugendsprache, sowie mit möglichen Zusammenhängen zwischen Sprachpurismus und Globalisierung.

This volume contains a selection of ten papers based on lectures which have been given in the Language & Linguistics section of the Centre for Anglo-German Cultural Relations (CAGCR) at Queen Mary, University of London, since autumn 2006. The first paper discusses the position of Linguistics in British German Studies; subsequent papers discuss not only the influence of English on Swiss German, Austrian German, and German in Germany, but also the German influence on English. Other papers deal with the integration of anglicisms in the German language, problems of the grammatical gender of anglicisms, their position in Luxembourgish, their role in a multi-ethnic youth variety, and the connections between linguistic purism and globalization.